The Death Brigade

STATEMENT OF PURPOSE

The *Holocaust Library* was created and is managed by survivors. Its purpose is to offer to the reading public authentic material, not readily available, and to preserve the memory of our martyrs and heroes untainted by arbitrary or inadvertent distortions.

With each passing day the memory of the tragedy of European Jews, the greatest crime in the annals of mankind, recedes into history. The witnesses and survivors of the holocaust are still alive, their memories remain vivid; yet, a malicious myth about their experience keeps rising before our eyes, distorting and misinterpreting evidence, perverting history.

As new generations arise, so grows the incredible ignorance about our tragedy. Millions of men and women, Jews and Gentiles, are unaware of the basic facts of the tragedy, many have never even heard the word "holocaust." This is a seed of a new disaster.

The holocaust story should be untiringly told and retold making the world aware of its lessons. This can contribute to that moral reconstruction which alone may prevent a repetition of the catastrophe in our hate- and violence-stricken world.

THE
DEATH BRIGADE
(The Janowska Road)

LEON WELICZKER WELLS

HOLOCAUST LIBRARY
NEW YORK

First published in 1963 by The Macmillan Company
under the title "The Janowska Road."

094347

Library of Congress Catalog Card Number: 77-89068
Publication of this book was made possible by a grant
from Benjamin and Stefa Wald.

Cover designed by Eric Gluckman
Printed in the United States of America

Contents

Acknowledgments

The author wishes to express his gratitude to the many people who helped him in the publishing of this book.

My warmest thanks to Rabbi Arthur Herzberg, to Mr. Clement Alexandre of The Macmillan Company, and to Philip Kassel. I also thank the following publishing houses: The Macmillan Company, New York; Albin Michel, France; Carl Hanser, Germany; the publishers in Italy, Spain, Portugal, and in all the other countries, as well as all the translators.

I am particularly indebted to my wife, Frieda, not only for her encouragement to me in writing this book but also for her devoted assistance.

I especially thank my friend Leonard Wallace Robinson for the editing of this book and for his deep and sincere interest in this work.

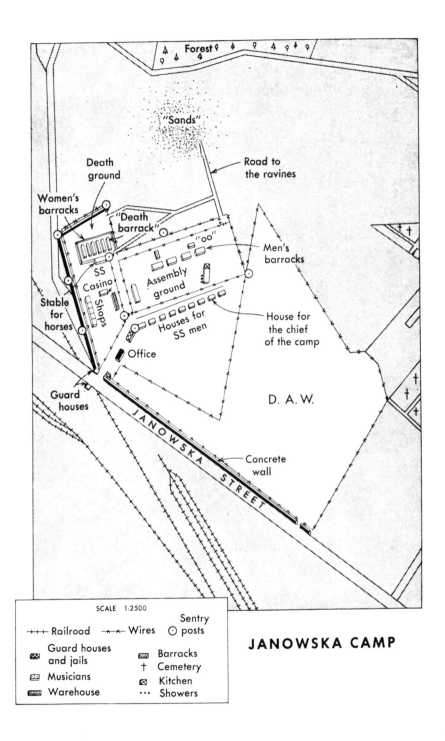

JANOWSKA CAMP

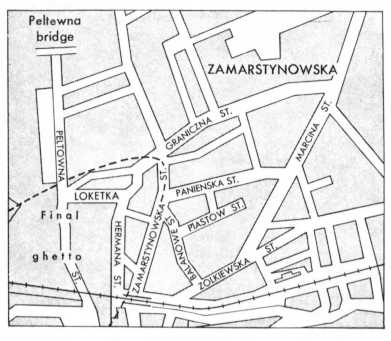

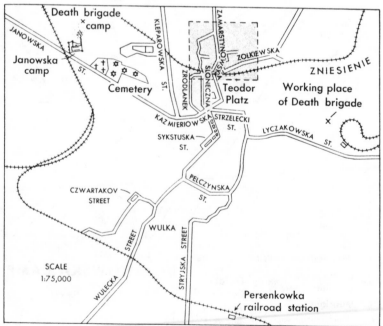

STREET PLAN OF LVOV

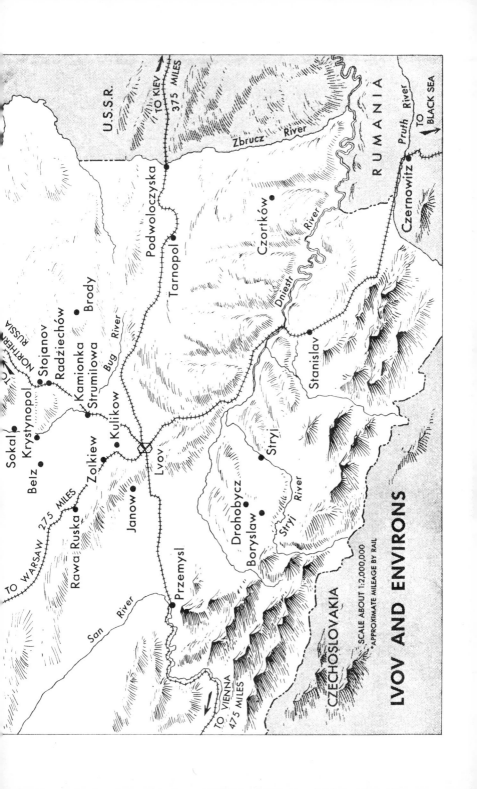

LVOV AND ENVIRONS

SCALE ABOUT 1:2,000,000

APPROXIMATE MILEAGE BY RAIL

My face is red with weeping,
And on my eyelids is deep darkness;
Although there is no violence in my hands,
And my prayer is pure.
O earth, cover not my blood,
And let me cry find no resting place.

                        —Job. 16: 16 to 18

PART I

Time
of
Peace

1

I SHALL BEGIN with the time of peace, before the Germans came.

On Saturdays the inner part of the city was deserted. Hardly any grownup walked on the streets, and if one did so, he was filled with the silence. He would hurry to get quickly to the outskirts, where there was more life.

Here and there, one would see children playing in front of their homes or in the marketplace, and their voices were muffled. Laughter was rarely heard from the windows.

Only, from the nearby synagogue, the old songs of the pious ones: a thin monotone threading the silence.

"A psalm, a song for the Sabbath day."

The Sabbath really began on Thursday. That afternoon Mother would go to the stores and markets to shop for the weekend. In the evening the poor came to those who were better off to borrow money for the Sabbath supply. On Thursday, too, Father would cut the children's fingernails, and his own, wrap them in a piece of paper, add wood shavings, and burn them. Because, as it was said, fingernails resume their growth on the third day, it was the custom that the paring of the nails be done on Thursday. Therefore, the nails wouldn't start to grow on the Sabbath, but on the first day of the week. It was also believed that the nails must be burned so that one's soul would have peace after death. Otherwise the soul would have to gather up all its lost fingernails.

The whole of Friday was taken up with preparations for the next day. Mother arose early—in the winter, when the day is short, as early as two o'clock in the morning—to bake, cook, and clean for the next day, for Saturday, our Sabbath day. On Friday the food was different from that of any other day. In the morning there was a fresh buttered *pleztel*, an oval-shaped, baked, thin dough covered with seeds and onions. I especially liked the *bube*, a potato cake one ate with meatballs and sauce for lunch.

The younger children did not have to go to cheder (the lower grade of religious school) on Friday. After lunch we boys accompanied Father *schwitzen* (sweating) in the steam bath. This bath with its

3

steam, its *reisigbesen* (the scrub brush) to rub our hot bodies with, the people lying on the wooden boards, sighing, enervated by the steam, was an ever-new and exciting event for us boys.

On our way home we passed a stand where we would stop for a glass of fruit juice and seltzer. We could see the little girls in front of their houses, already dressed for the Sabbath, their hair freshly washed and combed, and shiny from the kerosene used to wash it.

At home Mother, dressed in her holiday outfit, greeted us, and we felt the house filled with a holiday atmosphere. We hurried to change from our everyday suits into special ones.

Then came the evening. About half an hour before sundown the *shames* (sexton), a short, long-bearded old man in a shabby *bekeshe* (a long, silky black coat), ran hurriedly through the streets and rapped on the house doors with a wooden hammer as a signal that the Sabbath had begun.

Our house now came to life. Everybody ran around trying to get ready to "bench the lights" (the benediction over the Sabbath candles) exactly on time. On the street one could see belated business people desperately hurrying to reach their houses for the ceremony.

Now the candles were lighted. My mother covered her head with a white kerchief, went to the table on which two covered *chales* (Sabbath bread) were placed. Also on the table were two silver candlesticks and one three-armed brass candelabrum in which candles were burning. She covered her eyes with her hands and said the blessings. For a while there was complete silence in the room; then we heard her soft voice saying "Good Sabbath."

The lighted candles within the houses shone out into the street, and the entire inner part of the city was illuminated by thousands of candles one could see glimmering through the windows.

We boys now left with Father for the synagogue. He was dressed festively in a black coat with a velvet collar and a black velvet hat. Each of us boys carried a prayer book and marched solemnly abreast of Father without exchanging a single word.

All the Jewish men of the city were assembled in the synagogue, which was aglow with candles. The faces of the people shone from beneath their velvet hats or the *Strameln* (velvet hats with squirrel tails worn on Sabbath or holidays only by orthodox Jews). The beards, which practically all the married men wore, were shiny and combed, and some were freshly trimmed. Some of the men even wore black silken coats, as festive as their mood, carefree, happy, ready for the coming Sabbath. We children, too, felt the holiness of this hour which elevated us above everyday life.

After the prayers the out-of-town beggars gathered at the exit. Father always took one of them home; he was the *oirach* (guest) for the Sabbath.

In front of our house Mother waited for us, sitting on a bench with her daughters and neighbors, discussing the hard work all of them had done in preparation for the Sabbath. When she saw us coming she would rush in ahead of us. We greeted everybody with "Good Sabbath," and, following Mother into the house, we all sat down around the table. Father poured the raisin wine into the tiny silver cups that stood next to each of our plates, and began to sing "Shalom Alaichem" (Peace be unto you), the greeting of the Sabbath angels. Next the song of "The Woman of Worth" was chanted. We children joined in the singing. Afterward Father made *Kiddush* (the blessing over the wine) and drank the wine. After him each child made the blessing and drank his wine.

Then Father poured water over his hands and spoke the blessing over the *chale* (Sabbath bread), cutting it, dipping each piece in salt, and giving everyone a piece of it. The dipping of the *chale* in salt symbolizes the salty Red Sea that divided into two parts, letting the Jews pass through on their exodus from Egypt.

My Mother served gefilte fish, which we children liked especially, followed by a wonderfully aromatic soup with noodles, then meat and dessert. Father and we children sang *Smires* (Sabbath mealtime hymns) between the courses. Tea was served last, and after it we said "After-Meal Grace."

When dinner was over, my parents liked to sit and read. My father usually had his newspaper, while my mother read a book which, when I was older, she would send me to get for her on Friday from the library. We children ate nuts and played until it was time for saying our night prayers and going to bed.

The next morning, on Saturday, after breakfast, Father again went with us boys to the synagogue. Here, sometimes, there was excitement during the morning prayers. It was an accepted custom that if anyone had any grievance against the community or any member of it he could step up to the podium just prior to the reading of the Bible, with the Holy Scrolls lying on the table on the podium. The man had the right to announce that he wouldn't let the scrolls be read until the entire congregation listened to his grievances. Everyone would sit down, and there would be grave silence in the synagogue. Everyone knew that it must be a serious grievance; otherwise no one would take the responsibility for stopping the reading of the Holy Scrolls. The grievances varied. On one occasion a friend of a widow accused the community of not taking proper care of her; on another, a man complained that a member of the community had opened a store next to his and was taking away his already meager livelihood.

I remember a time when the butcher, with his loud and raucous voice, complained that there was gossip that he cheated with his scales; that would mean to everyone, of course, that he was not true to the Jewish religion, and therefore could not be trusted to be selling truly Kosher meat. He could lose his livelihood through the rumor of dishonesty, of course, and wanted to know who was responsible for it. He wouldn't leave the podium until the community leaders promised to investigate the whole problem.

The airing of grievances was employed mainly by the poorer members of the community, because the well-to-do and influential had other means of letting the community know of their complaints. When grievances came up at the synagogue, they became the chief topic of conversaion for the whole of Saturday, and often for weeks to come. This method of laying one's problem before the community is very ancient; a description of it can be found in the Talmud of two thousand years ago.

Sometimes a *Magid* (storyteller) came to the synagogue. He spoke in fables or in instructive parables. The *Magid*'s visit and what he had said were a basis of discussion for weeks. He would go from town to town, preach in the synagogue on Saturday, and on Sunday would collect offerings from house to house. This was his livelihood.

When my father and we boys returned home at noon on Saturday Mother took the *tschulent* out of the oven. This is a type of bean and meat casserole that is cooked on Friday and kept in a hot oven until the next day. On Saturday, too, we ate a special dish, the *kugel* (round), so named because of its shape. It was normally made of macaroni and raisins or grated potatoes, and in rich homes sometimes out of rice and raisins. The *kugel* was a symbolic dish showing that in life everything is round—today one is rich; tomorrow one can be poor, or the reverse. After the meal my parents, as did all the others in the city, took their naps.

Now we children rushed out to the street to play with the neighborhood children. We were never as noisy on Saturdays as on other days, so as not to awaken our parents; moreover, we were permeated with the holiness of the day. We could play until about four o'clock.

As much as we disliked parting from our playmates on weekdays, today's parting was even worse, because we knew that the *rebbi* (religious teacher) would be waiting for us in the house, ready to test us in front our father to find out how much we had learned during the week. If we couldn't answer the *rebbi*'s questions, a good beating awaited us, followed by reproaches from my father that lasted all the next week.

After the "testing" we all visited my father's parents, for Mother's parents didn't live in the same town. Grandmother sat in front of her house in a long black dress, with a white scarf on her head, reading the Bible. When she saw us she would get up, greet us with a happy smile, and lead us into the house. Here, too, it looked different than on weekdays. The floor was scrubbed, and the table, which boasted brass candlesticks, was covered with a white tablecloth.

Grandfather, who was a tall, well-built man with a long white beard, was sitting, in his black silken coat, his *Stramel* on his head, in front of a Talmud, studying. When he saw us he would get up and invite us to the table where all my other uncles and aunts were already sitting. Grandfather would then inquire about our lessons in *cheder* and about the portion of the Bible we had studied that week. Father shone with pride when I knew the correct answers.

Then we children would go into another room, and Grandmother would give us sweets and fruits. Generally there was great fighting among us, everyone thinking that he didn't get the right share. Grandmother, who was smaller than some of her grandchildren (being a tiny four foot eight) smilingly would try to satisfy everyone. Then, the quarreling over, we would start to play while the ladies, sitting on one side of the table in the next room, conversed in low tones in order not to disturb the men, who liked to revive old memories or discuss politics. Sometimes we stopped our games and gathered around the adults to listen to their talk. Even though we usually didn't understand much of it, we felt grown-up being able to listen at all.

On Saturday evenings Grandfather and Father and the rest of the men went to the synagogue. We went home where we waited impatiently for Father's return. When he arrived, he poured wine into a cup, making *Hawdale* (meaning separation—the separation of the holy day and the workday), and so the Sabbath ended.

The festive hours are now over, and "everyday" life begins. Another week has begun. Mother now makes a fire in the oven, and my older sister Ella, who goes to school, has to do her homework.

The next day Father, as usual, will take the train from Stojanov, the name of our town, to Lvov on one of his various business enterprises.

2

STOJANOV was a little town. It had a population of about two thousand, of whom over one thousand were Jews, and it was situated about sixty miles east of Lvov. The center of the city was populated almost exclusively by Jews, while the non-Jewish population, most of them Ukrainians, lived on the outskirts.

The streets were not paved except in the center of the town where lumber boards were laid out end to end. Except for two stone houses, all the others in Stojanov were wooden ones, some of them having straw-covered roofs. Our town had one seven-year grammar school, one Roman Catholic church, one Greek Catholic church, a synagogue, a police station with a jail for a maximum of two men, and a post office. There was neither a pharmacy nor a doctor, and until 1945 there was not a single radio in the entire town. Who knows—perhaps it is still the same today. There was no industry. It was mainly farm-land, producing wheat and potatoes, some poultry, and eggs. Some timber was felled and sent to the neighboring towns to be cut into lumber.

The standard of living was very low. About 50 per cent of the Jews couldn't afford any meat except on Saturdays. The main dish for most of the people was potatoes. Quite a few people sat in darkness in the evenings because they couldn't afford kerosene for their lamps. I believe that the idea of gefilte fish was developed to make the most out of the smallest amount of fish possible; fish was quite a delicacy.

My father was a timber merchant. This was his main business, and he was an expert at it. But he also had business associations with a company that exported eggs and was a partner in a cement-pipe com-pany. In Stojanov we were one of the richest families.

My father was born in 1894. He was tall and slim and had very dark black hair. His large, penetrating brown eyes were deeply set under a high forehead, and he wore a short, pointed beard. He walked with a slight stoop. His interest in charitable organizations was great and his support of them constant. And he deeply respected learning. He be-lieved that with schooling we children could get what he had been

9

unable to but wanted so much. He respected knowledge, both religious and secular, for its own sake.

My father's father worked as manager of the timber-felling grounds in the forest. My father, at the age of twelve, went to work as an assistant to his father in the forest. During the First World War he served in the Austrian Army, and became a corporal.

In 1919 my father married and began to work as a manager at the felling grounds. The shavings from the trees that fell to the ground were sold for heating purposes. After working for a few years, my father, in addition to his salary, also obtained the right to sell the shavings.

In 1928 there was a severe winter, and wood for burning purposes was at a premium. That winter he made enough money to go into business for himself. His former employer, knowing his capabilities, went into partnership with him, and within two years my father was a controlling partner in three lumberyards in three different cities, and a sawmill factory, and was able to buy timber-felling grounds of his own. He often said with regret that his "good year" was a year when so many people were freezing from the severe cold.

His intelligence was far above average. Later on, when we moved to Lvov, my father actually designed houses for people, laying out all the plans, and mastering all the building codes. Hard-working, peaceful, never complaining, he always tried to tell us that one should be able to adjust to all circumstances in life, the hardships as well as the good times.

My mother was considered a comely woman; she had dark hair and eyes, was a little shorter and two years younger than my father, and was slightly plump. Her parents had fourteen children, of whom eleven died in their infancy. Only mother, her sister, and a brother remained alive. Her mother ran a drygoods store while her father spent his life studying the Talmud and Cabala. He had the reputation of being a great scholar, and people who knew him have told me that his knowledge of the Hebrew grammar and the Aramaic language was unsurpassed. I remember as a child hearing people say that he knew the whole Talmud and commentaries by heart. He and his family lived about seventy miles away from Stojanov, but everyone in Stojanov, as well as the other neighboring towns, knew the name of Josel Moshe Reiss from Kristonopol—of his greatness in Talmudic studies. He was one of the first orthodox Jews to go as a pioneer to Palestine, taking a group of young people there with him. That was in 1920. But after a short while he had to return to Poland because of sickness, and so, unhappily, the family never migrated to Palestine as he had hoped.

My mother was well read. I would often play in the room where she read. Sometimes she would interrupt my playing and call my attention to some part of the book she was reading which she thought would be useful for me to know. She taught me much. That I was a good student, interested in learning and reading, is surely to her credit.

But as much as she liked to read, it was hard for her to find the time for it. With seven children there was little time for relaxation. Though she had a hired girl to help, most of her time was taken up with the latest baby. The cooking, baking, shopping, serving of the meals, in addition to other tasks, remained exclusively Mother's domain.

In spite of the hard work, she was happy and thankful to God for having a big healthy family. In later years, when we moved to Lvov, all the beggars "worked" certain streets on certain days. Our street's turn came on Wednesdays. Every Wednesday morning mother would get up earlier than on other days to cook for the poor. Huge caldrons of soup were cooked, and every beggar received a plateful with some bread. Mother served as many as forty beggars; and, including her own family, she would cook for and serve fifty people on those Wednesdays. On that day we children knew we must not bother Mother too much, because this was, as she used to say, "her day." She too, had the right to do something for herself.

3

My FAMILY, as did most of the Jews in Stojanov, belonged to a religious sect called Chasidim. This sect, founded in the eighteenth century, appealed greatly to the poor, and eventually became one of the strongest movements in Eastern Europe, especially in the southern part of Poland. Chasidim, a kind of Judaic Renaissance, taught the enjoyment of life and the belief that the greatness of God can't be appreciated by constantly sitting in a room studying the Talmud. One should go out into the forests and gardens to enjoy the beauty of nature. Through this His greatness can be seen. Chasidim taught that "Everything that comes from the heart will reach the hearts of other people." The phrase "a Jew in heart" was often repeated to us children, and it meant a feeling for your fellowmen. Emotion was above knowledge.

As a child, my mother often told me the story of an orphan boy who became a shepherd. He was poor and uneducated and couldn't even read from the prayer book. He was never taught about God; but, spending all his time in the fields, he felt God through nature. Whistling tunes and playing a variety of melodies on his flute was his way of praying.

Once, during the High Holy Days, according to this story of my mother's, the entire town was in the synagogue, praying. But something was wrong. The wise men felt that the prayers were not being received by God and that the doors of heaven were closed to the Jewish community. Everyone was silent. Fear pervaded the synagogue. What would this mean? Disaster for the community in the year to come? At this point the simple shepherd boy entered the synagogue. Sensing the disquiet of the community, he began to pray in the only way he knew, by whistling. The entire community was shocked by this act of sacrilege in a place of worship. But the rabbi's face lightened and he called out, "Let us rejoice; with his whistling that comes from the depth of this boy's heart, the gates of heaven are opened, and our prayers have gone through to God." And so, it was believed, this boy saved his community.

Another Chasidic belief was that if one looks deep enough he can find good in every human being. We were told of the Jew who was rid-

13

ing a horse and smoking a cigarette on the Sabbath. These are two heavy and shocking sins according to the orthodox law. A pious one approached the man and said to him, "You are probably committing these sins because you forgot that it is the Sabbath."

"No," the man answered.

"Then you are probably riding to a doctor and smoking a cigarette to quiet your nerves which have been jangled by pain," continued the pious one.

"No, I don't care about religion," came the answer.

The pious one then raised his eyes toward heaven and said: "See, God, how holy your people are. Even a lie they won't tell."

Other stories already written in the Talmud were greatly stressed in the Chasidic philosophy. One, for example, was the legend of the "thirty-six." It held that there are thirty-six pious men, thanks to whom God does not destroy the world. No one knows who these "thirty-six" are, but it is known that they are among the poor and the meek and that they have a deep and vast knowledge but appear to the people to be simple and plain. The moral of this story was: Don't look down on the poor man who seems to have no learning, and don't turn away a beggar, because it might be by their grace that you are alive. Either may be one of the thirty-six.

This Talmudic story found a modern counterpart in tales we learned about the founder of the Chasidic movement. He was called the Baal Shem Tov—the Master of God's Name. We were told that he was an orphan and that as a young boy he worked as a "helper" to a religious teacher. Since children began in religious schools at the age of three, such a helper often had to carry the young ones on his back to and from school, especially in bad weather. The teacher himself was usually one of the poorest people of the town, so one can imagine the utter poverty of such a helper. The Baal Shem Tov at length married a village innkeeper's daughter, one of the simplest and most untutored girls one could imagine. He became the innkeeper, and slowly the inn became a pilgrimage place. He performed miracles, and gave sage advice, and the story is told that when he died there were forty thousand converts to his philosophy.

The Baal Shem Tov's closest students became spiritual leaders after his death and actually set up rabbinical dynasties in different cities. The leadership of each dynasty was passed on from father to son.

These Chasidic leaders had a tremendous influence in our lives. If one of us were very sick, or couldn't make up his mind about a business deal, or if a woman were barren—whatever serious problem one might have—one went to these rabbis for help. We had implicit faith in them.

I remember that when I was eleven, I was taken by my father to the rabbi of Belz, a town near Lvov, to get his blessing. I stood in line from seven in the evening until three in the morning. When I finally got in, the rabbi shook hands and said, "God bless you," and the audience was over. It was swift, but it was enough.

We loved Chasidim, with its emphasis on the goodness of the heart of man. As young people we liked to hear Chasidic stories and legends. They made us feel grown up; they were religious stories always with a moral. We children would relate them to each other, and never got tired of hearing them again.

They weren't the only stories we children were told. We were also told about the hungry wolves in the woods that attack people, about the gypsies who steal children and raise them as their slaves. And the fact that gypsies used to set up their tents each summer on the outskirts of our town lent credibility to these tales. There were also stories about "lost souls" who were embodied in cats, mice, or rats, and as such came to the synagogue at midnight to pray. These souls were said to have tortured animals during their lives.

The better educated women liked to read and discuss poetry. When our parents were in school our part of Poland belonged to Austria, and the language that they were educated in was German. The poets most often discussed were Schiller, Goethe, and Heine. The hearts of the women went out to Heine. He was pitied rather than condemned for renouncing his Jewish religion, and the women liked to recite those of his poems that sounded most tragic, especially the poem where he wrote:

> "Nor the Holy Mass will be sung,
> Neither Kaddish [Jewish mourning prayer] will be said,
> Nor will it be sung,
> Neither will it be said
> At the moment of my death."

Songs, also, were a very important part of our life. Singing and rejoicing were part of the Chasidic credo. Whatever elevated one's spirit was considered "food for the soul"; including good melodies, snuff, dancing, a drink of vodka for all sorts of occasions, such as births and weddings; or, if someone were very sick, one had to bring a bottle of vodka and a cake to the synagogue. After prayers, everyone, rich or poor, got a small glass of vodka and a piece of cake. We all would wish the donor much happiness, the speedy recovery of his loved one—or whatever the occasion called for. If the donor gave the vodka because of a happy occasion, the men sang, and very often danced in a circle, rolling their eyes as if they were trying to enter another world, a world of pure joy. It used to be said, "What could be a better deed than to make a congregation, even for a short while, happy?"

All kinds of music delighted us, and a man with a good voice was very much looked up to. Or if a man had composed some small melody on a religious theme, he might sing it himself on the Sabbath or Holy Days at the synagogue, and the whole town would discuss the new composition.

The women, in addition to the religious songs, liked the more worldly ones. These varied from love songs about a Prince Charming to those with social themes. The songs came to Stojanov from the big cities, where streetsingers had made them popular, singing them and also selling sheets printed with words of the song for a few cents. If anyone brought such a sheet to Stojanov, it would pass from house to house, and be copied, while the melody would spread from mouth to mouth.

I remember one new song a young girl brought back from Lvov after a trip there. It was called "Srulek." She came over to our house on a Saturday afternoon, and all our neighbors got together to listen to the new song. It told the story of a young boy—Srulek—born to a poor Jewish tailor. How happy the father was as he watched Srulek grow up! The son became a rich man and married a girl from "high society." The father wasn't invited to the wedding, so he stood under a window outside the house, looking at this big wedding and saying: "You are rich today. I am only a poor Jew, but I wish you much luck, my dear Srulek."

Tears streamed down the women's cheeks, and their faces were filled with pleasure as they listened to this new song and nodded their heads, implying, surely this can happen. Looking at these women, one could understand how some people receive pleasure through pain.

The kinds of songs that were most popular in Stojanov were those that gave one the deep pleasure of a good cry.

4

THERE WERE seven children in my family. First to come was my eldest sister, Ellen Lea. She was born in November, 1923. She was a sensitive, quiet child, liked to study and read a lot, and seldom played with us. I was the next one, born on March 10, 1925. My brother Aaron was fourteen months younger than I. He was a timid and weak child and didn't want to study. Three years later came Jacob Michael, the rugged individualist of the group. Later, each about fourteen months apart, came the two blond and blue-eyed girls, Rachela and Judith, and at last delicate Bina.

In spite of the many arguments which naturally occur among children, we were a very close-knit family and truly loved each other.

It was the custom (dating back to Talmudistic times) to let the boys' hair grow until about the age of three, and then to have it cut off communally on the thirty-third day from the first day of Passover. At the age of three, exactly on his birthday, a boy started *cheder* (religious school). I was no exception. Together with ten or twelve other children, I was, from three on, taught how to pray and to read Hebrew. Those lessons took place in the home of the teacher, an old long-bearded Jew. The house consisted of one large room. On two sides stood beds, in the middle a long table. On one side of the table was a long bench and on the other side the bed was used to sit up on. The teacher sat at the head of the table; in another corner was the stove, where the teacher's wife busied herself cooking, washing laundry, or feeding the baby. In wintertime the goat was kept inside, too.

We all feared our teacher. He kept his *kantshug* (whip) ready at hand at all times. When we didn't understand quickly enough, he put his *kantshug* to use. I must admit that I wasn't whipped too often, as I liked to study and was mostly ahead of my study group. Some children were constantly up to some mischief, and felt the teacher's whip often.

Once, a boy, sitting on the bed, took out his small penknife and cut a hole in the big feather pillow. All the feathers flew around the room and even into the soup that was cooking on the stove. The teacher's beard was white with feathers. The *kantshug* was in use that day.

About the middle of January there is a Holy Day called "Fifteenth Day of *Shwat*." This holiday is the "New Year for the Trees"; it is the day the trees in Israel are supposed to start blooming. On this holiday it is the custom to eat various fruits. In our *cheder* the teacher arranged a party for the Saturday afternoon nearest to the Fifteenth Day of *Shwat*. Every child contributed a few pennies and the teacher bought some prunes which were cooked on Friday and kept in the oven until Saturday when the day came. We children sat around the table dressed in our Saturday outfits, waiting for the big moment. The room was cleaned up. The table was covered with a white cloth, and in front of everyone was a small glass plate. The teacher in his black silken coat, for once without his *kantshug* nearby, stood, looking very serious, at the head of the table. We all followed him in the singing-chanting voice used for the blessing. After the blessing the teacher went over with his dignified, slow "Saturday walk" to the oven to get the pot of stewed prunes. He brought it over to the table. There was an expectant silence. The teacher uncovered the pot, and his face bloomed red. We immediately knew something had happened. In the pot, except for a few prune pits, there was nothing but juice. It soon became obvious that the teacher's daughter, about nine years old, who slept near the oven, had eaten it up during the night. Right there and then in front of us all she got a good beating, and with her screaming the "party" came to an end.

The little girl was our teacher's child by his first wife, who had died when she gave birth to her. It was not unusual for such poor people to have eight or ten children, the first few coming from a mother who would finally die in childbirth. Then the husband would remarry and have more. It is amazing that such children, in spite of deprivation and hardship, often grew up with deeply sensitive natures. When, later, during my wanderings in 1942, I met this same girl, the teacher's daughter, she was married to a man who had four children by a wife who had died in childbirth, too. She lived about forty miles from Stojanov, and she was very happy to see a "student of her father." She talked about her "great, pious" father with deep love and respect. I was made to feel very welcome in her house simply because I had been her father's student. Her father by that time had been killed by the Germans. While I was listening to her talk, I saw him in front of me, his patriarchal beard, his kind eyes, and I could hear the low singsong of this poor man who, in spite of his hard work, could barely supply his family with bread and soup.

Time passed, interrupted by the excitements of "growing up," Holy Days, and "additions" to our family.

When I was five, I became the "big boy." On winter days, as an "older student," my religious schooling started in the afternoons, and by six o'clock, when school was over, it would be dark. We made our own lanterns, we students, against the darkness. Each would cut the insides out of a big pumpkin; small windows were carved, a candle was placed inside, and a string tied around it for carrying. There was competition among the boys for the best lantern. Everything had to be done by the boys themselves, even to selecting and then picking his pumpkin. The very first night, going home from school in the total darkness, seeing the road only by the glow of the candle, I felt really grown up; my pumpkin lantern took away all the fears of the dark.

At the age of six I began public school. Normally the starting age was seven; so, during my school years, I was always one of the youngest in my class.

In the middle of March, 1933, a few days after my eighth birthday, we children were surprised by the announcement from my father that he had bought a house in Lvov and that we were going to move there soon. My father began to look for a buyer for the house in Stojanov. But when he found one, and everything was settled, our next-door neighbor suddenly told us he didn't like these new people. The neighbor took my father to the rabbi, who decided that we must sell the house to people acceptable to the neighbor but that in case the next buyer should pay less than the first one would have, the difference must be equally shared between my father and the neighbor. The house was sold a few days later, and packing and preparing for the move were begun.

Mother told us children about life in the big city, about the electric lights, streetcars, running water, elevators, and similar things we couldn't even imagine.

The day of departure arrived. On a nice Sunday afternoon the whole family went to the railroad station, where we left by train for Lvov—to our new home—a new life.

The trip was very exciting; it was our first trip on a train. In the evening we arrived in Lvov and went to a hotel to sleep. Next morning my father, my sister, and I walked to our new house. My mother, with the other children, came later by taxi.

I was very much disappointed by the big city. The people, the streets, and even the horses somehow looked sad; nothing was as it had been in Stojanov. We approached our new home. It was a two-story building. Our apartment was on the second floor and it had three large rooms and a kitchen. The house, of which my father was now the landlord, had six apartments in addition to our own, and each consisted of one room and a kitchen. The families living in these apartments had between two and four children. The people belonged to the middle-income class. The poor ones couldn't afford such "big" apartments in a nice house like ours.

A week later I started school. In Lvov the public schools in strictly Jewish neighborhoods were attended by Jewish pupils only, and of course had Saturdays off. We lived in a "mixed" neighborhood and on the border of an exclusive non-Jewish one, and so we had to go to a non-Jewish school, and had to attend on Saturday. In our class there were about fifty pupils, of which about six were Jewish. My father came to an agreement with the principal that while I would attend school on Saturday, I wouldn't have to write on that day. I was often beaten up by the non-Jewish pupils while some of my teachers looked the other way.

My father, and everyone else, knowing that a small minority cannot fight force with force, repeatedly told me, "A Jew doesn't fight." When I pointed out that I was strong and not afraid, the answer was, "How about the other Jewish boys who may not be as strong as you are?" It would be pointed out that violence could sometimes lead to a pogrom. Every Jew, we were told, is responsible for all other Jews.

I finished one term only, and for the next one was enrolled in a private Jewish school.

In 1938 I took the entrance examination to the Gymnasium (high school), which I passed very easily. Now a new period started in my life. The Gymnasium was a co-ed school, and all the students wore dark-blue uniforms with light blue stripes at all times, even out of school. On the left arm we wore a light-blue heart-shaped emblem on which was embroidered, with silver thread, the school number. We were Number 213. The school hours were normally from 8:00 A.M. to 2:00 P.M. I also studied in a higher Talmudistic school—Yeshiva—from 3:00 to 8:00 P.M., and six days a week, except Saturdays. On returning home at eight-thirty in the evening, I had dinner alone. Then I did my homework, which normally required one and a half hours. To catch up with my Yeshiva work I studied on Saturdays and on the Holy Days when there were no classes. I enjoyed studying. At the age of thirteen, I knew by heart 130 pages of one of the most difficult parts of the Talmud, in its complicated Babylonian-Hebrew language. I believe this rigid training gave me the desire for learning in my later years.

5

In the summer of 1939 I finished my first year of Gymnasium with good marks. My elder sister and I then spent three weeks of our summer vacation at my uncle's in Grzymalow, a handsome city with many parks and beautiful avenues. It never occurred to anybody that these would be the final carefree weeks we should ever know. It was the last time that I was to see my cousins, my uncle, and my aunt.

This was my first vacation without my parents; it was a high point in the closing chapter of this part of my life. After our return, general mobilization began.

There was no chance to share the excitement of our vacation. The look of the city had changed. People were depressed. A dark, heavy cloud of uncertainty seemed to hang over everyone.

On the evening of August 30th there was a complete blackout. For the young it meant only something new, a change, excitement. In the night the air-raid alarms were tested, and everyone ran to the basement. We were all told that a gas mask would be the most important thing in the "next war." Everyone was warned about gas bombs and told what to do if they fell. The basement of our house, our "air-raid shelter," was sealed up so that only the minimum outside air could come in. Most people knew that near the end of the First World War the Germans had used gas bombs on the French front.

Next day, column on column of our soldiers went marching through the town. They were all carrying gas masks in addition to the other supplies. The streets were full of people, mothers, wives, and sweethearts crying, throwing flowers. Others from time to time cried out "To Berlin!" One could sense from the tone of the voice that there was no belief that Polish soldiers would ever get "To Berlin."

On the night of August 31st, there was a blackout again. There were more test "air raids," but no one went down to the shelter that night. One night of "no sleep" was enough.

Next morning, September 1, 1939, the radio announced the German attack on Poland. At nine in the morning the sirens announced an actual air raid. Nothing happened, and many people could not believe that we were actually at war.

That night, around eleven, the real enemy air attack began. Bombs fell, and fires broke out all over the town. Now no one doubted that the war was real.

We were raided nightly, and then on the fourth night a tremendous air raid occurred at midnight. Everyone in the house ran down to the basement. While the men tried to look brave, the women were crying, pressing their children to them. In a few minutes we heard the noise of planes and the detonations of bombs. The house and the ground vibrated, and we heard the cracking of window glass and the crash of collapsing houses. At one point a woman yelled "gas." The hysteria became indescribable. Others started to smell it, and began choking. It took quite a while to quiet the crying children and the women, to convince them that this was a false alarm. The biggest air raid so far went on for several hours; then, suddenly, it was over.

When we came upstairs and looked out, it seemed as if the whole town were on fire.

For the three days preceding this tremendous raid the radio had played sad music, announcing only every so often the course of the heroic battle the Polish soldiers were putting up against the Germans at Westplate, near the German border. On the fourth day the radio announced that the last soldier had fallen there and that the Germans had taken it over.

The day after the raid my parents decided to leave Lvov and return to Stojanov. With much difficulty my father found a Polish farmer who owned a horse and a wagon and who agreed to take us, and some of our belongings, to Stojanov. As we left town the entire city was still ablaze. Our neighbors looked at us with reproachful eyes, implying that we were deserting them.

Our driver was frightened. En route, he neither ate nor drank. He cried, and kept repeating that he wanted to get back to his family.

We drove steadily on through the night. The next morning, having arrived at a city eight miles from Stojanov, the driver decided that he would not take us any farther. Talking and pleading didn't help any, so my father went in search of another driver with a horse and wagon. He found one, and by lunchtime we arrived in Stojanov.

We moved into my grandparents' house, which by no means had enough space to accommodate us, but somehow we managed. There was never an air raid on Stojanov.

The first round of the war was nearing an end. Day and night

Polish soldiers passed through Stojanov in the direction of Rumania. They were in full flight. The Jews knew from past experience that during governmental changeovers, while the city was without law enforcement, there were always pogroms and plunderings. Therefore we started to prepare some shelters and hiding places to survive the "changeover" period and to bury our valuables, such as silverware, clothing, jewels, and so on.

There were many rumors as to what the fate of our town would be. Some people said that the Russians were going to occupy those Polish territories that had been under them until the First World War. This would have excluded Stojanov and would have meant subjection by the Germans. Our suspense was soon over, however. The Red Army marched into the city, and the changeover went very smoothly and peacefully.

The Russian soldiers were extremely friendly, though they wouldn't get involved in any discussions. They would trade *machorvke* (very coarse Russian tobacco) for things they wanted. They also brought with them many newspapers, pamphlets with articles about Communism, Lenin's and Stalin's speeches, pictures of Stalin, Lenin, Kalinin, Molotov, Beria, and so on. The soldiers, as well as the officers, though not elegantly dressed, were neat and clean and behaved well. People, remembering the Russian soldiers of 1919 and that then they were called "the barefoot ones" because of their lack of shoes, were pleasantly surprised by the complete change in the Russian Army. The fact that these soldiers again and again repeated that they believed in the equality of every man immediately won them the respect of the minorities. Left-wing Polish groups now began to point out that Communist justice was superior to the capitalist concept of justice. Little did they know.

Everything was peaceful and orderly. We couldn't find out anything from the soldiers about life in Russia. Their answer to every question was, "U nas wsho i mnogo." (We have everything, much of it.) When, as a joke, we would ask, in Jewish, if in Russia they had *zures* (trouble) the soldier, without even understanding the word, would answer, "U nas wsho i mnogo."

A few days after the entry of the Russian Army, the stores in Stojanov opened again. The soldiers immediately started to buy everything and anything without regard to cost. This caused prices to soar, and soon the store owners began to hide their merchandise for speculation. A soldier would come into a store to buy a bar of chocolate. When he got it, he would ask if he could buy a second bar. After he got the second bar he would look around to see if anyone from the army was around, and then, in a low voice, would ask if he could get a whole box.

In late September, 1939, we returned to Lvov. By this time the Russian Army had taken over there, too. The city was peaceful, and we found our home in order just as we left it. In view of the new social and economic system, with little knowledge of what this new system represented, one thing was sure, and that was that owning an apartment house and a lumberyard would not be an advantage.

Slowly life started to become normal under the Russian system. Socialization of the new territories, Russian-style, progressed rapidly. Four weeks after the entrance of the Red Army, everyone over sixteen had to get a passport. These passports were given out for a five-year period, after which they were renewed. On certain passports so-called "paragraphs" were stamped. According to these paragraphs, one could tell if he were one of the "favored" people. It was said that those with unfavorable paragraphs would not in the future be allowed to live within a radius of sixty miles of the German border; they were considered to be security risks.

There were many Jewish refugees, especially men from German-occupied Poland, who got passports with unfavorable paragraphs. The same thing happened to the "capitalists," as well as to people who had been members of certain political parties before the war.

Nationalization of private property began. First to be nationalized were big businesses and apartment houses. The nationalization was, we were informed, "voluntary." When the officials came to our house, my father, without a question, signed the house over to the government. There was a "chief" superintendent for about twenty-five houses, and every three houses had their own individual superintendent. My father became the superintendent of his own and two neighboring houses. Everyone living in apartment houses had to be registered, and no outsider was allowed to stay overnight without permission and registration at the nearest militia post. There were night inspections by the militia to check on whether any unregistered people lived in these apartments.

The time was changed to "Moscow Time." All moved their clocks two hours ahead so that no one would say they were counterrevolutionary. The new time didn't fit our geographical location.

Very soon, except for a few small items, one couldn't buy anything except by queuing up. For a loaf of bread, the normal time in line was two to three hours. For two pounds of sugar it could be four to five hours. Because the price of sugar on the black market was twenty-five times the official price, there were "professional" linestanders, experts at pushing their way to the front of a line. With drygoods and shoes the situation was at its worst. Normally, people started to line up in the evening for the next day. But it would have been poor propaganda to admit that people had to stand in line all night for a pair of shoes, so police on horseback would disperse the crowd; when they rode away, the people would run back into line and the militia would return to disperse them again. Often this would go on till midnight; at other times, till six in the morning. Even if one stood up all night in the line and most of the next day, he wasn't sure to get anything, because by the time he got into the store there might be nothing left. At other times the black market "professionals" would stand at the end of the line and start pushing. The line would start to bulge, and people would fall out of it and then not be let back in. Soon the "professionals" would be in front of everyone.

More and more Russians, with their wives and families, began arriving at Lvov. There were either the families of top officers or of high-ranking party members who had come to take over our industries. They had their own supply stores. On the black market they would buy anything they could afford. The women would buy nightgowns and wear them as evening dresses; even at this "high" level they were so unused to consumer goods they could not tell the difference.

In the schools collections were taken up for MOPR (International Organization for the Support of Revolution). We were told the money would go to poor children in the United States, and we were shown headlines from American papers stating that four million were unemployed. We interpreted this as meaning four million families were dying of hunger in America.

Strikes are not allowed in Russia, for, after all, everything belongs to the people, and how can anyone strike against himself? To make sure that no one sabotaged the "people's property," the law read that if one were over fifteen minutes late to work more than three times, one could get a jail sentence. The working week was forty-eight hours, but very often after working hours one had to attend a political rally. Before Russia's national holidays, such as May 1st, or October 7th, the people, after working hours, had to prepare slogans, posters, and large banners for the members of the parade, which was usually a whole-day affair. One also had to march in the parade.

I remember when I once came back dead tired from marching in a parade, I found my father relaxing on the couch. When I asked him why he was already home, looking so relaxed, he told me that while marching in the parade, carrying a heavy poster of Lenin, he stepped out to a public lavatory, left the poster there, and disappeared through the other door. The big problem was not how to get out of the parade, but how to get rid of the poster.

For something like that, one could have been sent to Siberia as a counterrevolutionist.

After a while my father lost his superintendent's job. It was given to a more "trustworthy" person. My father then got a position as manager of a notions store. Many items allocated to the store never reached the customer. They went straight to the black market. The proceeds from such items on the black market were split between the "trustworthy" general manager of all the notions stores and my father. This was a universal practice among store managers for several reasons. In the first place one couldn't live for more than a few days on the monthly salary one got. Second, the general manager had to make a living, too. And, finally, if you wouldn't go along (risking five years in Siberia for black marketeering), the general manager would refuse to assign supplies to your store; if there were no supplies, the store, of course, would have no turnover and would soon be closed down. Against the general manager one could do nothing, because he usually was a Communist party member sent to Lvov from Moscow or Kiev.

We accepted the economic as well as the other limitations by trying to make the best of circumstances. We got used to the lines for bread and sugar, and the strict travel limitations which had been imposed. As for freedom of speech, people stopped talking politics, even pro-Soviet politics, and stopped reading the newspapers. The best thing was to be as ignorant as possible.

In April, 1940, about eight months after the Russians arrived, nightly arrests of the "enemies of the people" began. These, of course, were so-called former capitalists, such as factory and real estate owners. Some of these "capitalists" were poorer than some of the workers. In this "enemy of the people" category, former officers, refugees from western Poland, policemen, and all kinds of political party leaders were also included.

The militia would come, always in the night, to arrest the men. Then a few days later the militia would come again in the night and take away the rest of the family. Shortly after their arrest, all were loaded into animal trains and sent to Siberia. The details of their arrests and their further fate is described in Part IV of this book.

During the arrests of the heads of the families, my father and I hid every night in our basement, for we did not know whether we belonged to the "capitalistic" group or not. When we found that our families would be arrested too, we gave up hiding, for we did not want to be separated; and to hide our whole family, seven children and two parents, would have been impossible.

During this period all of us would sit up all night, dressed, packed, so that if they came to take us away, at least we'd have with us all the essentials for the "trip." This went on for a few weeks. Then the arrests quieted down.

In a few cases it happened that whole classes in the upper grades of a school were taken away. This, in addition to the night-long tension of waiting, really put a great strain on the people. On the other hand, not sending the older children to school, for fear they might be on the "enemy of the people" list, could prove even more dangerous, and antagonize the government by implying the schools were not safe.

Though everyone knew about the trainloads of men, women, and children going to Siberia, officially it was only a "local resettlement," and no one dared to talk about it.

From West Poland, which was under German occupation, we had no official information. We heard from a few people that though there were some labor camps and ghettos, most of the men, after a hard day's work, were allowed to return home in the evenings. Some of the men refugees who had left their families to escape the hard labor the Germans imposed on Jews decided now to return to their families instead of facing Siberia.

The "action" against the "enemies of the people" lasted only a few weeks. It was over by the end of April, 1940, and life went back to "normal." In the autumn there was an election. All the candidates were on a single ballot. You had no choice. There was a big publicity campaign with pictures of the candidates all over the city. Registration was not necessary, since everyone had been permanently registered when the Russians came in. On election day people were already in line to vote at six in the morning, though the polls did not open till seven o'clock. The first people in the line were those who felt that they were none too popular with the regime. Not voting could mean being counterrevolutionary.

All of us began getting new "values" in life. Being "happy" could now mean you had had a successful day in the sugar queue, or that you had not been interrupted by the police during the night. Above all, we were satisfied as long as the family was together. We children continued our school. Some of us had ambitions—to become professionals or scientists, the groups that were not only the most respected but also the highest-salaried. To give some comparison of incomes: a store manager's salary was about 200 rubles a month; an engineer's salary was 1,200 to 1,500 rubles. In addition, engineers got their supplies through special stores, without waiting in lines. They were also given bigger and better apartments, and many other fringe benefits.

Schooling was not only free, but at the university one's scholarship could be as high as an average worker's salary. Getting into the university was a matter of merit, and there was no racial, religious, or social discrimination.

In 1941 my older sister and I made an application to take a special examination to enter the Technical Institute in Moscow, and we were accepted by the local department of the Ministry of Culture. All our papers were sent to Moscow for final approval, but it was more or less a formality. It was then June, 1941. We looked forward to our studies in Moscow, which would begin in September, with great enthusiasm, and with the sense of a new adventure opening up ahead of us.

PART II

Time
of
Tragedy

6

IT IS SUNDAY, June 22, 1941. We are still asleep. Suddenly I am awakened by artillery fire. My immediate reaction is to close my eyes and to try to get back to sleep. But the din continues steadily. I sit up in bed and glance at the clock. It is still very early, five o'clock Moscow Time. My mother, seeing that I am now awake, calls me to join her at the open window. My father is already standing there, and so also is my eldest sister. Their gaze is directed at the sky, as if they are expecting something there. Full of curiosity, I join them. There is nothing to be seen. One hears only the droning of airplane engines and the rattling fire of antiaircraft batteries. Somewhat uneasily my mother asks me what it means. Is it merely practice or war? I peer out through the window and leave her question unanswered.

Gradually activity becomes evident in the street outside. People go hurriedly toward the center of town. Their chatter is agitated. No one has definite information.

Outside the grocery store queues have already formed. People are anxious to lay in supplies against they know not what. A few passersby laugh the idea off. "One shot and the whole town goes running for grub! Why don't you get sense? It is you who are setting the place topsy-turvy with your panic."

It is now 6:00 A.M. I must join my father on his way to work. Outside, I am amazed to find the street suddenly filled with the military. Tanks line behind tanks; vehicles stand bumper to bumper. Countless soldiers are standing around or running about. Slowly the thought takes shape in my mind. "This is the beginning of a new war."

Am I afraid? I just don't know. The turn of events has taken me so much by surprise, and the overnight change is so incredible, that I can't give an accurate account of my feelings at that moment.

With difficulty we make our way nearer to my father's place of work and see that here, too, a queue has long since formed. The people are waiting for the shop to open.

My father gives me two rubles and sends me to the baker's, as my mother hasn't time to take her place in the queue. Here, too, there is an immense crowd waiting. At last the shop doors are opened. The

33

people storm in in a confused and heaving mass, jostling one another and making an unbearable din. Against the clatter of smashed window-panes, one distinguishes the helpless cry of the shopkeeper: "That's enough, that's enough! The shop can't hold any more!" Quite a long time elapses, however, until it dawns on the crowd that a bit of order and discipline will get things moving much faster. They finally draw themselves up in orderly fashion and each one gets 2.2 pounds of bread. Joyfully I carry the booty back to my father.

Nothing can now stop me from going to the center of town to find out what really is afoot. But there, too, nobody knows precisely. Opinion is still sharply divided. "War," say some. "Practice," declare others; but neither side can produce proof.

Then, about ten o'clock in the morning, the hours of uncertainty are brought to an end. Radio Moscow brings the numbing announcement that, during the night, the Germans have crossed the border and invaded Russia.

At two o'clock in the afternoon, Lvov is bombed. When evening comes, no one dares to set foot outside his own house. We lie on the sofa, still fully dressed. Mother and Father have no thought whatever of going to sleep. In the street outside, it is dark, as the lamps have not been lighted tonight. Then the air-raid sirens sound again. All dash to the air-raid shelter: the earth is already trembling. The light goes out. The window panes burst asunder. The doorframes are blown out. A bomb has fallen on the street directly outside our house. So passes the first night of war.

Next day it becomes common knowledge that the Russians will withdraw from Lvov. On the streets one sees them already forming up in preparation for their departure. Gradually the scene grows quiet again. Toward evening, however, shooting is heard—fascist Ukrainians have turned their fire on the retreating Russians.

A few Jews tried to leave with the Russians. They were the ones who were in the Communist party. (It was hard to leave with the army—the retreating Russians did not have a chance to evacuate their own troops completely.) Others even thought that the changeover to German domination would be for the better. Their reasoning went as follows: What had been done, indeed, to the Jews in Germany? Their belongings had been confiscated. The men had been put into labor camps. Hard work. Cleaning streets, wearing Jewish stars. The women and children had been forced to move into smaller apartments. Some pogroms. But if anyone could get a visa to another country, he was still free to leave Germany, in many cases even taking his household belongings with him. One might have a chance to start a new life.

But under the Russians, too, everything had been taken away. Our accommodations had been restricted—nine people in two rooms. My father, as well as others, cleaned the streets "voluntarily," through fear of being penned with wife and children in livestock wagons and sent to Siberia. Everyone was then sure that Hitler would lose the war within two years. Hence one would rather endure real hardship for the present than to be sent to Siberia, to be lost in that wilderness forever. I mentioned before that there were Jews who, in 1939, fled from the German conquest of West Poland to the Russian side, and who had escaped back to the Germans in 1940. Anyone talking about the Nazi crematoria at that time would have been laughed at. The Germans were considered the most civilized people in the world.

By Tuesday, two days after the first German onslaught, we thought things had returned to normal. But Friday brought a still heavier air raid. The city was no longer protected by antiaircraft guns. Bombs showered down relentlessly. We no longer had water. An ominous new chapter had opened in our lives.

On Monday, June 30, 1941, the Germans march into Lvov. Many cheer the incoming soldiers. We Jews know that hard times are in store for us, but no one guesses what horror is ahead. Hardly anybody will venture into the streets. Now and again a solitary individual appears, his head bent, edging his way along in the shadows of the houses. Jews who have formerly worn beards now shave them off, either completely or in part. Unless it's absolutely unavoidable, we, too, will not leave the house in the next few days.

The other occupants of our house join us in our apartment. The time is passed in discussing politics and in making conjectures as to our immediate future. But not one among us can indicate with the slightest authority what our fate is to be.

Across the street from us a German patrol has put an end to the plunder of Hazet, a candy factory. Two Jews are put to work to get things in order again. In uneasy anticipation, both of them—and indeed others besides them—wait to see what will happen when the work is finished. Finally, the tension ends; they are rewarded with chocolate and sweets that remained over in the factory. Then they leave for home.

One assumes, accordingly, that anti-Semitism is not such a threat.

We shall, of course, be forced to work, and shall have to sacrifice some of our freedom, but we shall at least live. And one day the war will end.

On Tuesday, in our part of the city, everything is just as it was on the previous day. The men again collect in some house or other, play cards, and discuss politics. Today, however, they have reason to feel unsettled. For, beginning as mere rumors, and gradually assuming authority, has come the dreaded news that persecution of the Jews has begun in the city; they are being beaten, arrested, murdered. House-to-house interrogation has begun; whole families have been taken out; the pogrom is, apparently, being carried out by Ukrainians. We sit around in suspense, keeping a conversation going, while, outside, many who have gone into town today will come back no more. None of us dares to face up to the truth.

But news of the formation of a Ukrainian militia removes any further doubt. The persecution is now in full swing, and goes on relentlessly all day Wednesday; but for the present we are left in peace.

Then comes Thursday. Seated in the living room, I am trying to concentate on reading a book. Suddenly my mother rushes in, extremely upset, exclaiming: "The Ukrainian militia have arrested your brother Aaron. He was out on the balcony!" Shaken as I am, I try to console her. "It'll be all right—they'll make him work but he'll be back again by the evening." I myself would welcome a chance to do some work. Sitting around and waiting is exhausting. On the other hand, though, it seems inadvisable to go ahead and offer my services voluntarily. Before long the doubts I have are dispelled.

It was just two hours after my brother's arrest that the Ukrainian militia came to our house. There were two of them. Standing outside the front door they shouted, "How many men are in there?" Without waiting for an answer, they burst into the outside room. I myself was in the second room. My father, who had been ill and in a weak condition for the past two weeks, was in bed in the third room. The two militiamen entered the room where I was. "Identity card!" one demanded. "He is too young," exclaimed the other. "Where would he get an identity card?" Those who, not being of the necessary age, had no personal identity card were not recruited for work. I had one, however. It had been issued two months earlier. There was no point in hiding the fact. It was obvious to me that sooner or later it would be brought to light. "So he has one all right!" said one to the other in Ukrainian, and then to me, "Come on!"

"You'll have to eat something first," my mother said to me, and in obvious distress she pointed to the meal already set on the table. "There's no need to," answered one of the Ukrainians; "he'll be back shortly."

They searched about to see if anyone had hidden himself on their arrival, and finally went into the third room. Here they saw my father lying in bed.

"What's wrong with you—sick?"

"Yes," answered my father.

"Doctor's certificate?"

"I haven't any."

"Get up, then. Come on!"

As my father made no move to rise, one of them drew his revolver. My father got up, gave the men his identity card, and came along with us as we went down the stairs and onto the street. Weeping, my mother stayed in the room behind us.

We went along Piastow Street. The militia entered each house, and returned after a few minutes with the male occupants to where we, unsupervised, stood waiting. They well knew that no one, having handed up his identity card, would dare to escape. On the assumption that this would go on for another two hours or more, none of us was prompted to try anything unpleasant.

Gradually we worked our way nearer to the Ukrainian militia buildings, which stood in an open railed-off space at the corner of Chodkiewska and Zolkiewska Streets. We entered the yard. We saw a crowd of men already assembled there, all over thirty years of age, and separated into groups of five. We, too, were now divided up. The older men, among them my father, were also separated into small groups.

The younger men, including myself, were led through the front entrance of the building and down the cellar steps. Terrible cries rang out in the cellar and filled me with apprehension. The cellar was divided into a number of rooms. We were lined up by our Ukrainian captors before the door of one such room. One of them commanded us to proceed into the room. We stepped over the threshold, and as we did so, each one was punched indiscriminately by our guards.

A spectacle such as we could never have dreamed of awaited us. A huge heap of men, one lying on top of the other, lay helpless on the floor of the room. Militia men with truncheons in their hands moved among them. At first I thought that the men on the floor must be corpses and that we had been fetched to carry them out. The story had indeed got around that the Russians, prior to their withdrawal, had shot all the inmates in the city jail, as well as in the small police jails. It is true that inmates were shot in the main jail, but by whom and whether all or only a number of them, I don't know. This basement had been used before as a temporary jail—which explains my immediate belief that the men here were dead. In this confused state, I reached for the foot of one of them in order to draw him out of the heap. As I did so, a savage blow on the head stunned me, and I toppled among the bodies. Instinctively I buried my head among them for protection. Then, unable to fight it off, I sank into unconsciousness.

7

How LONG I lay there, and what transpired in the meantime, I have no idea.

Suddenly I heard someone bark, "Get up!" Those who had the strength to do so obeyed the order mechanically. Many who were buried under the heap were destined to remain there. The cry arose from others, "We won't!" They were beaten; cold water was thrown on them. I could no longer look on. I turned my gaze away and found myself looking into my father's face. It was covered with blood which streamed from a head wound. Out in the yard he had heard the terrible cries within, and, thinking that we were about to be killed down here, had volunteered to join us in the cellar so that his son and he might face death together.

The Ukrainian militiamen now searched each of us thoroughly. They then enumerated the different ways in which we might die: by shooting or hanging or by being beaten to death. The choice would be ours. At last they led us back up to the yard, punching us as we walked along.

On the way up to the yard we could see into another cellar room. Here a number of Jews were seated. They were wearing beards, and their Ukrainian captors were cutting these off with blunt scissors. The agonizing cries of the unfortunate fellows were drowned in the guffaws of their torturers, who were hugely amused at the agony they inflicted on their exhausted victims.

The yard outside was now perfectly still. No one was to be seen. We were ordered, for the amusement of the guards, to perform various physical exercises. Finally we were commanded to line up in marching formation. We were then marched off, heads bent, hands folded across the nape of the neck. In this posture we made our way through the city, the guards moving up and down among us, striking out indiscriminately.

We reached Pelczynska Street. Here we were led through a wide gate into a field that was perfectly enclosed on all sides—the former hockey field. We were ordered to halt. A large number of Germans were already assembled there. One of them addressed us: "Those who belong to a special trade or profession, and who are under sixteen or over sixty, fall out!" He checked the papers of those concerned and, having established their validity, gave the order for dismissal.

The rest of us remained there. One of the Germans approached us— a tall, thin man with a fleshy nose, wearing a white apron. He called one of our group forward and led him into a hut. Then a piercing scream rang out. A few minutes passed and, with a smirk on his face, the tall man appeared again. His apron was smeared with blood. He called a second forward. The process repeated itself. Then he called a third, and then a fourth, and so on. The ordeal made us quake.

Meanwhile, German officers were fixing ropes on a pole with a cross-beam. When this was done, a swaggering German officer confronted us with a gruesome choice: "Those for stabbing, to the right; those for the gallows, to the left!" No one made a move. . . . The officers then called forth one of our number from the front line. They led him to the gallows and placed the noose about his neck. At the last moment one of the officers took pity on the unfortunate fellow, and allowed him to rejoin our ranks.

It was the next morning before I found out that those who had been led into the hut had not, in fact, been murdered, but had been released on the far side of the hut, once they had complied with the request to utter a piercing scream. The butcher had then smeared his apron with the blood of a freshly killed goose and had proceeded to fetch his next "victim." This process, as well as the drama at the gallows, had been enacted only in order to give the officers a chance to witness the horror we felt. By all appearances they derived real satisfaction from it.

Gradually the night came on, and at last we were led to another nearby field. Thousands of men were lying here in rows. They lay on their bellies, their faces buried in the sand. Around the perimeter of the field searchlights and machine guns had been set up. Among them I caught sight of German officers standing about. We were ordered to lie flat like the others. We were pushed and shoved brutally, this way and that. My father was separated from me, and I heard him calling out in despair: "Let me stay with my son! I want to die with my son!" Nobody took any notice of him.

Now that we were all lying still, there was a hush that lasted for a moment or two. Then the "game" started. We could hear the sound of a man, clearly one of us, stumbling awkwardly around, chased and beaten by another as he went. At last the pursued collapsed out of sheer exhaustion. He was told to rise. Blows were rained down upon him until he dragged himself to his feet again and tried to run forward. He fell to the ground again and hadn't the strength to get up. When the pursuers were at last satisfied that the incessant blows had rendered him unable to stir, let alone run, they called a halt and left him there. Now it was the turn of a second victim. He received the same treatment. Now a third was hauled out. The Germans, in pursuit of their sport, tramped up and down over our backs as we lay there. No one dared to raise his head. The dread of being picked out for the next turn almost drove me crazy. Every few minutes I touched my neighbor to see if he was still there or if he had gone to face this merciless ordeal. Where could my father be? Was he already among those now lying stunned, with the ordeal behind them? And what of my brother Aaron? Had not he, too, been recruited for work?

Thoughts raced in order and confusion through my mind. I was so exhausted that I fell asleep. Not even the agonizing screams, the sound of savage blows, or the continual trampling on our bodies could prevent me any longer from sinking into oblivion. I dreamed of home—the whole family was there, sitting happily together. . . . I dreamed that my brother has been sent home.

The welcome state of unconsciousness passed all too quickly. I came to, and was startled by a painful stab of dazzling light. Powerful searchlights were focused on us. We sat up, one beside the other, so close that we could not stir. Directly in front of me sat two men with shattered skulls. Through the mess of bone and hair I could see the very brains. We whispered to them. We nudged them. But they did not stir. They just sat there, propped up, bulging eyes staring ahead. They were quite dead.

The sun rose slowly. The day promised to be heavy and oppressive. Thirst was already making itself felt among us. Ten at a time we were allowed to go to the toilets. The greater number, however, were so apathetic, still so full of numbing dread, that they declined to budge. An almost stupefying stench arose from the many battered bodies of the dead.

I was sitting near my father, who, in the course of the night, had found his way back to me. There was no sign of my brother. I finally learned from one of the men nearby that he had been released on the grounds that he was under sixteen years of age. My father and I heaved sighs of tremendous relief.

Around eight o'clock some senior German officers arrived and stood before us. One of them stepped forward and bawled, "I want seventy young men to fall in immediately!" In the hope of being sent to work and of later being released to go home, many of us found the strength to press forward into the front line, hoping to be picked out. The Germans selected seventy-five. For a minute or two those selected were convinced they had been more fortunate than we who had not been. But their elation was short-lived. They formed up in lines of four. Then they were beaten until many collapsed. Those who survived the beatings were marched off. We watched the departure of each group until it was out of sight.

A short time afterward a big truck drove up. "Let fifty men board the truck!" Once again there was a scramble for places. We had decided that it was a choice between forced labor and death. No one wanted to remain here any longer. I, too, was anxious to get out. But my father opposed the idea. "Don't volunteer when you don't know what it leads to." Seeing that he decisively balked at the idea of going himself, I naturally stayed by him.

In the course of the day a total of fifty trucks were loaded up. By evening there remained only a small portion of the five thousand men who had covered the field in the morning. We who were left squatted down one beside another. Pain and hunger were no longer of consequence. But the persistent thirst tortured us.

At one stage tradesmen were again ordered to step forward; a few did so and were at once released. It didn't make any difference to us. We sat about—at least unmolested—and waited.

More prisoners were brought in. Now my apathy left me. I reproached myself bitterly that I hadn't joined the truck squads, and hadn't persuaded my father to do so also. We faced a night that would be no different from the unforgettable previous night.

Suddenly the order was given, "Let fifty men step forward!" It no longer mattered where we would be taken—even if it were to death itself. Anything would be better than repeating the agonizing experience of the previous night. I stepped forward with the others. My father, thinking along the same lines, joined us.

We were made to form a huge circle. Then, driven on with truncheons, we were forced to run about in a circle. Our captors bawled out abusively that we still had plenty of running in us and that we'd had it too easy all along! Indeed, I had to confess to myself that our strength, greatly diminished though it was by torture and by burning thirst, was something for which I could find no explanation.

Then we were subjected to repeated turns of "Up—Down! Up—Down!" the truncheon blows accompanying each action.

And then, suddenly and miraculously, the order was snapped out, "To the gate—on the double!" The voices of angels could not have meant more to us. A "farewell stripe" from the Ukrainian whips as we made our way through the exit left no impression whatever on us. All I could see was that beyond the gate my mother was waiting, and all I could feel was that, weeping copiously, she had her arms about me.

We went down the street, my mother, my father, and I, and not one of us spoke a word. It was half-past eight in the evening.

We are home at last. Bitter tears flow when we undress and they wash my own and Father's back. Then Father throws himself on the bed. I drink tea first—lots of tea. I can't eat anything. Then I, too, get into bed. Deep moans show that my father is very restless. He can neither lie flat nor sit up. I myself am not much better. I am stronger than he, however, and will recover from my pains—which are now really making themselves felt—much sooner than he will. My eyes grow heavy and I fall asleep. It is a deep slumber, undisturbed by dreams. So the night passed, after a day of experiences such as I was destined to repeat many times.

8

I awoke. It was almost four o'clock in the morning. My mother was standing at the foot of the bed. She was weeping, and the words she uttered choked in her throat. "You'll have to get up and go away into hiding."

She took me to the apartment, in the same building, of a neighbor of ours with whom she had made the necessary arrangements the day before. The woman of the house, taking her children with her, went to our house with my mother; her husband and I remained at her house. She locked us in. The idea was to give the appearance that the house was unoccupied. This was a fairly safe gamble, for until now, inexplicably, there had been no attempt to enter any house that was obviously untenanted.

We sat there till the evening. Then the woman returned and released us, and I went home. I was still exhausted, stunned. My whole body ached. Mother brought me my meal in bed, and sat down by my side. From the next room, I could hear my father's moans. I asked my mother if he had been examined by the doctor. She nodded, and then added that one of his lungs had been injured.

Then she went on to tell me what had happened during our two days' absence; of her fear, and solicitous inquiries as to the place of our detention, and how much it had meant to her to see us both alive again. She spoke softly, and, without noticing it, I moved toward sleep. Her voice trailed off, and then, after a moment, I felt the impression of her lips on my forehead.

The next morning I went again to our neighbor's apartment and stayed with her husband. After a while the woman, who had left us alone, returned to fetch a few belongings. She left her young daughter keeping watch outside the front door of the apartment house, so that we would be warned in time if the Ukrainian militia should approach. We three, her husband, the wife, and I, were talking when we were suddenly startled to hear the excited call of the little girl below, exclaiming loudly, "Mummy, a militia soldier!" The latter could not but hear her, too, and sensing that there was something suspicious afoot, he followed her as she raced up the stairs. He came upon us in an instant, and

45

grasped the situation immediately. "Get to work, you!" he barked gruffly, tugging me by the arm. My mother had heard the disturbance, and rushed from our apartment next door and implored him to let me go, but the soldier replied that I would be required for only an hour's work at a flour mill; brooking no interferenece, he took me with him. I had hardly recovered from the previous ordeal, and my legs were very weak under me.

He picked up a few more men on the way. One of them told me that on Friday Dr. Rab Levin, the chief rabbi of the local Jewish community, had been killed. Rabbi Levin had gone voluntarily to the authorities to intervene for his community, even though he knew that his chances of ever returning alive were minimal.

We arrived at last in Zolkiewska Street where the flour mill stood. A terrible sense of alarm gripped me suddenly when no halt was called here and I realized we were continuing on in the direction of the militia building, back to the same awful spot we had been brought three days ago. Once again we marched in through the great wide gate. I could hardly keep a grip on myself; I was trembling all over. If we were subjected to the same brutality, I felt that this time I would not leave this field alive. It was at least some relief to know that my mother was ignorant of my fate, for I knew that she, too, couldn't have borne a second such ordeal.

To my amazement, however, I saw that the field was empty. My hopes began to soar. Our soldier-captor spoke for a while with the porter at the field, and then, to our great relief, led us back to the mill. Here, under the supervision of two soldiers—the first to treat us like fellow human beings—we were put to work sorting sacks of flour. The work had been going on for about half an hour when my mother appeared, anxious to assure herself that I was really with the working party. She brought me my breakfast. I stuffed it into my pocket, convinced that we were shortly to be dismissed.

Suddenly, however, a German dressed in black overalls came and requisitioned a working party of six, including myself. We had to carry cases of beer along the tracks leading to the town of Zolkiew. From a distance we could see Jews hauling rails, their guard striking at them brutally with truncheons. The beer was intended, of course, for the Germans supervising the work.

As soon as we had delivered the cases of beer, we too were put to work on the spot. We began by hauling rails, coming every bit as much under the blows of the Ukrainian and German guards as the other men we had seen carrying rails. I had, indeed, already experienced worse than that, and it seemed to me that these armed guards—who, incidentally, outnumbered us 120 to 100—administered their punishment not through any motive of cruelty but simply as part of their routine supervision. Brutality seemed to be part of their natures. The work itself would have been punishment enough.

After a time we were called away to unload heavy artillery pieces from wagons—twenty men being assigned to each piece. The unloading of the guns was much more exhausting than hauling the rails, for these were many hundredweights heavier and were tightly wedged in the wagons. Moreover, we got in one another's way, thus provoking the guards to even more brutality.

At last the guns were ranged side by side on the ground. We then had to pull them for about two hundred yards over uneven ground. Dragging them up and down the steep slopes was particularly strenuous. The truncheon blows increased accordingly.

As soon as one gun was drawn up into the desired position, we were marched back without a second's pause to fetch the next one. So the process repeated itself, until I was gripped by the conviction that this was in no way less than the unbearable ordeal three days previously.

Our respite when we had completed the task of drawing up the guns was short-lived. Almost at once we were ordered to collect all the scraps of paper lying on the ground within a wide radius of the site. Scarcely had we finished this when we were marched off to a wagon to load cement.

Such tasks made impossible demands on our exhausted physical condition. But eventually our guards got tired of this meaningless work, although obviously they still had no intention of releasing us. A fire was lighted and we were ordered to toss cement on it—a senseless procedure. To do so, we had to approach so close that the flames leaped around our faces. The already parching thirst brought on by the heat of the day now reached an unbearable degree.

We were next ordered to gather up those who had been knocked down or who had succumbed to the interminable beating or to sheer exhaustion, and to lay them all together in one place. For this purpose we drew up in ranks of four. Out of a round hundred men, only about thirty-four could engage actively in the work. The others lay in an area where we had put them, and in such condition that expert medical attention would have been needed to restore them to health. Their collapse sealed their doom.

Within earshot of us the Germans deliberated as to whether they would shoot us now or wait until the following day. I was convinced at that point that the battered creatures around me who had been stripped of the last vestiges of human dignity shared my thoughts. "Go ahead! Do it now—immediately! Can anything be nicer now than to sink slowly into death, to lose all sense of pain and to find relief at last?"

And all the while mothers and wives sat at home believing their sons and their husbands had merely been rounded up for easy work and would shortly arrive home safe and sound.

Our guards now led us down to a stream to wash ourselves. It was nothing but a big puddle, with dead rats and other animals in it. We drank the water greedily. Our thirst slaked in the horrible slime, we then washed. After that, we sat around for about half an hour, trying to recover some strength. Then, again miraculously, we were allowed to go home. Every two men had to bear between them a third one who was no longer able to walk of his own accord.

It was about four o'clock in the afternoon when I reached home. The makings of my breakfast were still in my pocket.

My mother broke into tears on seeing the awful effects on me of the "light" work. I myself could think only of how happy I was to reach home again. What did it matter if I could scarcely move a limb? But even now I dared not dally idly about, for there was always the danger of being recruited for another work party.

I had to find a hiding place. After much thought I remembered a Jewish friend of mine who lived in a house that was otherwise occupied only by "Aryans," and was not therefore searched by the Ukrainian militia in their hunt for workers. I went to him and found just the refuge I had been looking for.

In the early morning my friend and his sister would leave, locking me in. They were out most of the day. He went to work. She was seeking her father, who several days previously had been taken—like myself—to Pelczynska Street, since then there had been no trace of him. Toward evening the two of them would return. The girl was continually fatigued, for she was on her feet all day, tramping from worksite to worksite, inquiring if anyone knew where her father was.

My older sister, Ella, came in the evenings to bring me some food. She told me how difficult it had become to procure even the bare necessities. It frequently happened now that some could not even bring home the desperately small rations—the Jews received only half the quantity granted to the Aryans—for if a woman in a family could not queue up for some reason, it was too dangerous for a man to do so; a passing German or Ukrainian might seize him and dispatch him to "work." And not even the women could be sure of reaching the shop counters, for it sometimes occurred that they, too, were shoved out of place in the line and forced to go to the very end of the queue, so that everything was sold out by the time their turn came.

For five days I enjoyed a respite in my new hiding place and could recuperate somewhat in reasonable security. It would have been expecting too much, however, to have been left in the enjoyment of such shelter for long. On the next Sunday morning, at about four-thirty there was a sharp knock at the door. My friend's sister opened it. A party of Ukrainian militia and Germans stormed in.

"Get up! Get to work!" bawled one of them, and, scarcely fully dressed, my friend and I were hustled out into a truck where a number were already detained under guard.

The soldiers then entered neighboring houses in search of more workers. At the end of half an hour, a total of fifteen Jews had been rounded up, and were guarded by five policemen. No one spoke; all were pale. For none of us was this the first time that we had been recruited for "work," and we knew that anything could happen. For once, we had a surprise in store for us.

The truck took us to Strzelecki Street, and we climbed out at a school building that had been turned into a barracks. Without being excessively ill-treated, we had to clear out the building and then clean particularly the stairways and the corridors. Two hours later we were dismissed. We could scarcely believe our luck.

On the way home my attention was attracted by placards which proclaimed that, as of the middle of the month, all Jews must wear a white armlet with the Star of David on the right arm, above the elbow. This provision extended also to half-castes as far as the third degree; that is, one was a Jew if he had one Jewish grandparent. It was stated in addition that failure to comply with these provisions would result in the imposition of severe penalties.

My mother was clearly startled as she saw me standing so unexpectedly and at such an unlikely hour before the front door. A torrent of questions was directed at me before she had overcome her surprise.

With a laugh, I said, "Unless I'm much mistaken, I've got my day's work behind me!"

She really didn't know whether to laugh or cry, for she knew already only too well the scope of the term "work." Finally I told her the story from start to finish. Overjoyed that my task had taken such an inexplicably mild form. Mother forgot for the moment her anxiety over the loss of my hitherto secure place of refuge, and all our chatter gave her a chance to unburden her heart, until Father brought her down to earth by remarking, "Don't make a session of it, but give him something to eat and bring him down to the cellar, for these fellows can come at any minute and whip him away again."

Darkness had long since fallen when I emerged from my shelter and came up into the house. I got into bed immediately, for I was still quite weak. Mother sat by my side. She sat there without stirring, and watched me with tears in her eyes. With an almost shy gesture, she smoothed my hair back from my forehead. All her love and all her fear found a simple expression in such tender petting. Then she turned to face the stern reality of our circumstances again, and full of solicitude said: "Thanks be to God that all has turned out so well today. But who knows what tomorrow will bring? You have no longer any place in which to hide, and if you stay in the cellar you're bound to pick up some infection. Perhaps it would be best if you reported for work tomorrow morning in the Hazet factory across the street." She kissed me on the forehead, and I felt her tears falling on my face.

9

I AROSE at five o'clock, hastily got myself ready, and reported to the factory a few minutes later. Although it was a full hour before opening time, there were already many Jews lined up there. Everyone was afraid to remain in his own house, for in the early morning the chances of being hauled off somewhere were greatest. The soldiers at the Hazet Candy Company knew this and were decent enough to let the Jewish workers enter the factory grounds before the official opening.

By four in the afternoon the work was finished. I hastened across to our house, where my mother had my dinner ready, but I took it with me down to the cellar again in order not to run the risk of being rounded up. After eight o'clock I ventured up into the house again.

My sister had brought home a newspaper in which it was stated that the Russian armies had been wiped out and that hundreds of thousands of Bolsheviks had been taken prisoner by the Germans. This was bad news for us. Considering all that had happened here under German domination, the elimination of her enemies by Germany could well mean the end for us, too. I had no desire to think further about the matter. I went to bed with a sense of foreboding.

Next day I was again at work in the Hazet and had the good fortune to be selected as mate by a glazier who had been commissioned to restore all the windows in the building and who proposed to make me his apprentice. So, when it was decreed that Jews were no longer to be employed in the factory, and after a notice had been hung on the entrance gate, "Jews forbidden to enter," I was able to continue working there as "glazier's mate," and so spent a further two months in circumstances which, if not altogether gratifying, were at least bearable.

At the beginning of August, 1941, we heard that an order had been issued to the Ukrainian militia to arrest all the respectable and well-known Jews in Lvov and to drive them into the courthouse yard in Loketko Street. After being tortured terribly, most of the Jews were shot. The rest were placed in the courthouse jail only to be led out a few days later to the same fate. Though nobody had any reason to doubt this horrible story, nobody wanted to believe it had actually happened. Thus the rumor persisted that the men were still being kept in the jail.

At about the same time a "Jewish community" was organized in compliance with an order from the German occupation authorities. At the head of the group were representatives of the Jewish community which had existed before 1939 under the leadership of Dr. Parnes. (Shortly thereafter Dr. Parnes was shot by a German officer when he told the officer that he was not to be ordered around.) Everyone had to register. With the establishment of this "Jewish community" the occupation forces had created a responsible instrument for carrying out their orders regarding the Jewish population. For instance, manpower was no longer chosen and distributed by the Ukrainian militia but by the Jewish community. To carry out these measures, a Jewish militia was organized, made up of volunteers who were later given uniforms. Those who had any self-respect did not join this group, and it was composed essentially of those from the Jewish rabble.

Official doctors were appointed to control the health of the 150,000 Jews in Lvov, but the Germans saw to it that their practice remained mostly in the realm of theory.

Two months later, at the beginning of November, 1941, it was announced in the newspapers and on posters that, beginning in the middle of the month, all Jews from the four different parts of the city would have to move to the Jewish quarter within five days; the exact borders of this Jewish quarter were indicated. The Aryans living in this district were ordered to leave immediately. At the same time the Polish people were given a district in the western part of the city, the Ukrainians and the White Russians another part, and so on. The Germans were told to live in the vicinity of Strijer Park. In practice, native-born Germans were free to move about the entire city, but non-German nationals living in the German district and Jews living in the Polish district were restricted to their own areas.

A new office, the Lodging Office, was established in the Jewish community. Its task was to provide the Jewish population with quarters in the newly assigned district. Its first activity was to make an exact disposition of the Jewish population according to their ration cards, and to estimate the available living space. The officials went from house to house in groups of two, measuring and writing down the results, after which it was computed that each Jew could be alloted two square meters of living space. Each person looking for a house or apartment or room was given a certificate on which was indicated how much space he was entitled to rent.

Such moves on the part of the Germans marked a decided step-up in their policy of persecution. A real ghetto was now clearly in the process of being formed. And now one can see how their moves foreshadowed the "final solution" of the "Jewish problem."

Policemen were posted at all three railway bridges the Jews had to cross in order to get into the new section marked out for them. Everyone was checked. Many of the Jews who came from other sections to look for apartments in the new ghetto were never seen again. We knew only that they were last seen being led, individually, into the yard of a nearby power plant. In one case a group of thirty men crossing one of the bridges was loaded into a truck and driven off, never to be heard of again.

Even those Jews already living in the section were constantly molested. Soon few dared to leave their houses. The men stayed in their cellars. The route to work which most of them had to traverse could be the way to death. For urgent errands children and old people were sent, but they were not spared either. It was impossible to help those who were moving. Thus, women and little girls plodded through the streets carrying heavy pieces of furniture.

I sat in the cellar while this new wave of terror spread out over the city. Work now ceased entirely in the Hazet and I chose to remain in my hiding place all day long.

After November, 1941, a German named Weber became head of the employment office. An exact registration of all the manpower on hand was now carried out, and each Jew received a registration permit. This permit was stamped by the firm where he worked. The most-desired permits were those from firms employed by the German Army, for they appeared to offer relatively good security to their possessors. And a large number of these firms were authorized to issue permits to the workers' wives, allowing the wives to remain at home. The passes were placed under a rigid monthly control. Weber examined and stamped them.

Finally, because it had become extremely dangerous to prolong an illegal existence (that is, one without a work permit) I decided to look around again for work, but in an essential industry. I learned from companions that it was still possible to find employment in a certain road-construction firm without too much difficulty.

c

I went to the construction firm my friend had told me about. By great good luck I was not accosted on the way. And by even greater good fortune I obtained a work permit. We were overjoyed at home. Inspired by my experience, my father also applied at the same place. And he too was given a work permit.

Both of us had to work sixteen hours a day, doing the heaviest kind of construction work, building a railway. But for the time being we were safe. Those who had jobs of a "necessary" nature would not be molested—at least for the present.

PART III

Janowska Concentration Camp

10

UNTIL NOW our family had been lucky, or so we felt. Such feelings show how quickly human beings adjust to the most terrifying circumstances, the most grinding tyranny. But our hope sustained us. We still firmly believed that somehow the Germans would be defeated and we would be free once again. Free to return to the happy days of—when was it? Over a year ago? No. It was hardly more than six months since the Germans had marched in. It seemed like a lifetime.

We felt we were lucky because we were all alive, Father and I were working, and none of us had been unbearably molested. Then, suddenly, our "luck" deserted us permanently. I was interned in the Janowska concentration camp.

Three months had passed comparatively calmly. It was now March 2, 1942. At the end of that workday the head engineer at the construction job read out a list of those who had missed more than three days of work. My father's name was on the list. But he and I were not frightened, for we knew he had an excuse from the workmen's sick fund. Those whose names were called were told to remain together and to report to the supervisor's office. It was pointed out that if anyone did not report they would be assigned to a forced-labor camp.

In order to play it safe and protect my father from difficulties, he and I quickly decided that I should go to the supervisor's office in his place to see what it was all about. After all, we had the same name, and if they should demand it I could present my perfect attendance card and maintain that there must have been an error. I had great difficulty persuading my father, but finally he let me go.

Everything happened so fast then that I was at first unconscious of the danger to which I had exposed myself. The supervisor suddenly appeared and led the men who had reported to his office into a room, locking them in. At the very last moment I felt that there was something not quite in order and had sprung unseen to the side of the door and so did not go into the room with the others. From my position I could see everything.

The supervisor had barely locked the door when a truck full of Askaris drove up. (Askaris was the name given to Russian prisoners of war who had volunteered for service with the *Schutzstaffel* or Black-shirts, the SS.) They rushed from the truck as if they were about to put down an armed revolt, and lined up in single file while two German SS officers unlocked the door and brought out the men and made them climb into the truck. They found that four men were missing. Since I still stood near the gate in view of the SS officers, they came without a word and made me also climb into the truck. I was so frightened that everything went blank. I crouched against the gate of the truck, paralyzed, unable to think, my head bowed.

They drove in the direction of Janowska Camp, and drew up in the big yard there. We were ordered to get out of the truck and line up facing the wall, and to press our noses against it. We obeyed. It was very cold. Two Ukrainian guards walked back and forth behind us, hitting us without mercy when we made the slightest movement. Then we were called one by one into the office. When I entered I spotted near the desk a Jewish woman, a stenographer, who asked me in a pitying voice what such a young fellow as I was doing there, because prisoners of my age were seldom seen at Janowska.

I told her what had happened, and she advised me to report myself as a skilled worker. Then I had to hurry on into the office. There sat the camp commander and the speaker for the camp. I was ordered to empty my pockets, and was asked my name and my profession. I stated that I was a glass worker, the only skill I could think of. Then I was sent back to take my old place against the wall. When all of us had been "interviewed," they took us into the camp through a door that was covered with barbed wire. This was the real Janowska.

In the middle of the compound was a wooden barrack that was divided into three parts, a living area, an empty area, and a kitchen and washroom; each section was separated by a wall. Ukrainian sentries led us into the washroom, where some Jews were at work doing repairs. They showered us with questions about what was happening in the world outside, how the war situation was, and so forth. They were not surprised, nor did they even seem disappointed when we told them that we in the city did not know any more about the war than they did.

After I took off my clothes, I had to go to a barber who shaved my whole body. Then I took a shower. It was not possible to wash oneself thoroughly because the water was ice cold. So everyone bathed hurriedly in order to put his clothes back on.

"Hey there, take it easy! Everything here is done in turns, except dying," one young fellow prisoner called out. He was clearly a veteran of the camp. "Take one set of underwear, a shirt, suit, hat, one pair of socks and shoes; the rest of your clothes remains here." We were standing in a space outside the showers. I had on a sweater, a second pair of underwear, and a coat.

"But," I said, "can't I at least keep my sweater and my second pair of underwear? One can die in this cold weather."

"Do you think I will risk *my* life for *your* sweater?" inquired the young prisoner. "You are making a big mistake. When an order in here is not carried out exactly, you hear a shot, and again there is one more in heaven. What I have told you about your clothes is also an order."

That was enough for me. I finished dressing, shivering from the cold.

In the meantime, everyone had washed. The cook and an SS man came over and told us it was close to suppertime. After about twenty minutes, these two returned with a five-pound loaf of bread and a can of coffee to feed the twenty of us who were there. The SS man asked us ironically how we liked it here. He was quiet for a while; then, suddenly, he went up to one of the group and said: "Show me how your are dressed. Have you put on too many clothes so that you cannot work properly?"

The man to whom he had spoken unbuttoned his jacket and had to undress down to his underpants.

"That's good," said the SS man, satisfied that the prisoner was clothed according to the regulations. He turned to the young man who had spoken to us before, and said, "Show me what clothing is left over."

"As ordered, sir, I have seen to it that everything has been carried out in accordance with the regulations." He pointed at the heap of clothes.

"Well, that's nice," said the SS man. "Take this stuff and come along with me." Then he said something about our quarters for the night and went away with the young boy, who was now laden down with our clothes.

The cook divided the bread and coffee among us. Later, when the SS man came back again, we were led into the part of the barracks the SS man said had been designated for the dispensary. He locked the door behind us. It took some time before we could see anything, because the entire room was lighted by a single very dim bulb hanging from the middle of the ceiling.

We did not even think about sleeping because we would have frozen. There were cots, but these had neither straw mattresses nor blankets. So we walked around all night long or jumped from foot to foot in order to warm our stiff joints at least a little bit. Above all, we thought of home, where our parents and brothers and sisters were caring for their loved ones.

My father rushed home. My mother, knowing immediately that something had happened, dared to ask the question that would bring confirmation of her thoughts. My father sank down on the sofa and wept. Until this moment my mother had never in her life seen him cry. He whispered, "In the camp."

Then my mother left the house and rushed to the construction company to seek clarification of what my father had said. But of course no one there was interested in the burning sorrow of a Jewish woman, and they consoled her, with assurances that I would be back quickly, just to get rid of her as soon as possible.

All were very sad at home. No one wanted to eat. When they went to bed, my mother and my sisters put aside their blankets in order to feel closer to me; they did not want to be better off than I, and they spent many more nights renouncing each comfort.

The next morning, which was Sunday, my mother went to the firm again. They were not working there on that day, but she was not discouraged, and dared to go to the apartment of the construction supervisor, only to be turned away with meaningless words of consolation. As she finally lost her courage and returned home, she received the news from a member of the Jewish community, who had heard it from the camp speaker, that I was in the Janowska Camp.

They all knew now that they would not soon see me again. They fasted the whole day, and even my little sister Bina knew the extent of the great misfortune that had fallen upon me, and said, in her small voice, "Leon is in the camp, and I don't want anything to eat either...."

It seemed as if the night would never end. At five o'clock in the morning the door was finally unlocked, and someone growled at us, "Get up!" We rushed outside into the fresh air.

Tired, emaciated figures moved slowly through the yard. One could hardly believe that these were people who just a few weeks ago had gone about well dressed, healthy, and full of strength, tending to their respective jobs. Now their feet were wrapped in straw, held in place by pieces of cloth and string, their clothes ragged and torn. Around their waists were cords with dirty eating utensils attached to them. So they trudged along toward the mess hall, where they joined the already waiting breakfast line. The bitter-cold weather had driven all humane expression from their faces.

Terrible disorder prevailed in the latrines. Everybody crowded wildly about, and some dirtied others. Two overseers with clubs attempted, but with little success, to keep a semblance of order, and they were furious when they caught someone who had dirtied the floor or the wall. I heard one prisoner say, "But, Herr Director, I really did not do anything on the floor." I turned around, amused, in spite of the horrible situation, for I wanted to see just who this "Toilet Director" was. He was a fat, greasy old man, and someone told me that he had at one time been the owner of a well-known chocolate company. Because of his association with brown materials, the Germans, always efficient, had put him in charge of the latrines!

This was the *only* case of real, even if somewhat raw, humor that I encountered in the camp.

At 6:30 A.M. we had inspection, for which we had to line up in groups of twenty. His brow moist with perspiration, the camp senior, Kampf (the Germans appointed certain prisoners as group leaders*) strove to get these living corpses into line. Then, as two SS men approached—the camp commandant, Obersturmführer Gebauer, and his deputy, Unstersturmführer Wilhaus, the same two who had brought us into the camp on the previous day—Kampf bawled: "Attention! Caps off! Herr Obersturmführer, I beg to report 140 men, and 20 newcomers, in all 160 men ready for work!" At that moment, two more SS men— Scharführers and a civilian—arrived on the scene. The Untersturm-führer now bawled out "Caps on! Number off!"

---

* Thus there was a barrack leader, work leader. washroom leader, etc. The prisoner put in charge of all these leaders was called the Camp Senior. The American Army equivalents of the German ranking system that concern us here are:

Sturmbannführer—Major
Haupsturmführer—Captain
Obersturmführer—First Lieutenant
Untersturmführer—Second Lieutenant
Sturmscharführer—Warrant Officer
Hauptscharführer—Sergeant
Scharführer—Corporal
Sturman—Private

Now a gruesome charade began. Any of those ill and intimidated wretches who made a slip of the tongue or who didn't number off quickly enough when his turn came was set upon by the two Scharführers and beaten with rubber truncheons until he was unconscious. Then the numbering off began at the very beginning again and continued until a slip-up brought another beating. This was repeated about twenty times; then Kampf was ordered to put us through an exercise of "Caps on! Caps off!" twenty times. In this case, too, the two Scharführers were no less diligent in using their truncheons. This, as I soon found out, was more or less the routine procedure at inspection. At last, when the two SS officers had exhausted their anger against us, the order came for us to line up in brigade formation. The old camp inhabitants now formed themselves into columns and marched off to work.

We twenty newcomers stayed behind. After breakfast, we were led off to the doctor for examination. The doctor's room was down in a basement that was in a complete shambles. In a partitioned section that served as a waiting room, we stripped to the waist. Then, one after the other, we went into the adjoining cellar room where there was neither flooring nor panes in the windows. It was unbelievably crude. The doctor, who himself was freezing, scarcely looked at those who presented themselves before acquitting them. The "examination" of the entire twenty men—many of them in seriously impaired health—lasted only a few minutes. All were found to be fit for work.

On our way back to the hut we passed a work party that was engaged in extending the inspection ground where we had been worked over earlier. A huge number of stakes had to be driven into the frozen ground. The mechanical motions of the prisoners were under the scrutiny of an Askari, a Russian prisoner of war named Sklarow, who dealt out blows of his stick with almost clockwork regularity. He gave the impression that this was purely reflex action on his part; or, if there was any motive at all, it was simply the desire, perhaps, to keep himself warm. The prisoners took their punishment with an equal lack of passion or reaction. It was taken for granted, like any natural phenomenon—the unpleasantness of a cough, for example, or the sensation of hunger when one has not enough to eat. And just as they accepted the blows without demur, so the fulfillment of their task elicited not the slightest spark of interest from the prisoners. If one of them had been asked what sort of work he was engaged in, or what piece of equipment he had in his hand, he would undoubtedly have had to reflect for a few seconds before finding an answer. For these dehumanized creatures the great world outside no longer existed. They lived only within the rhythm of the camp routine.

When we arrived at the hut we found that the living room was being cleaned, so we had to wait in the washroom. There we met a new batch of prisoners. Like us, they had had their hair shaved off, and were now taking a showerbath. They told us that they had been taken from their homes on the previous evening and brought to the camp.

At twelve noon dinner was served—a repulsive, foul-odored broth made of slices of half-rotten turnips. After dinner we spent about two hours on the inspection ground undergoing the prescribed brutal treatment. As it was Sunday, further work was dispensed with.

Each of us was now given a plank bed by the hut seniors, but there was not a stitch of anything to place on it or to cover ourselves with. However, we availed ourselves of these relatively peaceful few hours to relax, to sleep, or to chat. So it was that I came across a former acquaintance who had been at Janowska for more than three months. He did me an invaluable favor by giving me a rundown on the important elements of camp life.

A burning question for me was how I might establish contact with those at home. But to this question he could give me no encouraging answer. Personal meetings with my family were out of the question, he said, and letter writing was forbidden; anyone found with a letter on his person faced certain death. In spite of that, my friend told me, letters were in fact written; for what reason had anyone to fear death? Would not death simply be a shortening of their suffering? Aryans from the city, who worked in the camp, acted as messengers. I would like to be able to say that they were motivated by altruism, but it was not so. The messengers saw to it that they were rewarded for their risks by the relatives. Anyone caught smuggling out a letter from a prisoner would, of course, have been mercilessly beaten, and the prisoner himself would be shot.

My informant then told how food parcels could be brought in if they were addressed to the Jewish community and had been forwarded for distribution in the camp. It was senseless, he went on, for one's family to send clothes, as these would be confiscated—and I should make these points clear to relatives.

That I had put myself down as a glazier was very satisfactory, he thought. Since glaziers were continually in demand, and could not always be found, I had good prospects of being allocated to a workshop where it at least would be warm and where constant beatings were not a fixed part of the day's work.

Thus acquainted with the rudiments of life in the camp, I took to my "bed" after a very frugal evening meal. Toward eight in the evening the main light was switched off and the hut locked.

Tired though I was, the thought of how things were at home gave me no peace, and I decided without further ado to write. I had scarcely begun when there was a sudden uproar, the door was thrown open, and two Askaris, so drunk they could scarcely keep upright, reeled in. They immediately proceeded to run amock, striking out left and right at us with the butts of their rifles. They pursued this amusement for the best part of two hours, then cleared out, locking the door behind them. The prisoners showed not the least sign of anger. They had long since been broken to such treatment, and their fate was clearly so irrevocable that reaction was futile.

As soon as I had to some extent calmed down, I began to write. To write a letter home! The very thought brought the utter hopelessness of the situation before me again. This horror camp—so many battered bodies and broken spirits about me! Then I realized how insignificant all that was, compared to the awful uncertainty about my fate that plagued the minds of those at home. I finally banished confusion from my mind and concentrated my thoughts on writing the letter. But even then my hand seemed loath to respond. I was able, finally, to put down the bare facts of what had happened, and with it consolation, as much consolation as I could muster, for those at home. Tears blotted the words I had written. I lied to them, saying that the blottings were the marks of my kisses.

I stuck the letter into a shoe. Then I fell asleep from sheer exhaustion. My last thought was: Hold out! Hold out! You *must* see your parents again!

At that time I was not yet seventeen.

11

BECAUSE we were not allowed to leave the hut until morning, two large buckets had been placed inside the locked door to serve as toilets. Many of the prisoners suffered from dysentery and the buckets were soon filled. The overflow then spilled out, covering the floor with a stinking mess. This had the inevitable result of adding to the already prevalent sickness.

Early morning again brought the order: "Get up! Fast!" The barrack leader, a prisoner himself, as I've said, told me to rouse my neighbor, who had not stirred. He was dead.

"The poor devil is dead," I said. My sympathy in calling him "poor devil" was misplaced. The others thought my expression was a huge joke. He was a "damn lucky devil," they corrected me.

I gave my letter to my informant of the previous evening, who agreed to pass it on.

This morning we were divided up among twenty different brigades. I joined the painters' squad. This consisted of house painters, sign painters, lacquerers, and glaziers. We were led to the section where the workshops, office, and administrative buildings stood. This place was railed off, and was surrounded by watchtowers, which were manned by Askaris. Ukrainian militia mounted guard at the gate.

The workshop was quite big, and had small yellowed windows such as one sometimes sees in factories. A long table, with seats around it, stood on one side of the room. The sign painters worked there. Opposite that stood a small table, which had been provided for my work. The work leader, a prisoner himself, asked if I had really mastered the glazier's trade. He told me that I was the only glazier there. I would have had it considerably easier, he said, if I had put myself down as a painter, as there were enough good painters there to cover up for me. But I was not worried. I felt lucky to have got into the workshop, for I knew that I could not have stayed with the outside work for more than a month. For the present, in any event, there was no glasswork to be done, and I was able to assist the painters.

The brigade leader had set up an elaborate sentry system to guard against being surprised by our captors. It operated as follows: A "sentry" was posted for the duration of the work period at a window that afforded a clear view of the yard, and therefore facilitated the issuing of a timely warning, for if one of the authorities should discover that one of us was not diligently engaged in his work, he had nothing to expect but a beating and tranfer to outside work. Therefore, according to the rank of the approaching officer, the sentry would call out "Half-six," or "Six," or "Big six." The last two numbers signified the approach of the Sturmführer or Untersturmführer.

It wasn't long until we heard a call from the window. "Half-six!" Each of us now occupied himself with some piece of work, and gave the appearance of having unbounded interest in it. An SS Scharführer entered, a whip in his hand. He was the supervisor of the workshops, an Austrian named Czekala.

He first turned his attention to me, the newcomer, and asked me how I had come to be here. He listened to my story with such an open expression of dejection, his head nodding in such sincere regret, that I simply could not regard it as a pose on his part. I learned later that he was a very good sort, and had never been known to strike a man in the workshop. It was only outside, in the course of inspection, that he struck out like the others, and then he did it only to save his face in the presence of the senior authorities.

After his departure, the "six watch" was again taken up at the window, and shortly afterward came the warning, "Big six!" We got to work, playacting as before. The Obersturmführer entered, accompanied by Czekala and two civilians. The brigade leader snapped, "Attention! Caps off!" Everyone dropped his work, stood stiffly to attention, and whipped off his cap. The company commander nodded in acknowledgment, and then ordered, "Get on with the work!" We put on our caps and were immediately engrossed in our work. He moved slowly from workbench to workbench, took a brief look around, and then departed.

A fellow prisoner called me to the window to see for myself how the work of the other brigades was progressing. In front of our windows one brigade was engaged in rooting out and collecting small car parts that had been frozen into the ground. The work in itself was not too difficult, but the prisoners had to labor without gloves, and suffered relentless blows from an SS man in civvies, a certain Rerich, who had a deservedly infamous reputation. At a distance I saw a column of men bearing a dismantled truck body on their shoulders. Even from where we stood, we could hear the blows that fell on the heads and shoulders of these unfortunate fellows. Without sense of purpose they were forced to carry the truck body around in a circle. The sole object of the work was to make the men suffer. I could see other brigades at work, too, and the pattern repeated itself everywhere, wringing out the last drop of energy from the captives, and all to no purpose other than to give our captors pleasure. Their pleasure in inflicting suffering on us was inexhaustible.*

Our "lookout" finally called, "Lunch-time!" He had seen the heavy work outside come to an end and a cookhouse queue form up at the hut. We too formed up and headed in the same direction. On the camp road ahead of us stood several SS men, apparently waiting for us to come by. As soon as he saw them, the brigade leader called out: "Attention! Caps off! Eyes left!" Holding ourselves erect, caps in hand, heads turned to the left, we marched by.

But of course there had to be inspection, too. We were just falling in for the inspection, when the Untersturmführer, with several SS men, suddenly appeared. At first we were subjected to a rough beating up, for we should have stood still at the approach of our superiors, instead of falling in.

After the inspection, we were led to the camp entrance where a van stood, loaded with packages. The Untersturmführer, assisted by the camp senior and some work leaders, undertook the distribution. The names of those receiving packages were called out. The Untersturmführer stood by with drawn revolver, for once previously the men had crowded in an undisciplined manner around the van, each trying to secure a parcel for himself.

A spot check was made on some parcels to see if they contained prohibited objects, such as knives, bootbrushes, clothing, and so on. Each name was called out only once. If the individual for whom the package was intended did not claim it immediately, it was laid to one

---

* It is said that people get "hardened" to pain. I believe from my own experience that this is so. Without realizing it, one gradually begins to apply what is called "self-hypnotism" to shut off certain connections between the brain and the body. In time, one begins to witness the most brutal and degrading scenes without reacting; a person may be killed before one's eyes, and one views it without reacting emotionally, simply records it as a machine might. The same process applies to personal beatings. As the amount of the beatings increased, one consciously felt them far less. Hunger, however, did not diminish so dramatically; it was felt by most as the greatest pain, and in time even twenty-five lashes for a bit of bread did not seem too high a price to pay to assuage one's appetite.

side, and finally ended up in the kitchen, where it was divided up in the evening among those who had got relatively little or who had got only some contribution from the Jewish community.* The latter contributions were sent in for those who had received nothing from home.

There was a particular reason for reading the name of a receiver of a package only once. It very often happened that those for whom packages were intended had died. That, however, was something that should not come to the notice of the van driver, who, on his return to the city, might well set "rumors" afoot.

I stood there full of impatience, waiting for my name to be called out. I was convinced that there would be some communication from home. Then the moment came. My name was called. My heart seemed to be choking me. I ran forward. The work leader handed the package to the Untersturmführer. He inspected it, looked at me searchingly, and then, as I stretched out my hands to retrieve it, struck me two blows with his stick on the head. He thrust the package to one side, and said, "Get back."

In a daze I returned to my position and had to fight hard to hold back the tears. But I pulled myself together, and determined to leave no stone unturned in the effort to gain possession of my package, my own package which had brought with it so many tears from my dear ones at home. After the distribution had been completed, I hurried to the camp senior, Kampf, and asked him to give me the package. He said nothing by way of reply, but conveyed to me with his eyes that I should accompany him to the kitchen where it had been taken. Here he sought it out and looked through the contents. It contained homemade bread, some butter, a package of saccharine, some garlic, which was an essential requirement on account of the lack of vitamins here, and—two sets of underwear. It was forbidden to receive underwear. Now, at least, I had the explanation of the Untersturmführer's behavior. Kampf let me keep one set of underwear, and he himself kept the other, as he had to hand up to the laundry as many sets of underwear as there were confiscated packages. I was, of course, overjoyed to have

* As I have mentioned, the German authorities appointed a known Jewish leader to head each Jewish community. This leader had to choose, subject to approval by the Germans, other well-known Jews to administer various aspects of the Jewish community. Jews were appointed, for example, to administer a labor department, a Jewish police department, food and supply department, etc. Such departments were under the absolute control of our captors, needless to say. The enormous personal and moral problems such compulsory duties raised for the Jewish community leaders were, because of the merely token authority they were allowed, spiritually crushing.

my package at last, but even here my happiness was short-lived. For my name had been inscribed on a white satchel (which contained the food) that had been made out of a linen towel. The writing in blue crayon was that of my mother. The letters were blotted, as if tears had fallen on them. The name of the sender was written below—in my sister's writing. I took it that she had brought the package to the Jewish community, for there the signature had to be applied.

It was now too late to go to dinner, but what did it matter! Was not this the first occasion since my arrival in the camp that I was with my beloved ones, not through torturous thoughts but through something really tangible?

The afternoon's business in the workshop was just the same as that of the forenoon. One of the group was detailed to take up the "six watch" again.

The others engaged in animated conversation about the distribution of the packages, always on the alert to swing back to industrious activity should the warning call be sounded. I stood at the window, observing those engaged in heavy work outside. Presently the Obersturmführer made his appearance on one of the work sites, accompanied by several SS officers. There was one unfortunate individual among the working party who was obviously straining every nerve and sinew in the effort, but failing, for all that, to keep pace with the others. The Obersturmführer walked up to him, and asked, in an unforced, menacing tone of voice, why he was working so slowly. The man replied that he had not the energy to work any faster. The Obersturmführer thereupon drew his revolver unhurriedly—almost nonchalantly—and shot the man in the head. As unmoved as if he had merely crushed a beetle underfoot, the officer passed on.

Work ended at six o'clock. Inspection then took up an hour. After supper, there was a general move to the lavatories to avoid a repetition of the awful mess of the buckets the night before. The scene inside the hut was somewhat different—many sat with their packages in front of them, eating by themselves. In one corner stood a group of those who had received either no package at all or else very little. A commission consisting of work leaders had been set up to see that the packages sent in by the Jewish community were distributed as fairly as possible among the men. Sugar was being exchanged for bread, bread for saccharine, until each man had got what he thought would give him most satisfaction. Some scrupulously ate only part of their food. Others didn't raise their heads until they had eaten all that they had. The latter were in the majority, although they knew that they would be sick on the following day. Their main concern was to see that nothing was left over. Who could know, they felt, whether such an opportunity would ever offer itself again?

The business with the buckets was worse than ever that night.

12

In the workshop next day I was entrusted with keeping the "six watch." Outside, on the grounds, the same scenes repeated themselves. From my window I could keep an eye on the lavatories, before which a row of men stood. Suddenly the Obersturmführer appeared, with a whip in his hand, and lashed out among the men who were waiting there. Then he went inside, and I could hear him venting his rage on those he found in there.

After the Nazi had gone, a man with a battered skull crawled from the lavatory, barely able to drag himself along. Now I could understand why one of the men in the workshop had said to me he was afraid of going to the lavatory. But, indeed, in the long run, it was all the same whether it was the lavatory, the kitchen, the workshop, or the hut in which we were accommodated—the worst could happen at any time and in any place.

Someone at the window with me drew my attention to the notorious "half-six" Rerich. He appeared to be over sixty years of age, and was dressed in civvies. He had Czekala, the workshop supervisor, with him to conduct him around, and he noted with obvious satisfaction how the latter—anxious to make the right impression—struck out a blow here and there indiscriminately. At that moment Bleines, the German foreman of all the work brigades but who was not a member of the SS, passed by. He was a little over thirty years of age, and a distinctively handsome man. My comrades had told me that he, like Czekala, was a very decent sort of man—that is to say, he was when he was by himself, for he shared Czekala's fear of the Obersturmführer. On one occasion, so the story went, he caught one of the men smoking in the workshop, and warned him off: "Look here: personally, I've no objection to your having a smoke, but I'll tell you one thing—if it comes to the notice of the Obersturmführer, I'll step in myself and beat the life out of a few of you. . . ."

At the evening inspection, which again lasted over an hour, the Untersturmführer selected six men who were of haggard appearance and clearly very ill. He forbade them to go into the hut that night. In fact, he told them, they were to spend the night in the open. Then he imposed on the Askaris, who would be doing duty on the watch-tower, the responsibility for seeing that his order was carried out. To us he explained that the action he was taking was in our own "best interests," in order that we might not pick up any infection from these six ill comrades. For them, of course, his order meant certain death.

Since there was a strict prohibition against any movement in the yard after eight o'clock, these men had to lie down on the ground and remain still the whole night. If there was any movement, the Askaris on the towers had the right to shoot. It was an easy way of shooting people, as it didn't involve a barefaced transgression of the regulations against unmotivated murder. Until now there had been rules that people recruited for work should not be killed. The concentration camp was, officially at any rate, only a working place in which the workers were accommodated.

There was no doubt but that the six men would freeze to death. On the following morning we saw six small snow-covered mounds over by the railing.

Workers suffering from illness, according to the Nazi regulations, should have been sent to the hospital. Arrangements for this were supposed to be made through the director of the Jewish community. But only corpses ever reached the hospital. Those who had been shot were buried hurriedly, and their names still remained on the list of the Jewish community.

A few days after our arrival in the camp, we received the camp badge. One was sewn on our clothes over our hearts, and the other on our backs. The badge consisted of a yellow triangle, with a red or a white rectangle underneath. The rectangles bore various inscriptions in black, which corresponded to the designation of the prisoner. I had, for example, the inscription "FA 63." That meant that I was a *facharbeiter,* or tradesman, and that my identification number was 63. Others bore the letters "HA" in addition to the number. That signified *Hilfsarbeiter,* or tradesman's mate and meant that one was employed in the workshops. In these two cases the rectangle was red. Those engaged in heavy manual work, on the other hand, wore a white rectangle, marked with the letters "HA" and the identification number.

What little time there was between supper and "lights out" I generally devoted to chatting with my friend, Feder, for as such I now looked upon the comrade through whom I had opened up a contact with home, and had learned the salient facts of camp life, as well as the ups and downs of his own three months' experience here.

"You came into the camp at a fairly good time," he told me. "At the beginning, when the Ukrainian militia were doing full sentry duty in the camp, the circumstances were much worse." And he went on to tell me how the Ukrainians distributed the packages and what the outcome was like: They took for themselves any foodstuffs of value that were in the packages, such as butter or sausage, and as a rule they left only the bread, for they had plenty of that themselves. Then they'd leave the packages open for days on end, without distributing them, so that finally what was left over was scarcely edible.

When the relatives outside learned that the dear ones, for whom they had at personal sacrifice put aside some of their food and clothing, were being denied access to these hard-won offerings, they no longer handed up their packages to the Jewish community for distribution, but began to bring them to the camp personally. This meant trying to pass the packages in through the railings that skirted the road, to the workers inside. This was, of course, strictly prohibited. For the first couple of days the guards did no more than to fire a few warning shots. But then, as these attempts became far more extensive, and the women—for it was nearly always women who came—took no heed of the warning shots, the guns were trained on them, and a number of them were fatally wounded. The women were now thrown into a torment of anguish and hesitation. They wavered in uncertainty between fear of death and their love for their husbands and sons, all of them knowing that a close approach to the railings brought with it certain death. Nevertheless, a few continued to press forward. Their love more than outbalanced their fear and the sense of reason that should have bade them exercise discretion if only for the sake of those other members of their families at home. Not until the distribution system in the camp had been revised, and the prisoners got the greater part of what was intended for them, did the personal transmission of packages come to an end.

On another occasion, Feder told me what the water situation was like at that time. There was no "washroom" then. This was built later, and there was only barely enough water for the kitchen, making it impossible for the inmates to wash themselves or their underwear. Many of the prisoners were literally eaten alive by bugs and lice. And for all that, everyone had, of course, to present a clean and neat appearance.

"It was much the same as happens now with shoes," said Feder. "No one was allowed to possess boot polish and brushes. The only way of getting water of any kind was to retain half of our coffee for washing ourselves."

He recalled one bitterly cold January day when the Obersturmführer picked out seven quite healthy and hardy young fellows and, ". . . since you swine won't wash yourselves otherwise," ordered them to undress and to get into a vat of cold water which had just been freshly filled. After two hours, chunks of ice could be broken off the corpses of these unfortunate youngsters.

"As you can imagine," said Feder, "such miserable, unhygienic conditions contributed to the spread of sickness. Above all, there was a serious outbreak of typhoid which claimed many lives."

Then he went on to tell me of an occasion on which fifty men were allowed to go home for the day. As the event had passed without any unpleasant incident, and all the men returned in due course to the camp, it was expected that fifty more would be allowed out some days later. Each prisoner heaved a sigh of relief, reckoning that, having been out of luck up to now, it would surely be their turn next time. But something different turned up. Leave was canceled. The camp remained cut off from the world outside. The reason was that the men who had been granted leave from the camp had infected their relatives with typhoid, and the latter, in turn, had spread the infection among the Aryan part of the population. Such a danger had to be countered by strict isolation of the Jewish population. A strictly enforced ghetto was ordered. That indeed was a heavy blow for the Jewish community, and it was not too difficult to see what the consequences of such a restriction would be. The Jewish community leaders were faced with the unenviable choice of putting the whole Jewish population into an unbearable position, that is, exposing them to infection, or, alternatively, of depriving the camp workers of the last shafts of light from outside the prison camp. The latter alternative was the one they decided on, and they accordingly requested the camp commandant to withdraw leave from the prisoners. "This," said Feder, "was the ironic fulfillment of Hitler's prophecy that the Jews would make of themselves a means to their own destruction. . . ."

So passed my early days in the camp. After a short time I began to observe to my disgust that I, too, was coming very near to developing the indifference and apathy of so many others. I was saved from succumbing to these feelings only by the thought of those at home, and the determination that my mother should see me alive. These ideas kept me from yielding, and gave me a positive ideal to strive for.

In the first week of my captivity, my people at home went to the office of the firm where I had worked every day. They left no stone unturned to get me out. The boss, a Pole, made promise after promise, but put them off one day after another. The relatives of the twenty of us who had been interned together at that time joined together, sold what they could for ready money, and made the boss a very handsome and costly present, with the request that he take the matter in hand more positively and more earnestly. But it was all in vain. In one letter to those at home, I told them that every cent of what they had laid out was to be regretted, for the influence of the boss here in the camp where we were interned counted for nothing. But they persuaded themselves that that was not so, and kept up their efforts. Finally, the boss promised them that he would get us out in the coming week. Reading their letter to this effect, I could feel, almost physically, the hope which rose in them from these words of his. But, my God, I knew better. . . .

13

Even at the time when I had not yet been interned, there were rumors going round that an "emigration" project was being planned for the Jews. No one rightly knew what such a project would entail; consequently, the opinions were as manifold as those who held them. It now appeared that the planned project was about to be implemented. As a preparatory measure, the Jewish community was required by a German commission to draw up a list of fifteen thousand Jews. These would be allowed to emigrate, the Germans informed us. No one had the slightest idea that this "emigration" was just a euphemism for the killing of the entire fifteen thousand. In order to hoodwink those concerned, the Germans said that each person would be allowed to take up to fifteen kilograms of baggage with him. The list, as finally constituted, was made up of elderly people, women and children, of the lower classes.

Once again it was the poor among us who were called upon to make the sacrifices. One may well ask, Why was it precisely these people whom the community chose? The question is easily answered: The community required money, a great deal of money, to pay the penalties, bribes, and countless other forms of extortion the Germans forced on us. If the rich were removed, who would be left to provide these monies? If no more money were forthcoming, the rest of the Jewish community would soon be got rid of.

Another, and more interesting, question was, Why did the Germans consider it necessary to carry on protracted discussions about the "transplanting of the Jews"? Why were not the Jews wiped out at one swoop? Why were they not all collected together and liquidated *en masse?* That wouldn't have caused the SS to bat an eyelid. It so happens that this question can easily be answered. For propaganda reasons, it was desired to make it appear that Jew had listed Jew for extinction. Afterward the Germans could claim that the Jews had actually wiped one another out.

The "emigration" project began on the night of March 14, 1942. It soon became clear that following the list would be impossible, for many on it had gone into hiding. The numbers were made up by hauling people arbitrarily out of their houses. People who were engaged in work for the armed forces, and the women who looked after them, were spared. It was mainly old people, girls, and young children who were taken away. Relatively few young men were called.

In the first week the *Aktion* (that was the word the Germans used) was carried out only at night. In the second week it was carried out during the daytime as well. The roundup was carried out by the "Jewish militia," assisted by the Gestapo. As the militia entered each house, a car, occupied by Gestapo agents, was drawn up before the door, and into it were bundled those who were being detained. Once the car was full, it was driven to a school in the vicinity of the Jewish quarter and its contingent dropped off. A commission had been set up at this collecting point for those to be "transplanted," and it saw to the registering of the victims handed over to it, and made arrangements as to provisions for the "journey." Then, when night had fallen, the "émigrés" were brought to the railway station, loaded aboard a train, and the journey began. To what destination no one knew; no one ever saw them again.

In the school, however, the work was not restricted to selecting those who were to be transported. It was also used to recruit young, able-bodied workers to perform the senseless labor we did at Janowska. In general, this group consisted of young women and grown boys. Some horrible scenes were witnessed here: young mothers still carrying children at their breasts were roughly torn away from their children; brother and sister clinging to one another were separated; little children ran about, forlorn and crying in anguish. It seemed as if every human impulse had been banished from the world.

In the course of two weeks, during which the Aktion lasted, about forty new prisoners each day were delivered to Janowska. Soon there was a tight squeeze indeed in the huts. The rate at which prisoners were murdered increased greatly, as we could not disseminate information among the newcomers about the strict camp regulations fast enough. In the first few days a number of the prisoners received twenty-five lashes of a whip, beatings severe enough to kill them, though most of them survived. One of them had done no more than to come into the workshop to us, to warm himself a little. The other offenses were no greater.

The Germans now planned to extend the camp. Hand in hand with this went an extension of ill-treatment and brutality that gave rise to fear and terror on all sides. The following incidents took place within a short time of one another.

A Jew named Zudyk, a former street singer, stood on the edge of a pit, mixing lime. Convinced that Zudyk was working too slowly, the Obersturmführer went up to him and pushed him into the pit, where the poor wretch burned slowly, agonizingly, to death in the corrosive lime.

On another occasion, at a checkup on all work brigades, it was noted that one man was missing, and the brigade leader was commanded to present the man at the evening inspection. When the man presented himself, they made short work of hanging him over the hut door. His body was left there for forty-eight hours. We were all forced to witness the execution.

Not a night passed now without several being sent out into the snow to freeze to death.

Again, a so-called compulsion brigade was formed. If one were forced to join it, certain death followed. One need have committed no "fault" to be forced into this brigade. Members of the compulsion brigade were forced to pick up huge stones far too great for an ordinary man to lift, much less to carry. The inability to lift such stones was considered sufficient justification for inhuman punishment. The brigade leader whose duty it was to beat and drive these unfortunates on was a certain engineer named Schanzer. He made every effort to lay his hands on poison, so that he might relieve himself forever of such work. He had no chance to do so, however. As a result of the beating that he himself had to take from the Untersturmführer, owing to his alleged leniency with his men, he languished away. In the last few days of his life this frail man went about with both arms broken and in bandages. Two weeks later he was dead.

Not one of the thirty men who ended up in the compulsion brigade could endure the exertion for more than eight or ten days—that is, provided he was not shot in the meantime.

Such shooting was not uncommon now. All subterfuges, all hiding behind regulations to kill were now going fast. When the Ober- or Unter-sturmführer wished to practice "sharpshooting," they stood at the window of the office building and used the workers of the compulsion brigade who passed by as targets. But targets were also provided by any other workers who had to pass the windows.

It was the aim of these Germans to strike the hand, the nape of the neck, the knee, or the nose. Once the practice was ended, the Untersturmführer went about the camp, seeking out those who had been wounded, and giving them a "mercy shot" in the head. A wound on the finger sufficed as justification for this treatment.

Our workshop was not spared such scenes either. It happened that one of our men had fallen asleep on his feet and did not hear the warning that announced the approach of the Obersturmführer. With a callous smile, the latter went up to him and strangled him there and then. In this way it came about that, at the end of the Aktion called the "transplantation of the Jews," the total number of prisoners had not increased beyond 550, despite the fact that large batches of new prisoners were brought in every day.

What happened in Lvov under the guise of transplanting us was repeated throughout eastern Galicia, though the Aktion did not take the same form throughout the whole province. In the town of Sambor, for example, the Jewish community was slow to make up the required quota of eight thousand Jews. Therefore, the Aktion was carried out by the SS themselves, and claimed finally not eight thousand but twelve thousand lives. Then, in some small towns, like Grodek Jagiel-onski and Przemysl, only men were rounded up, and they were brought into the camp. A number of them were shot immediately, and the others a little later. About twelve hundred men from Przemysl, a town of some twenty thousand, and about five hundred from Grodek Jageilonski, another town of about ten thousand, came to our camp. A large table was set up between the garages and the office building, and around it sat a commission of senior SS officers whom we had never before seen. The prisoners were lined up in a row, facing the table. Then they were told that if anyone moved his hands—which were held across the back of the head—he would be shot. All had to give up the private possessions they had brought with them. They were led in groups into the washroom where all articles of clothing "not strictly needed" were taken from them. When that had been done, they were led out to the ground outside the railing. Here they were forced to remain three days without food, under the observation of SS men and Askaris. At the end of these three days, many were eating grass, in their desperation. Then they were sorted out; the weak ones—the majority of the group—were shot. The rest were returned to the camp for work.

Among a group of about a hundred people who had been brought in from the town of Stanislav were twelve children between the ages of twelve and thirteen years. They were put to work as apprentices in the workshops. The remaining one hundred adults were transported out of the camp. The next thing we learned was that our heavy-work brigade had been sent out after them. We asked ourselves what this could mean, but no clue was forthcoming. About three hours later the brigade returned. Many of the men in the brigade now wore different clothes. At supper they were served double rations. To our question about where they had been they gave the most evasive answers and asked us not to press them.

Not until the next day, when I happened to meet one of the brigade, did I find out what had happened. "We were brought to a site not far from the cemetery of Janowska," said the brigade man. "A group of SS men were there, entertaining themselves with schnapps and music. Round about them lay a countless number of corpses. These were the people from Stanislav. We were told to collect the bodies together, dig a mass grave, and bury them all in it." He said that anyone who had been spattered with blood in the course of this operation was provided afterward with a change of clothes from the depot. "Before we left the spot," he concluded, "it was forcefully impressed on us that the whole brigade would forfeit their lives if as much as a whisper about this Aktion leaked out."

It was the first time that prisoners had been called in to do this kind of work.

One of the twelve Stanislav children was allocated to our workshop. In answer to our inquiries as to where he came from, and what he had seen, he told us that he lived in a town in Hungary, on the Polish border, and that his father had been "sent off to war—for the fatherland, they said." (It was obvious that, as in Poland at the beginning of the war, Jews were also called up in Hungary.) "The rest of us," he went on, "my mother, my two sisters, and my young brother and I had to leave the town when the time came—just like the other inhabitants—and we crossed the border into Poland. There was a big group of SS men waiting for us on the other side with farm carts, many pulled by people." And then he went on to describe how the old people and the small children were put into the carts, while the others—from ten to fifty years of age—were herded together and driven along like cattle, forced to keep to the middle of the road the whole time. It was nighttime, and pitch dark, and no one could see another. From time to time a flashlight threw a beam of light from the side of the road—the SS men keeping guard. And the sudden lash of a whip could be heard as someone fell down.

"At one stage the horses shied, and my mother and one of my sisters were hit by the flailing hooves, and killed," the boy continued. "We were hardly given time to lay them in the ditch on the roadside before we were herded on again. I was separated from my other sister in the throng and never saw her again. My young brother was lost too. He was no longer with the crowd when we reached Stanislav on the following morning."

He told us how in Stanislav they were enclosed in a large railed-off area, and spent four days tightly crammed together without any food worth talking about. The people were packed so tightly that they could not even stretch their legs. On the fourth day all the men—actually only old men and youngsters—were collected together and loaded onto a truck for transport to Janowska.

"So, my father is somewhere in the war, my mother and sisters and brother are left somewhere along the way behind me, and I am here. What is there in store for us?" His head sank onto his breast with these last words, which were scarcely audible.

The child was twelve years old.

14

As a result of this Aktion in the province, the number of internees at Janowska soon rose to two thousand. The hut was so overcrowded that many had absolutely no place in which to rest. They had no alternative but to spend the night squatting on the ground. A few were lucky enough to be able to squeeze in under the plank beds, which were about six to eight inches from the ground. This meant that once they had squeezed themselves in, they could not move in any direction during the night, but had to lie flat on their backs or on their bellies the whole time. And there could be no thought of getting out of such a position until the morning, as they were hemmed in by bodies on all sides.

Similar difficulties arose in connection with the distribution of the meals. Just as was the case when our number was only a quarter of its present level, the mealtimes were restricted to one hour. This meant that every day quite a number had to go without meals. Food packages, which formerly offered some compensation in such cases, were no longer available; they were now forbidden. In the end, the hunger was so great that many were forced to barter a shirt or a pair of socks for a ration of soup or even a ladle of warm water. An internee named Stock was shot dead by an SS man who noticed that he had come up a second time for a helping of soup. A painter from Lvov, named Schneck, suffered the same fate when he pulled a head of lettuce from the camp garden to alleviate the pangs of hunger. Similar cases followed. The SS became noticeably more brutal. It seemed that their one object was to cut down, by any and all available means, the excessive number of internees at Janowska.

Around the beginning of April it was rumored that one of the internees had escaped. Such a thing had never been known to happen before, and we could think only that the consequences would be unpleasant for us. At our evening inspection the escape was reported to the Untersturmführer. He remained strikingly unruffled, and merely ordered that we should remain standing as we were until the person concerned was found. Then he returned to his office building.

The inspection had begun at 6:00 P.M. It became 10:00 P.M., and then

11:00 P.M. We stood quite motionless in formation. The rain was now beating down upon us, and a chill wind cut through our thin clothes. If an unexpected order for dismissal had been given us at that moment, I doubt if we could have reacted. Another hour passed. It was now midnight. At last the Untersturmführer strode out of the office building and allowed us to get our supper and retire to the huts. Slowly we worked the stiffness out of our limbs. Everyone hoped that the case was now closed; but that was a hope that was not fulfilled.

On the following evening we had to line up on the inspection ground again. From the brigade in which the escapee had been employed, five men were ordered to stand forth, and were shot without further ado. Among them was a nineteen-year-old youth. His stomach was cut open by a bullet, and the intestines gushed out. With an inexpressible, benumbing horror on his face he gathered them back to him. Then he staggered a step or two, like a stricken animal, until a second bullet put an end to him. At this point an SS man suddenly recalled that he had, on one occasion, caught an internee smoking during work hours and had inflicted no punishment on him at the time. Intoxicated by this impromptu blood spilling, the idea of pouncing on his victim appealed to him. He subjected the whole sector to a close scrutiny. Then he found the one he was looking for, and beckoned him out with his revolver. The man, white as chalk, had scarcely stepped forward when a bullet pierced his skull and he dropped to the ground. Once the execution had been completed, the Untersturmführer made it clear to us that for the present occasion he had drawn the line at five victims. If anyone else should get the bright idea to "skip it," we could count on ten victims in reprisal. This threat left us unimpressed.

What did impress us, however, was the fact that the escape had been successfully accomplished. Two days later another attempt was made— one of the newcomers staked his life on freedom. He was shot down on the far side of the railings. On the following day a third attempt was made. It proved successful. Following this, a truck drove up to the man's house, and the entire family, with the addition of some others who happened to be there, was brought to the camp. They were detained for three days without food, in complete darkness. It was not until the escapee, his conscience tortured by this turn of events, had given himself up that the family was released. The man himself, however, was beaten so mercilessly that he never regained consciousness. The fact that the family had been released without being further molested outweighed the fear of having such treatment repeated, and a fourth man made his escape. When he failed to give himself up after three days, his mother, his sister, her child, his sister-in-law, and a neighbor's child, all of whom happened to be in the house at the time, were shot. This vehement reprisal evoked a feeling of horror among the internees that was sufficient to banish all thought of escape for a long time.

Around that time three hundred Poles were arrested in a raid on Teodor Platz (an important square in Lvov), and brought to the camp. As a result, the number of internees increased to such an extent that not all could be put to work. For this reason the Germans began to send prisoners into the city to work. The first working sites selected were the Persenkowka railway station and Sykstuska Street, where houses were to be demolished. It was not long until other working sites were agreed upon outside the bounds of the camp; for example, in the Jewish cemetery where tombstones were to be removed. Often we were guarded by the Jewish militia—answerable with their lives if we escaped—or by the Askaris.

A few days after this city work began, I was sent to glaze windows in a house—24 Wloscianska Street—which was not very far from the camp. An Askari conducted me to the work and then left me pretty much on my own. I was amazed, and immediately the thought occurred to me that here at last was an opportunity to see my family again. After weighing the idea briefly, I asked the woman occupant of the house— who was allowed to have only one room—to let my family know that I could be caught sight of at 6:00 P.M., when it was time for me to be conducted back to the camp. Any time before that was out of the question, as Askaris were guarding the house. My excitement mounted as the hours went by.

It was shortly before 4:00 P.M. when I saw my mother, my brother, and my eldest sister coming along Janowska Street, and several women, whom I did not know, accompanying them. Would I have to wait a full two hours until I could see my dear ones at close quarters, and perhaps be able to speak to them? No. I took courage, and asked the Askari who was standing nearby, and who appeared trustworthy, to conduct me to a neighboring street. I said, in explanation, that the people down there were my mother and my brother and sister. He understood immediately, and my heart fairly thumped for joy when I saw that he would not put any obstacle in my path, but would, in fact,

D

be able to make a reunion possible. He led me out into a shed and then went out to the woman and said simply, *"Weliczker,"* indicating where I was. Their first instinct had been to turn and flee when they saw the Askari heading for them, but now they too saw that there were no grounds for such fear, and within a few seconds I was surrounded by my loved ones and by the strangers. A torrent of questions was turned on me. Each one wanted to know something about her interned husband or her son. How was he, or was he still alive at all? Many answers to such questions were given with deceitful reassurance, for there was a lump in my throat when I had to keep to myself the knowledge that the man in question had long since been dead. So it was that I had scarcely a chance of exchanging a few words with my own family when the Askari came and sent them all away, for fear that an SS man might unexpectedly appear. The women gave me more packages to take back, and then they departed. It was indeed high time, for I was no sooner back on the job than Scharführer Kolanko appeared. I was fortunate that it was he, and not another. On seeing the women withdrawing, still crying, he grasped the situation at once, and said: "It doesn't make any difference to me, but if the Untersturmführer was here, you can bet your life that I would have struck you down on the spot!"

But nothing could disturb me. I had seen my mother again. It had been the happiest day in my life for a long, long time.

15

As MEN, what were our German overlords, the commanders of the concentration camp, like? I cannot really tell. I can give only a prisoner's eye view of these human beings, and some of the facts about them that became common knowledge at Janowska.

The men who ran the camp were two SS officers, Untersturmführer Wilhaus and Obersturmführer Gebauer. These ranks, as I've said before, corresponded to the American ranks of first and second lieutenants, respectively.

Personally, these two seemed at swords' points. Although we internees could not know all the details of their private lives or of their relationship, some of it was thrust upon us. We were constantly aware of the fact, for example that Wilhaus would turn away purposely whenever he saw Gebauer approaching; and when they were together it was clear that they did not behave toward each other in the manner required by military decorum. Too, Wilhaus called his dog "Fritz," which was Gebauer's Christian name—small wonder this did not contribute to a better understanding between the two!

Fritz Gebauer was about thirty-five years of age, and came from Berlin. His overall appearance was striking. He had more than average good looks. He was tall and broad-shouldered. He usually held himself bowed slightly forward, which suggested an aristocratic stance. Most striking of all were his jet-black deep-set eyes, which sparkled, and his deeply line countenance. He had a very pleasant, melodic voice. with a pronounced masculine tone, and in general seemed to have some kind of inner life.

Wilhaus was a native of Saarbrücken, and was a few years younger than Gebauer. In many details his features were similar to those of Gebauer, but the overall effect was completely different. He had nothing to compare with Gebauer's expression of a deep interior nature. With such traits missing from his countenance and manner, the superficial appearance was uninteresting, not unlike that of a doll. His appearance was made all the more unsympathetic and even frightening by his persistent, cold, and ironic smile, as unchanging as that of a mask. His brother-in-law was Major General Katzmann of the SS, and also Police Chief of Galicia. The likelihood cannot be ruled out that this relationship played a certain part in the change for the worse that took place in the camp administration.

A few words would not be out of place here to indicate the extent to which those standard-bearers of National Socialism, the SS, were loath to put the principles of the Nazi racial theory into practice when their private lives were involved in the circumstances, despite the fact that they would kill indiscriminately for these same principles. Gebauer, for example, had amorous relations with a Jewess. Thus the girl succeeded, at least for some time, in making her future secure. Mrs. Gebauer found consolation in turning her attention to a Jewish chauffeur. Similar relations were by no means the exception in the case of other SS men. Murder was one thing, lust another.

The position of deputy to Wilhaus was filled by a newcomer, Untersturmführer Rokita. He was small, stout, about forty years of age, and made a very favorable impression. He was a native of Silesia, and a musician by profession. As such he had toured throughout Poland, and by a unique coincidence he found in our camp senior, Kampf, an old colleague, with whom he had, over a long period, played in the same band.

With Rokita's arrival in the camp, the situation, in a number of respects, took on less catastrophic proportions. For instance, he supervised operations in the kitchen daily, thereby effecting an immediate improvement in the meals. He also introduced proper order in the distribution of the meals so that, at last, each man got what was allotted to him.

That Rokita was, however, well schooled in the ways of the SS was amply demonstrated by an incident that arose out of the failure to have one of his reforms put into practice. He had ordered that, in relation to sleeping arrangements, no one would be allowed to occupy an area less than that determined by him, and accordingly, those who had hitherto been most comfortable were now compelled to forego a certain amount of space. The idea was, of course, praiseworthy, but in practice it could not be implemented, as he had grossly overestimated the space under the plank beds. He appeared for a supervisory visit in the hut one night and, perceiving that his orders as to the distribution of the space had not been carried out, he began to shoot wildly about him, and numerous internees were wounded.

He explained on one occasion that his concern about our food was necessitated by the smallness of the packages sent in by the Jewish community. It was, however, his intention to see that that situation was improved, and he had asked representatives of the Jewish community to come along during the day to see how the work was carried on in the camp. Then he put it up to us to stone these representatives in order to express our obvious displeasure at their miserliness.

About two hours afterward, I prepared to set out from the camp to the hospital where I had to put in some panes of glass. At the gate I met Rokita, who had already gathered together some representatives of the Jewish community. He called me over to him and asked me if it was not true that the food had improved considerably since his arrival. I stuttered out some remarks, and prepared to go my way. He held me back, however, and asked what was my hurry, and whether I was afraid of him.

"*Nein,*" I said, "but I have a lot of work to do and have to hurry away."

Then he called another internee to him, and told the Jews to take a good look at him. He leveled the accusation against them that this otherwise excellent worker was in poor health simply because they were so indifferent as to the well-being of the internees. The internee whom he called over confirmed this, and complained about the community's indifference. He had to say that it was true.

The general opinion among us was that the community took far too little interest in us. We had to bear the burden. The others were allowed to retain their freedom, together with their families. But when it came to excusing the community, one must bear in mind that the relationship between it and the Germans was completely a product of the SS. When the community failed to carry out the German's strict instructions, members were hanged without mercy.

As it later came to light, Rokita had merely made such a scene in order to impress on the Jewish community his benevolence toward the Jews in the camp to make them accommodating as regards apportioning presents to him.

More about these men after a while. For the moment a new turn of events absorbed us.

We learned that a new concentration camp was under construction, not far from our own, and that we would be sent there. It would accommodate ten thousand men. One day, at morning inspection, we were given the order to form into groups. Then we were marched out

of the main gate. In time we realized that our destination was, un-
mistakably, the new camp. We were filled with an agitated sense of
suspense, but with little hope. We now knew that we could expect
nothing but utter and increasing brutality from the Germans. All illu-
sion was past.

The new camp covered an area two hundred meters long and sixty
meters wide, and was completely enclosed by three concentric rings of
barbed wire. A chain of lamps, set up at intervals of two meters, served
to light up the whole site once darkness had fallen. In addition, there
was a series of watchtowers, equipped with searchlights and machine
guns, and manned by Askaris. The whole site was divided into two
equally large sectors by a barbed-wire barrier.

Entry into the first sector was provided by a gate from Janowska
Street. Standing near the entrance were the bunkers and the administration buildings. A path then led from there to the entrance to the second
sector, close to which a watchtower had been set up. About thirty
meters from the near side of the entrance, one found, to the left-hand
side, a large, railed-off area, measuring about fifteen thousand square
meters. This was the so-called *Todesplatz* (Death Grounds), where
those intended for liquidation were assembled before being transported
away. As mentioned above, the path then led through the entrance
into the second sector. In this sector were the inspection grounds and
the tall, gloomy-looking huts.

Once drawn up on the spacious inspection grounds, we were divided
up into brigades, and led over to a painter who was standing by with a
tin of red paint, brushes, and letter stencils. Each internee then had
his roll number painted on his right breast, his back, and his knees.

Finally, we were shown to our hut. A flight of stairs led to the first
floor and on up to the attic. A number of Aryan prisoners occupied
one part of the building; the other parts contained the kitchen and
the washroom. In our quarters there were three series of three-bed
bunks. These were numbered, and each man had to bunk down in
the bed that corresponded with his roll number. It is true that at first
sight the hut made a favorable impression, or at least a better impression than the hut in the old camp, but a number of deficiencies soon
came to light that made the nighttime something far different from a
period of peace and rest. During the day it was excessively humid and
heavily oppressive in the hut, whereas during the night it was so cold
that we often had to sleep with all our clothes on. The flooring on the
upper stories consisted only of thin cracked boards, and sand and dust
continually sifted through, and lodged in our bunks. It would blow

into our eyes, making them smart painfully. Nor was it unknown for one of us on a lower floor to get a free "shower" from above, as it was particularly difficult to make one's way to the lavatory once darkness had fallen. In addition to the Askaris on the watchtowers, there were others posted inside the camp during the night, and anyone wishing to go outside the hut had to give notice to a sentry.

On the very first night I myself experienced just what this "going outside" could develop into. From the door of the hut, I drew the attention of the nearby sentry. He called me forward, and sent me on to the next sentry, who was standing some distance away. When I reached him, I saw to my horror a whole line of men attired, like myself, only in shirts and shorts, lying on the ground. The Askari ordered me to lie flat on the ground like the others. For three hours we lay there, growing numb in the wet grass. From time to time the sentry passed up and down along the row, dealing each man a lash of a whip across the back. In the end, he allowed us to get up, one at a time. Each of us had to urinate across the heads of the others. Half an hour later, the process was finished and we retired to the hut. Such incidents did not occur every night, but we could always count on them when these particular Askaris were on duty. There was one night when they refined their treatment by making each man urinate into another's mouth. There was absolutely no possibility of doing anything against such revolting barbarism. Because we drank a lot of water during the day to stave off hunger, and because the soup we got consisted of practically nothing else but water, most of the men had to get up a few times during the night; and when they didn't resort to relieving themselves inside the hut, they ran the risk of falling into the hands of the Askaris.

After the first few days in the camp, seeing the way things developed, we had to confess that it was a toss-up between the old and the new Janowska. One day the recent newcomer to the Nazi Command, Untersturmführer Rokita, came into the workshop looking for craftsmen to renovate his house, a four-room dwelling near the camp. He asked me to join the work party, and of course I had no choice in the matter. As we dared not absent ourselves from the workshops during the day, Rokita had some Askaris conduct us to his house after the evening inspection, and here we worked right through the night. We were conducted back to the camp in the early morning in time for the inspection. This additional work afforded an interesting insight into Rokita's private life.

It had become well known in the camp that Rokita derived particular pleasure from shooting people. Scarcely a day passed without someone falling victim to his revolver. One evening after the inspection, at which he himself had been present, he led us himself to his house. We had to pass the *Todesplatz* on the way. A number of prisoners, bloated, practically rotting already, were crouched there, wearing dumb and forlorn expressions and waiting for the end to come. Rokita ordered an Askari to bring them food. Insofar as the unfortunate creatures could still think, they must have entertained some hope of being rescued, or at least of getting some enjoyment from the meal. But the moment the first bite was in their mouths, Rokita winked at the Askari and they both opened fire. After a few minutes, the prisoners lay motionless in a great pool of blood. Rokita rejoined us and, as if absolutely nothing had happened, grunted, "Come on, let's go."

When he saw how shaken and speechless I was, he said to me: "You needn't have any fear. I won't lay a finger on you—you're healthy, aren't you! These fellows were sick. It was a happy release for them. Anyway, I've my orders to carry out. What am I in the long run but an SS man—I'm no civilian."

We then continued on in silence.

Thinking it over, I had at least to concede in his favor that he had expedited the executions, and had not tortured them beforehand like Wilhaus, who made a rule of brandishing his revolver for a long time under the noses of his victims, holding them in suspense between dread and hope, before finally shooting them.

On our arrival at Rokita's house, we would get down to work immediately. At 11:00 P.M. we went into the kitchen provided for the Askaris to eat our supper, which was given out each day according to Rokita's orders.

Under these circumstances, we had an opportunity of making informal contact with these Russian war prisoners, who consisted of the most varied types of characters. There were some who were really worse than the SS, but, on the other hand, there were also many who merely filled the job in order to secure for themselves a better means of livelihood. They were quite restricted in their personal freedom. Anyone wishing to have some time off had to secure a pass from Wilhaus, and that was obtained only after considerable difficulty. They themselves were not immune from being beaten. I myself once saw Wilhaus strike an Askari across the head with a tile because the Untersturmführer considered that the latter went about his work at a lackadaisical pace.

After supper, sometime around midnight, we would return to Rokita's house. Then we took turns at sleeping, so that one of us was always left on guard to rouse the others if Rokita should approach. As a rule, it was very late when he appeared. But on one occasion, at about 3:00 A.M. I was so sound asleep that my friend could not wake me.

When Rokita saw this, he bent over me to wake me himself. He drew a flashlight out of his pocket, intending to shine it in my face and so rouse me from my sleep. My comrade, thinking it was a revolver, got the fright of his life, and woke me with a sudden and not too gentle kick. Rokita shouted at him; what did he mean by startling me so? But I was convinced, on opening my eyes and seeing Rokita bent over me, that my hour had come. He could see that in my horrified expression, and said reassuringly: "You needn't be afraid. Haven't I already told you that I wouldn't touch you?"

He was usually drunk, and slept with a different woman every night. When four o'clock came, we would return to the camp.

16

New huts were continuously being built at the new camp, and we were forced to assist in their construction at night, notwithstanding the fact that we had to work all day. Accordingly, we were packed off after the evening inspection to unload building materials at the railway station. SS men and Askaris patrolled the whole evening along both sides of the road that led from the camp and over the Kleparowska Street bridge; they were equipped with whips and iron bars. Between this lane of guards, to the accompaniment of blows and sudden cries, we brought our loads of bricks and beams and other building materials. That went on night after night. From morning till evening, we worked in the workshops; as soon as the evening inspection was over, we had to head for the station. It was too much. As we had nothing more to lose, the unbelievable happened—small groups banded themselves together and proclaimed that they would no longer carry out these extra duties. As was to be expected, the SS replied by firing at them from all directions. Many, who could not reach cover in time, were shot down. The majority received wounds of one kind or another. I myself suffered no worse than a superficial head wound. Then everything went on as before, day after day, night after night.

Had we ever revolted before? Was there ever a leader found among that host of oppressed creatures who was capable of organizing an insurrection against such tyranny? The answer is: Yes. Plans for a revolt were at one time formed. An organization was created, and at its center were several extreme protagonists who held that it was far better to make one definite choice between freedom and death than to languish in hope-gnawing, interminable imprisonment. Their object was to achieve freedom by means of a general insurrection.

The plan had penetrated to the outmost fringes of the prisoners' circles. By some it was approved. By others it was rejected, owing largely to the sense of responsibility of many influential individuals who chose to let present circumstances prevail. This sense of responsibility extended, first of all, to the families of the individuals themselves, and then to the families of their fellow internees, and ultimately to those of the Jews in general, who lived in the city. For one could only guess what consequences a mutiny in the camp would have for these people. Even on the basis of the pogroms previously experienced, I was doubtful if I could accurately forecast what the next pogrom would bring.

The project was therefore scrapped—a welcome decision. Perhaps if we had foreseen the treatment that in any case was to be meted out to us, we would not have been so hesitant to put the plan into action. When a considerable time afterward the last Jews in the city and its neighborhood had been liquidated, and there was no longer any reason for not revolting, insurrection was impossible. Mentally and physically battered, the prisoners now could merely vegetate in an atmosphere of despondency. There was no one left who was physically or psychologically capable of working out a revolutionary plan.

The persistent physical labor, the day and night overexertion, had to make its consequences felt on us in the long run. Typhoid and dysentery now spread unchecked, and finally became so bad that the camp authorities became worried, and resolved to disinfect the huts and to have us bathe ourselves thoroughly.

They did so, but typhoid and dysentery spread still further. Then, one Thursday, we were not allowed to go to work, but were enclosed in quarantine. We were led, a brigade at a time, to a pit in which a huge pot of Lysol solution stood. We had to strip to the skin, and immerse ourselves a number of times in the solution. All our clothes were burned. After the Lysol bath, we were marched to other grounds, and had to lie, stark naked, flat on the ground. Anyone who raised his head was shot. During the day, the sun beat down mercilessly on us.

When the evening came, and it grew cold, we were still lying there. Supported by the most meager rations, we were subjected to this ill-treatment until Monday morning. At that stage there were many lying there who would never again get to their feet.

Then came inspection. Before we were dismissed, each of us was given a shirt, a suit, and a pair of wooden shoes. At that time there were about six hundred out the camp complement of two thousand who were suffering from typhoid and dysentery.

I found that some infectious disease had caught hold of me also. I had opened a package from home, and suddenly discovered that all desire for food had gone. I wrote my family a letter saying that I was not well. My brother, on receiving this, brought me some invalid foods, such as sugar, light confectionery, and so on. In addition, my parents told me that they were making every possible effort to have me admitted to the city hospital. I held out little hope of that, however. My one concern now was to summon up all my energies, in order to be able to present myself for the inspections and not be put on the sick list. That meant certain death.

But now I cannot keep on my feet. I don't bother to line up for my morning coffee. I can neither eat nor drink, and I feel my energy sinking from hour to hour. When 6:00 A.M. comes, I drag myself to the inspection ground. I fall in in my usual position, but I cannot hold myself upright. I swoon and crumple to the ground and lie motionless. The numbering off begins, and my place is skipped. The brigades form up and march off to the work sites. I summon up my last resources of will power, trying to drag myself to my feet and join the others in the march-off. But limbs and brain no longer coordinate. I cannot move. I watch my fellow prisoners marching away. Finally the yard is cleared and I alone remain.

Then I am taken up and carried to the *Todesplatz*. Inflamed as I am by the fever, the morbid sight of five hundred fellow internees awaiting death swims unreally before my eyes. I am dumped in among them, but this scarcely makes an impression on me. My head slumps to one side, and I fall fast asleep.

A sudden prod in the hip brings me back to consciousness. Wilhaus is standing in front of me, his eyes fixed on me, his lips frozen in that characteristic ironic smile. I have the strange sensation that some of the superabundant health behind that countenance suffuses my own body, and a sudden current of energy draws me almost mechanically to my feet. I hold my stance. My thoughts are distant and intangible, and I gape like a puppet at everything that presents itself to my view. It is only when I recognize the Jewish doctor, hastening agitatedly about, trying to salvage what life is left in the bodies around me, that I am able to shake off my lethargy a little.

About 180 of these living corpses can still keep on their feet. I am among them, and we are now lined up in a row. Wilhaus goes around with a list of names, asks each man his name and the brigade to which he belongs, and then draws a line through the relevant entry. Whatever little hope we entertained up to now is dispelled when he crosses out our names. He has crossed us off the list of the living. Many of the men weep in heartbroken dejection. I cannot weep. I cannot think of home. Where my heart should be there is a boundless chasm, an emptiness. I can suppress this feeling only by a fervent prayer that God will send me a quick death.

We are handed over to an SS man named Blum, the officer in charge of the Askaris. We then march off. We encounter the *Scharrbrigade,* the squad of six which has the task of helping to dig graves for those who had been murdered in the camp. The six men join our column. We are led out onto the "sands," an open space outside the bounds of the camp. We obey the order to remove all our clothes, and then shovels are distributed to us. We must undergo the last extreme of mental torture that can be inflicted on us—digging our own graves. Trembling with fever and weakened by parching thirst, the men begin to turn back the sods, though they can hardly hold themselves on their feet.

All is quiet except for the scraping of shovels against the earth, and the dull thump of the clay falling to one side. There is not a sound from those who had been weeping. It is just as if they are already dead.

Now the pit is deep enough. The first two must now get into it, must lie properly side by side, and are shot. The next two are made to lay themselves transversely across them. The third pair must do as the first, the fourth as the second, and so on—a gruesome crosshatched pattern.

Since the first shots were fired, I stand there with eyes closed, feeling my life slip away from me piece by piece, as if I am stripping myself of my apparel a second time. And with each piece goes some of my pain, and it is replaced by a yearning, a desperate yearning for that moment when I will have been stripped of everything.

I hear my name called and know that the next step will bring me fulfillment and I can walk up to the grave with an indescribable sense of buoyancy.

Someone grips my arm sharply and I am brought down to earth with a shock. An Askari standing some distance away beckons me to him. He tells me to put on my trousers, which I do mechanically, and only when he leads me back to the camp do I finally regain my senses. We enter the camp through a small side door. He leads me past the kitchen where I get a hasty drink of water. Then he suddenly halts and, pointing to a corpse that lies there on the ground, says: "He has to be taken over to the 'sands.' He is to be buried with the rest of you."

For one fleeting moment everything goes black before my eyes.

The Askari orders me to drag the dead man behind me, and he himself starts out a few paces ahead. In my weakened condition I can make only very slow progress, and the gap between the two of us widens increasingly.

Suddenly, with lightning rapidity, all the impulses of life take hold of me again, and the thought of escaping flashes through my mind and becomes a living reality. I have nothing, absolutely nothing, to lose, but everything to gain. With a quick glance at the Askari, I drop the body and race back like one possessed into the camp, and mix in with a group of workers. My heart pounds so madly that it seems ready to burst. I can already hear my name being called by the Askari. Three . . . four times he calls. Then silence again. He is afraid to draw attention to the fact that he has let an internee slip through his fingers. Such negligence, if discovered, would have entailed severe punishment for him.

For the next few minutes I make my way about cautiously. Finally it is twelve o'clock, and the work brigades line up for dinner. My friend, Feder, gives me his shirt, and tells me that my brother is waiting outside with a package for me. After dinner, I head for the workshop with my friend. On the way I see that my brother is still waiting for me. I signal to him that I am in better health and that I don't need any package for the next few days. He is so overjoyed at seeing me again that he breaks into tears.

When I reach the workshop, my comrades tell me that the *Werkleiter* (overseer) knows, too, that I have been taken out to be shot. I dare not be seen here, in that case, and I conceal myself in a crate during work hours, trembling lest I should be discovered by some SS man.

It is now clear that I can't afford to hang around here any longer, unless I want to find myself again in the position I was in that morning. I want to find out, though, if it is known that I escaped from the Askari and was not shot. For, if that was the case, and I was not found, it is certain that reprisals would be taken against my family. I therefore stay in the workshop during the evening inspection, awaiting word from my comrades. If it should be announced that I have escaped, they have instructions to say that I am hiding in the workshop. I lie quite still, prepared to find the revolver of an SS man turned on me at any moment. But next morning, when my comrades arrive for work, I discover that I am assumed dead.

Now there is no time to be lost. As if guided by some provident hand, I avoid all danger. The Askaris on patrol take it that I have a pass to Rokita's house, and let me go unhindered. A few minutes more and, as if in a dream, I am out on the street, heading home to my parents and my family.

PART IV

The
Narrowing
Circle

17

As I MADE my way through the twilight streets—not guarded now and led captive, but free and following my own will—I could see that the face of Lvov had changed. It seemed overshadowed by silent grief. The streets, formerly vibrant with pulsating traffic at that time of day, were almost empty in the semidarkness. It seemed an eternity since I had walked here last. In reality it had been only three months from the day I had taken Father's place and gone to Janowska.

I paused before my house and glanced around suspiciously to see whether I was being watched. I must not allow anyone to see me, or all would have been in vain; my presence here could cause even greater misfortune to be brought about than my death at the camp would have been. I rushed upstairs, knocked at our door, and heard someone coming to the door amid a noise of tinkling crockery.

My mother opened the door. When she recognized me, there was a second's dead silence. But when the plates she had been carrying dropped from her hands and smashed upon the tiled floor, she who had been petrified came to life again. Quite unable to speak, she led me into the room—the only room that had escaped requisitioning. Almost timidly—as if I were a stranger here—I looked around. My father's hair had turned gray and he was very thin. I noticed how careworn my mother looked—because of her worry and constant anxiety about me. My father, too, was mute with surprise for a moment, and stared at me incredulously. When he regained his composure he asked me to tell him all that had happened.

It was my turn now, however, to be scarcely able to speak, for I was beginning to feel the reaction to the terrible strain of the past few hours. I was able to tell only the bare details of what had happened; then I fell into bed and sank into the deep sleep of utter exhaustion.

When I awoke I saw as through a mist my mother standing by my bedside and feeding me from a small plate. Then I dropped off again. Late at night I was wakened again. It was noisy outside, and there was a knock at the door. My parents feared some new Aktion. I had to hide under the bed, where I stayed for quite a time. But it was a false alarm, and when everything was quiet again I was allowed to return to bed.

In a few days it became very clear that I was sick indeed. Now I lay almost unconscious and with a high temperature. Typhoid fever and double pneumonia were soon diagnosed. There was no alternative but to send me to the city hospital (still not totally unsafe for Jews), although my father greatly feared I might, in my delirious ramblings, mention things that had better remain unsaid.

Somehow I was got to the hospital, and for many days I lay sick unto death, and I cannot remember anything beyond suffering from agonizing choking fits. Nineteen days passed before I fully regained consciousness. On a Wednesday I was allowed up for the first time and taken to the visitors' room to see my relatives. Just to see them, unfortunately, for patients and visitors were separated from each other by a glass wall because of the danger of contagion. My mother and my brother Jacob were waiting for me.

Mother was very pale, and when she smiled at me I noticed for the first time that her front teeth were gone. Later I found out that she had sold the golden bridgework she had been wearing. The money had enabled her to send me food parcels at the camp.

A few days later I was released from the hospital. I was still so weak, however, that I had to be carried downstairs to the car, which mother—God knows how—had managed to get hold of. At home I found only my brothers Aaron and Jacob, fifteen and thirteen years old then. My sisters had been staying at Stojanov for the past few weeks. In the evening Father returned from work. I was still very weak and was confined to bed for some weeks to come. Of course, there were never the real rest and quiet that I badly needed for my recovery. At night I was forced to lie under the bed far more often than on it. At every minute there was the very real danger that someone might see me and betray me. This would have meant the end, not only for me but for my family as well. Thus we lived in constant fear, made worse by the constantly renewed rumors of an imminent Aktion.

However incredible it may seem, there were still a number of Jews who would not admit the seriousness of the situation. They realized that there was hard forced labor in the camps, but they simply would not believe in the tortures and killings. They were the ones whose families had miraculously remained unscathed so far.

Soon we all saw quite clearly that I could not carry on like this. The constant anxiety was wearing us all down. One piece of furniture after another disappeared—sold for food. The constant worry delayed my recovery, and my health deteriorated still further.

I therefore decided to leave Lvov at all costs. The question was, Where could I go? Perhaps to Stojanov? Could I make it alone, in my weakened condition?

I asked my father's advice. He did not wish to advise me. "Whatever I suggest may bring about your misfortune. I should reproach myself bitterly all my life were I to give you some advice that would prove to your disadvantage. In such times as ours one cannot listen to anyone's advice; not even to one's own father or mother. Rely on your own sense as up to now. Trust in God as you have done so far, and all will end well."

So said my father, and I realized only too well how hard he found it to speak like that. I knew he could not speak otherwise.

While I was still considering what to do and envisaging all sorts of possibilities, my brother Jacob offered to accompany me to Stojanov. He would go with me and then return by himself. This unexpected offer, seemingly inspired by divine guidance, moved me to disregard all obstacles, all dangers, the bad roads, my physical condition. I now did not waste a single day in waiting and doubting.

At five o'clock next morning, thirteen-year-old Jacob and I said goodbye and went on our way. At that hour there was less danger of being caught on the roads, as so many Jews were on their way to work. The leavetaking was heartbreaking, and mother insisted on walking with us for several kilometers. Finally she could go no farther. In tears she gazed after us until we had turned the next corner.

Fear was our constant companion. As fast as my strength would permit, we marched along the highway; through forests, villages, and townships, for a roundabout way would have been too strenuous and perhaps even more dangerous. We felt we would arouse less suspicion on the open highway than on the byways. Toward evening we passed through Kamionka-Strumilowa, a small town that looked quite peaceful. We met several Jews. When we reached the next village after nightfall, we found a barn at some distance from the road, and crept into the hay. I felt very ill, but my last thought as I fell asleep was, I must keep going till we get to Stojanov.

At sunrise we continued our march, and by late afternoon we were near our destination. Four or five kilometers outside Stojanov a horse-drawn carriage suddenly appeared in front of us. This happened so quickly that we could not hide. An SS leader was sitting inside. What now? Before we could think, the man called out to us. We had to put on a bold front.

We crossed over to the carriage more dead than alive. The SS leader questioned us. He asked us our names, where we were coming from, and where we were going? I could see myself back on the way to camp with no hope of escape. So I did not make the least effort to make up a good story, but told more or less the truth: we were coming from Lvov and going to work at Stojanov where we had some relatives. The man looked at us searchingly. He made us open our bags, and seemed satisfied that they held nothing but some bread. He took down our names, scrutinized us from top to toe, and let us continue on our way. We sighed audibly with relief, and hurried on.

At last we reached Stojanov. We took a roundabout route to Grand-father's house for no one was to know of our presence; Grandfather would have been endangered. We had hardly entered the house and greeted my sisters and the others, however, when the eldest members of the local Jewish community arrived and brought the terrifying news that the mayor, a Pole, had learned of our arrival and wished to see us at once. I remembered our meeting with the SS leader in the carriage. A cold shiver ran down my spine. Was it just a coincidence?

My sisters burst into tears, and my relatives who, in the meantime, had gathered round us increased the general agitation. Much against our will, the news of our arrival had spread like wildfire. We debated about our visit to the mayor, but could not arrive at a decision. When my eldest sister got back from work, however, something was done at last. She set out at once to get in touch with the Jewish community to find out what the mayor actually had in mind. Long after nightfall she returned, a very dangerous thing to do, as Jews were strictly forbidden to venture into the streets after dark.

Fortunately, she brought good news. The mayor was willing to overlook our illegal stay in the town if we gave him some curtains and a sofa in payment for his acquiescence. At the moment we did not know where to get those things, but we didn't worry unduly. Such blackmail was an everyday occurrence and was usually settled by the Jewish community. At the moment the demands of our exhausted bodies were stronger than anything else, and, tired out by the strenuous walk, we soon fell fast asleep.

The following morning Jacob said goodbye to return to our parents in Lvov. Rachel and Judith, who were at this time twelve and ten years old, had to go to work. Little Bina, whom I remembered as a lively child, had completely altered. She went about sad and unhappy, and hardly spoke.

In the evening I asked my other sisters about Bina, and was told that the little girl had undergone this change since her separation from Mother. She would neither talk nor laugh nor play, despite all the affection the others showed her. We could hope only that time would gradually cure her melancholy. She was seven years old, and it was difficult for her to understand that Mother could not leave Lvov, for she had to look after Father, Aaron, and Jacob. But the sight of Bina made me feel the separation from my mother more from day to day. The fact that I was with my sisters and my grandparents did not help to overcome my longing for her.

Life at Stojanov seemed peaceful in comparison to that at Lvov. On the whole, the Jews had been left alone so far. A few had been shot when the Germans had first arrived, but those deaths were considered to be "mere incidents," which had nothing in common with the Aktions in Lvov.

All the Jews had to work, of course, and most were blackmailed from time to time, and then everything became quiet again. From time to time a certain number of Jews had to be allotted to a concentration camp. The Jewish community leaders usually settled this matter in such a way that as long as it remained possible only one member of each family was chosen to go. In this way the worst hardships were avoided, although the fate of those concerned was very sad.

There is not one known case, however, of a family complaining to the Jewish leaders about this method of selection. Everyone realized the necessity and even "efficiency" of the method. Thus the days passed, and there were quite a few of us who thought matters would remain like this and that the Germans would content themselves if we wore yellow armlets, submitted to the meager rations, the many prohibitions, and the forced labor. The more farseeing ones, however—and they were in the majority—knew what lay ahead. They lived in constant fear of an Aktion, the terrible results of which were—either through reports or through personal observation—no secret to them.

Beside the work in town, Jewish groups also worked in the surrounding villages. Those people stayed away all week, and spent only Sunday at home. Nevertheless, work in the country was much more popular than work in town. After a fortnight's rest and recuperation, I, too, began work and received a work card. With it I felt much more secure.

Friends took me along to a village, where I had to work in the fields. Each group of five to six Jews had a Ukrainian overseer. Ours was a brutal, bad-tempered man who dealt out many heavy blows, although this was forbidden. We therefore complained to the Jews' Council, who at once registered their protest with the German authorities and actually succeeded in having the Ukrainian removed from supervising any Jews.

A week later I was transferred to another village, Byszov, where working conditions were decidedly better. I was assigned to an elderly Pole, whose cows I had to herd, and who could not understand how anyone could have wanted to do anything else all his life. He was not at all pleased with my initial clumsiness. Every minute he found some new fault with me. He did not approve of the fact that I wore shoes. They made me too slow, he said. I had to leave my shoes off, and soon I could only limp painfully, and this bothered him.

He was at his angriest, however, when my cows invaded the adjoining turnip fields, which they sometimes did despite my best efforts. Even if I was lucky enough to get them back into their pasture after much shouting, the old man would belabor me with blows as soon as he got hold of me. But all this was not too bad, and I was even pleased to put up with it, for otherwise he left me more or less alone. An additional advantage was that every weekend I was able to take some fruit and wheat to Stojanov, and to ease our provisioning problems just a little.

Every Saturday night I returned home from Byszov like all the other workers. And always my first question was, "Any mail from home?" I had written to Lvov every day, but the weeks went by and no answer came. There were rumors of a large-scale Aktion. I feared the worst.

One day several Jews fleeing from the Ukraine came to Byszov. They reported that things had been very quiet in the Ukraine for a long time. Then, suddenly, out of the blue, SS men had arrived and had herded together all the Jews they could find, in the center of the town, shot them, and declared all those remaining to be "outlaws."

This report brought great anxiety and fear to Stojanov. There was an additional worry for us, for my grandfather was arrested on the eve of Rosh Hashana. During a search a millstone had been found in his house. This was strictly forbidden. But, fortunately, Grandfather was released the same night and was ordered to hand over some silver cutlery as "ransom." One of my uncles still had some, and we hurried to hand it over. Then we celebrated the Holy Day, indoors, of course, for it would have been too dangerous to attend the synagogue. But our prayers were no less fervent than in former days at the festive synagogue.

The general anxiety in which we lived since the report of the Ukrainian Jews, Grandfather's arrest, and rumors about a recent Aktion in Lvov made it very hard for me to return to Byszov. I wondered if I should not take one of my sisters with me—either Rachel or Judith, for Bina was too young, and my eldest sister was working—for doubtless it was safer in the village than in the town. But the two older girls didn't want to be separated. I left with a heavy heart.

The following night I had a terrifying dream which made my uncertainty sheer torture. I saw myself opening a letter from Lvov and bursting into tears. It told me that another Aktion had been carried out and that Mother had been taken away. I wanted to return to Stojanov at once to find out if this dream were based on reality—perhaps someone there would know. I had to wait, however, for it was strictly forbidden to leave one's work except on certain days. My day of leave would not be until the following Monday, a week's wait.

At midday on Monday I was back at Stojanov. The streets were deserted. Neither adult nor child was to be seen. There were only sparrows fighting for crumbs, and this increased the impression of paralyzing fear one felt in the atmosphere. I went into my grandfather's house and climbed the stairs. The place was deserted. As if pursued by furies I ran downstairs into the street. I headed for Lvov, blindly, determined to get there somehow.

As I passed by my Uncle Jacob's house, I decided to make inquiries there first. I opened the door and entered the room. At first I could not see properly, for the curtains were drawn and my eyes were still dazed by the midday sun outdoors. All was quiet. After a few seconds I saw that I was not alone, and I could make out my uncle and family, and Grandfather, who was sitting at the table.

No one spoke. Motionless, I stood in the doorway. I was choking. No, there was no need to say anything. I knew enough. Some minutes passed. In silence I sat down beside Grandfather. He looked at me sadly.

"Yes, my boy," he said brokenly, "we are the only ones here—the only ones to survive."

What could I say? I could not speak. Tears filled my eyes. After a while I asked Grandfather anxiously, "Any letter from Lvov?"

"Yes," he said, and fell silent.

"When?" I continued.

"A day before the Aktion," he replied.

By now I had guessed what I was going to hear, but I forced myself to ask, "Well, what has happened in Lvov?"

All were silent. Then Grandfather put his hand on my arm, and said, "Your mother, they took her away nine weeks ago."

What did I think? What did I feel then? I don't know. Unable to control myself, I seized a knife and tried to open the veins at my wrist. The others rushed up, took the knife away from me, and bandaged my wrist. I can remember only what happened two hours later. There was a meal. But I could not swallow food, and just drank thirstily. I think I would have choked had I tried to swallow any food.

After the meal Uncle Jacob sat down beside me and talked to me lovingly, trying to make it clear that I must not commit suicide.

"Perhaps," he said, "you are meant to be the only one of our family to survive. Perhaps you are meant to be the only one who will keep the family going."

I promised to be sensible; then we parted.

As Grandfather did not want to return to his old home, he stayed on with Uncle Jacob and I went to stay with Uncle Mordecai, who had lost his wife and two sons in the Stojanov Aktion. When we arrived at his house, he lighted two candles and began to pray. I sat in silence and stared at the open prayer book on my knees. But the letters kept whirling before my eyes. Uncle realized that this was not the right time for long prayers, and finished hurriedly. Then we went to bed.

I felt dazed and numb. I could not yet grasp the full extent of my loss. But one thought recurred again and again: I shall never see mother again. . . .

I fell ill and had to stay in bed for several days. When I was able to get up, I did not feel like returning to work. Surely my absence would hardly be noticed, and it would be presumed that I, too, had become a victim of the Aktion.

18

By AND BY the Jews of Stojanov ventured out into the streets again. It was found that in the whole town only thirty Jewish people had survived. Here is how it all happened.

One morning rumors had spread like wildfire: The Germans were planning an Aktion. My eldest sister and little Bina were hurriedly sent to hide on a farm owned by a Ukrainian. The other two girls had stayed with my grandparents. Then grim fate took its course. The Aktion was mainly carried out by Ukrainians and—sad to say—by our very own Polish neighbors. SS troops merely supervised and gave orders. They found enough willing helpers.

Early in the morning the Jewish homes were entered by force, looted, and destroyed. With lashes and blows the Jews were herded together in the marketplace. Only those working on the surrounding estates were spared. Uncle Jacob and his family had gone into hiding, Grandfather with them. The rest of the family had also hidden themselves, but were soon found. The Jews who had been herded together in the marketplace were then forced to walk a distance of twelve kilometers on foot, and were constantly beaten. Then they were forced to stand at the station for two days and two nights completely naked, without food or drink. Finally they were loaded into cattle trucks and taken to the gas chambers at Belzec, near Lublin.

Among them were all my four sisters, for the treacherous owner of the farm, who had agreed to hide Bina and Ella, had handed them over to their murderers and had betrayed, as well, my Aunt Hannah, her two children, and my grandmother.

Yes, there were only thirty of us Jews left in Stojanov—thirty miserable figures, more dead than alive. And yet, with all our grief and sorrow we were still not allowed to remain. Nearly all of us had to move to Radziechow, a small town where the surviving Jews of the district had been gathered together. The Aktion had been carried out simultaneously in the whole of eastern Galicia.

Before my forced departure for Radziechow I went to my grandparents' house to see whether I might find any souvenir. Even from a distance I could see windows and doors smashed in. Inside the house there was chaos. Beds, pillows, sofa—everything was slashed and scattered in confusion. No object of the slightest value remained. It was as if a typhoon had raged there. In dismay I hurried away and wrote a few lines to my father: "Don't send anything here any more; Stojanov is dead and so are my sisters."

Then, one night, I shouldered the sack that held my belongings and started out. It was a distance of only twelve kilometers to Radziechow, but I was exhausted when I got there next morning.

All the Jews in the entire district had been gathered in this town. As mentioned before, the Aktion had taken place throughout all Galicia. The tactics used by the Germans were the following:

At the start simple "Aktions" over a widespread territory were carried out. The survivors were then forced to move to certain towns. Then these towns were subjected to further "Aktions," and again the surviving Jews were forced to leave. In this way the circle around them became smaller and smaller. They lived within this circle. All of us could foresee that soon the circle would shrink to a single point.

I spent my first night at Radziechow with friends of my father's. On the following day I joined three brothers who had survived, and we found a room that had belonged to a Jew and now stood empty. There was even a spacious balcony here, and it would do even though the windows had all been smashed and all the furniture removed. We settled in as well as we could, closed the windows with cardboard, and managed to find some straw and a few blankets.

During my stay here two of the brothers worked, while the other brother and I did the housework. There was no kitchen, so we had to use the stove in the room for cooking. This was a little troublesome, but we managed. It was not too bad a time. No one took any notice of us. I did not need to work, and life seemed bearable, in spite of constant fear.

One morning, however, there was the old scare: an Aktion was imminent. What should we do? We decided to pretend that the room had been empty since the last looting. This was not difficult. We just had to hide our few cooking pots, throw the straw about, and leave the door wide open. But where were we to hide? Finally, we crouched in the small space between the double door that led to the balcony. We knew that this was rather uncertain safety, but we could not find anything better, and could only hope that our room would escape notice altogether.

We crouched between the doors the whole of that day. The slightest noise made our hearts beat faster. We dared not venture out at all, and remained hidden for two days. On the evening of the second day we crept out timidly and learned that the Aktion had taken place and was now over. Once again I had been lucky.

A few days later the "Jewish Zone" was considerably reduced in size, and we had to leave our room, as it was now outside the shrunken Jewish quarter. I moved to the house of one of my father's uncles. This change had great advantages for me, for once again I had regular meals, was one of the family, and—as far as possible—I felt at home. My cousin Chaim was staying with us, and shortly afterward Grandfather and Uncle Jacob and his family joined us. There were twelve of us now sharing a single room and kitchen, and yet, though we were certainly rather crowded, we lived in peace and harmony. I cannot remember a single quarrel.

Once more I went to work every day. We had to chop wood or dig turnips. Now and again someone, or even a whole group, ran away to hide in the woods, for we all lived in constant fear of a new Aktion. Some, whose looks did not betray their Jewish origin, enlisted for work in Germany under an assumed name and with faked papers. For it was rumored that nowhere else was a Jew—unless he was known as such—as safe as in Germany, the country from which all persecution stemmed.

Our life was quite tolerable. We were more or less left alone, apart from continuous demands to hand over this or that. But blackmail was the least of our troubles now. Cousin Chaim quite often went to Stojanov at nighttime and returned in the early hours of the morning. His father, my Uncle Mordecai, was still living there, and sometimes received provisions from the farmers. He shared these with Cousin Chaim, who brought the foodstuffs over to us. With these additional supplies we managed quite well.

Uncle Mordecai and five other Jews had remained alone at Stojanov. Uncle was an egg expert, and as there were large egg storehouses at Stojanov he was needed there. The other five also held positions in which they were hard to replace. This tiny group of Jews, the pitiful remnant of a community of over a thousand, shared lodgings.

One day I learned that a new Aktion had taken place in Lvov. My anxiety grew for Father, from whom I had not heard all this time. On the other hand, I realized that sending letters was almost impossible now. Formerly it had been easy to send letters from Stojanov to Lvov and vice versa, if you had some Aryan cover address. This was impossible now, for the Jewish quarters were—especially in Lvov—strictly separated from the Aryan quarters. I was well aware of these difficulties, and knew that I could not possibly hear from Father, yet my anxiety steadily grew.

We soon heard that Kamionka-Strumilowa had been declared "free from Jews." We knew what nameless sorrow lay behind this sober announcement. We had to send forty-five men for clearance of the ghetto there. Many Jews volunteered, for they thought this job would provide temporary safety for them. Uncle advised me to volunteer as well. I did not, however, for my experience at the concentration camp had taught me never to volunteer for any job, for nothing good ever came of it.

Then there were renewed rumors of an imminent Aktion at Radzie-chow. This time, however, our fears were in some degree unfounded. The preparations we could see going on were meant for the setting up of a ghetto, not for immediate extermination. But none of us had any illusions about the future. At first the strictly guarded ghetto fence; next, call-up upon call-up for the labor camps; and finally the machine guns as the last and decisive word. Therefore, quite a few of the men hastened to find a hiding place in the woods now. But this offered a chance for single men only, for neither women nor children were equal to the hardships of life in the woods. Thus, many men, whose families still survived, renounced this chance of safety.

I myself decided to stay for the moment in Radziechow.

On November 16, 1942, one of the six Jews who had remained at Stojanov, living together in the same quarters, arrived and brought us sad news. On the past Friday evening a Ukrainian policeman had come to see my uncle and told him to come immediately to the Landrat (County Councillor) who was waiting outside. Uncle went out to him without any misgivings. The Landrat demanded the key of the egg storeroom. Uncle handed it over and turned to enter the house. The Landrat then took out his gun and shot Uncle dead. Thereupon the police rushed in and killed the remaining Jews. One only, the bearer of the sad news, had been able to get away. Now Stojanov, too, was "free from Jews."

There was hard work in the new ghetto setup at Radziechow, but in spite of the strict watch, many escaped. Then, late in November, the expected order was issued. By December 1st all Jews had to leave the town. This time we would be allowed to move to three small towns, Sokal, Brody, or Busk.

This renewed persecution remained bloodless for the time being. There were now fifteen towns in the whole of Galicia where Jews were allowed to remain. Ghettos had been set up in all these towns.

The circle around us had narrowed considerably.

19

THE JEWS in Radziechow were afraid to leave, for no one knew what trick might be behind this order to move to Sokal, Brody, or Busk. No one wanted to make a decision, and most people waited until the last day. Then, as time was getting short, many people went into the surrounding villages to hire carts from the peasants. At night they removed their belongings, but had to be careful not to be caught in the act; otherwise they faced being beaten up. The following morning these families left with their hired carts. The Ukrainians, aware of this move, waited until the carts had traveled part of the way, then stopped them, and plundered and looted. They sent the peasants home, and the Jews had to travel on by foot, completely destitute.

My uncle and his family intended to move to Sokal, and left during the last remaining days. I was undecided where to go, and stayed behind. Perhaps, I thought, it would be best to take to the woods after all. But I still wanted to wait.

On the very last day the town provided transport to convey the Jews who had not yet left Radziechow to one of the three towns they could still choose. These were mainly poor people who could not afford to hire a cart. They were allowed to take their luggage with them, and arrived unharmed. Only forty Jews, all irreplaceable specialists, were allowed to remain at Radziechow. I finally decided to take to the woods with a friend.

Hiding in the woods did not, of course, mean absolute safety. Many Jews had been killed in the woods, too, not so much by SS bullets, but by Ukrainian and Polish underground partisans; though both were enemies of the Germans, they fought against each other as well. They made things even more dangerous for the fugitive Jews. The Ukrainians were fighting for a somewhat fascist national state, whereas the Poles were fighting for their fatherland, the ancient Poland, to which part of the Ukraine belonged. They were implacable enemies of each other. Both, however, hated the Jews just as much as they hated the Germans. The hatred of the Ukrainians for the Jews was an inveterate hatred, which they vented at every opportunity. The Poles hated the

E

Jews too, though here and there among the partisans were some exceptions to this hatred.

There was daily shooting and every step we took in the woods was dangerous. We had to be on our guard against everybody—Germans, Ukrainians, and Poles. And, occasionally, we were inadvertently fired upon by other groups of Jews. In the daytime I lay well camouflaged in a hole in the ground; at night I went out to forage for food in the surrounding fields or in a nearby village. My life was animal-like, and I had to exert all my willpower not to become completely demoralized. I was tormented by my constant anxiety for my father and my little brothers, Aaron and Jacob. I found it ever harder to bear the separation from them. Daily I grew more tired of being all alone. If only I could be with them again and share their fate, whatever it might be. The idea of returning to my family in Lvov took firm hold of me.

In mid-December I set out for Lvov. My shoes, which had not been in good condition before, had become completely torn and useless during my stay in the woods. Now I walked through the snow in my bare feet. By day I hid; by night I walked on towards Lvov. I arrived at the town of Busk. The ghetto there had not been closed up yet. I entered to get a little rest. In the streets I saw nothing but poverty and misery. Ragged children were begging for crusts; miserable starving figures lingered at street corners; and over all of them hung the fear of an even more uncertain, but dreadful, fate. I stayed for a day, then walked on, glad to get away from that dreadful sight. I arrived at the town of Jaryczow where there was a Jewish quarter. By chance, I met the mother of my Aunt Rywka. She told me that the family there, my uncle and his wife and four children, had been murdered too.

I marched on during all the following night, and toward dawn I reached Lvov. As if in a dream I went to look for our old home. No Jewish people lived in it any longer—only Aryans. The ghetto now began at the next street, Zamarstynowska.

I stood helplessly in front of the long fence separating the ghetto from the rest of the city. It was patrolled by armed guards at regular intervals. My head was whirling.

I saw Lvov as it used to be. Pictures raced through my mind: Stojanov, my grandparents' house, my sisters, my father's letter, that terrible letter which had told us of Mother's fate. There, behind that fence, was my father. How to get to him? A fence separated us. Where else was I to go? Father, what shall I do if they block my way to you? The world is so big, yet there is no room in it for us!

The guards kept patrolling. Night fell; it grew very dark. Searchlights were turned on. The fence was high. Lvov, Stojanov, Radziechow, Lvov again. The fence was not high any longer. No guard was near. Urged on by a strange force, I climbed up and up. Then I jumped. I was inside the ghetto.

I entered the ghetto under an unlucky star, for the very next morning there was another Aktion, during which I was promptly arrested. But not for long, for the guards were careless and I was soon able to escape. It was 4:00 P.M. I just stood about in the street now, not knowing where to turn. I had no idea where my father and brothers were staying, or whether they were still alive. Had I come here in vain? Despair overcame me.

And then, suddenly, as if in a dream, I thought I could see my brother Jacob coming along. I took a step toward him, and then he saw me. His face registered complete amazement, and joyfully he came up to me. But we greeted each other in total silence, and wordlessly my brother took me "home."

In the house we had to traverse a long, dark passageway, Jacob leading me by the hand. Near the end of the passage we entered a room. In dismay I looked round. The floorboards had been torn up, the windows broken. Three shabby beds, a shaky table, a damaged cupboard, and some wobbly chairs were all the furniture.

I could not see Father. I hardly dared to ask for him. "Five weeks ago," said Jacob. "In the November Aktion." I was petrified, unable to feel shock or grief, quite numb. First Mother, and now Father, too. All my trouble, all my hardships had been in vain. I sank into an indescribable melancholy. I sat down on a chair, unable to speak. After a while Aaron came home. He and Jacob stood in front of me, watching me.

Suddenly I felt life flooding back into me. My brothers needed me. I must not give up!

"Why are you not in hiding?" I heard myself asking them. "You may be caught any day."

"We didn't care any more," answered Aaron. "Father and Mother were dead; you were gone. Why should we expect a better fate than all the rest? So we sold everything and ate our fill of chocolate and sweets for once, and now all we are waiting for is the next Aktion."

Aaron was fifteen years old, Jacob, thirteen.

This was enough. I knew now where my duty lay, what I had to do. First I gave them a proper scolding. Then I looked round the room in dismay. The dirt was a grave danger to anyone's health. A woman was living there too, but she was ill, a physical and mental wreck, totally apathetic. A young friend of Jacob's, sole survivor of his family, shared the lodging as well. That evening I cut up a chair and made a fire in the stove. I heated some water, and a good wash for all followed. Next morning I fetched a barber. I still had a little money left from my labors moving the people of Radziechow in the night. Then I manfully tackled the dirt. I engaged a cleaning woman, and together we cleaned the room thoroughly. I was happy to notice that this outward cleaning revived my brothers inwardly as well. This proved to me that I was doing the right thing, and made me very happy.

The next morning the first thing to do, I realized, was to find work. Otherwise, I'd dare not leave the house at all, and would not be safe indoors either. I went to see the chief at the Ghetto Administration to inquire whether a glazier was needed. This sounds quite harmless: to go and inquire, to receive an answer, to work. But actually this was a daring venture, for now every day fifty Jews had to be handed over to the Germans to be shot at once. People who were not working were chosen first, of course. Had I been unlucky enough to arrive at the Ghetto Administration office before the fifty death candidates had been collected, my fate would have been sealed. And yet I had to risk it. I had no money to buy a job, and without one there was no hope for me. At least I had a chance this way.

The most unlikely miracle happened. A glazier was indeed needed, and the Ghetto Administration was glad to get me. I began work the following morning.

And now, once again, the days passed uniformly for a while. I worked until 4:00 P.M. or 4:30 P.M. Then I went home, tidied up, and was able to earn an additional bit of money by carrying water or chopping wood. Thus we led a fairly regular life, and were as contented as we could be under the circumstances.

I had to let a few days go by before I felt strong enough to inquire in detail about my parents' fate. In August, there had been a large-scale Aktion in Lvov in which sixty thousand Jews, all not working, had been exterminated. For two weeks nameless terror had hung over the city. My mother and one of my brothers and some other residents of the house had hidden themselves so well that there was hardly any fear of discovery; their hiding place was a sewer under a manhole.

On the very last day of the Aktion, when my mother thought all was quiet again, she left the hiding place. On learning the Aktion was still going on, she returned to her hideout. But she was noticed going down the manhole by a Pole; she betrayed my mother to the Gestapo and Ukrainian militia. The German policemen did not descend into the sewer; they just called, "Come up, all of you!" The unfortunate ones were intimidated, and obeyed the order. While the Ukrainian militiamen wrecked the house, the prisoners had to remain in the yard under Gestapo guard. As soon as the Ukrainians left, the Gestapo guards turned aside and allowed the children to flee. But Mother was taken away.

Father was caught on November 19, 1942, during a two-day Aktion in the ghetto. Confident that as a worker he was quite safe, he had gone to work that morning as usual. But at the gate of the working site entire work brigades were being taken at random and transported off. My father's group was among them. In those two days twenty thousand Jews were transported away to be exterminated. Only fifteen thousand souls remained of the one hundred and fifty thousand Jews of Lvov.

I had not worked as a glazier very long when a wealthy man came along and bought my job. I had to carry on as assistant. When I heard that a driver for a horse and wagon was wanted, I at once applied for the job. If a doctor or a dentist had been wanted, I suppose I should have applied for that post as well. The most important thing for me was to have a full-time job, and through it the greatest security. I was accepted for the driver's job, and began heavy work at once. I am sure the horses were not very pleased with me, for I did not know how to harness and unharness them, let alone how to drive them properly. When I at last succeeded in harnessing them after lengthy experiments, I left the poor creatures in harness for a full two weeks. I did feel sorry for them, but I was not at all sure that I would be able to harness them again. Had it been discovered that I knew as much about driving as the horses knew about glazing, my days would have been numbered. After some time, however, I got used to my new work, and quieter days followed, interrupted only by a small but upsetting incident: I had saved up 180 zlotys, the price of about ten pounds of bread. One day the money was gone. My brothers and I turned the whole place upside down—in vain. The money was never found.

Again a new Aktion was imminent. We feverishly began to build a hiding place. We bricked up the cellar underneath our room and filled the adjoining cellars with loose earth to hide our walls. We made a small opening in the floor of our room, through which we could get down into the cellar. A friend of ours, who had a good job and was therefore fairly safe and could remain upstairs, agreed to close up the hole behind us, and put the cupboard on top. According to information received, the Aktion was to start at 11:30 P.M. on January 2, 1943. With several fellow lodgers we sat in our room until about 11:00 P.M. and then went down into our hiding place. The cellar measured twelve square meters, and we were fourteen persons. Each of us had brought food for two days. I, however, had only some turnips. We spent two whole days in complete darkness, for the oil lamp, which we had brought along, would not burn because of the lack of oxygen. Then the Aktion was over, and we could return upstairs. Many houses in the town were on fire, and the smell of burnt flesh mingled horribly with the general smell of burning.

The following day we ventured out into the street again. It was an appalling sight. There were bodies everywhere. Many flats were empty. They were in a chaotic state, as if a whirlwind had raged there. Here and there we saw bodies still in their beds. Those had been people who were ill in bed. They had been shot dead then and there, and so had been given the most peaceful death. . . .

Two days later I began work again, as a pipefitter.

20

As at janowska, it was a rule in the ghetto, too, to wear a distinctive badge on the chest. Armament workers (*Rüstungsarbeiter*) wore an "R," those who worked for the German forces (*Wehrmacht*) had a "W", and the so-called specialists (*Facharbeiter*) wore "FA." The ghetto bosses, Oberscharführer Tiller and Scharfürer Mansfeld, had made it a habit to shoot at anyone in the street whose badge was not conspicuous enough, or who was not wearing a badge. Fortunately, I had received the FA badge at the workshop, where I was now working as a pipefitter.

One day our Lvov ghetto was renamed *Julag* (*Judenlager*): Jews' Camp. At the same time a new order was issued that everyone who was not working was to be exterminated. With this new ruling, paralyzing fear and silence entered the ghetto. No children were to be seen, and very few women. As my brothers were too young to work and could no longer risk going out into the street, I now had to buy all the provisions myself. Until now, this had been the boys' task.

Every day I was kept busy until midnight. The children were not allowed to leave our room at all and had to remain there absolutely quiet, for no one in the house must know of their presence. Even were there no treachery to be feared, a thoughtless word uttered in the wrong place might have dire consequences. But the Germans soon found out that in spite of their new regulations there were still nonworking people in the ghetto. Therefore the old regulation, according to which the Jewish militia had to round up thirty to fifty persons per day for extermination, was still valid. For the first time, the Jewish militiamen themselves were in a bad fix. So far they had been the only ones who were allowed to keep their families. A new ruling was introduced: if the daily quota was not complete, the militiamen had to hand over members of their own families for execution.

On February 19, 1942, an event took place that foreshadowed the final phase in the liquidation of the Jews in Lvov. Head Sturman Grzymek was appointed to rule over our ghetto. He was a German national who had been Chief of Police in the former Poland, and then changed over to the SS and had become a "ghetto liquidator" of evil repute. He came from Rawa Ruska, a Polish town where not one Jew had survived.

His rule over the ghetto began with a morning roll call of all workers. Each group of workers had to fall in separately. After we had been standing and waiting for a while, Grzymek drove up in his car, very elegant, and negligently dangling a leg over the door of the car. His driver was Jewish. Grzymek had brought him and his Jewish chief accountant as sole survivors from Rawa Ruska. Slowly Grzymek looked round. He noticed a militiaman who, in his opinion, was not standing properly. He called him out in front, and dealt him twenty-five heavy blows. There was gravelike silence. In silence Grzymek walked up and down. In silence he looked us over. For a whole hour we had to stand like this; then we marched off to work. There was no question but that this was the beginning of the end. No one doubted that the liquidation of the Lvov ghetto was imminent.

The first and foremost principle of our new chief was "order above all." We heard this phrase innumerable times during his rule, and it was put into practice immediately. Grzymek was the very model of German efficiency. The entire ghetto population was made to clean up and tidy up the quarter thoroughly. Not a bit of paper might remain on the pavement. All windows had to be clean and shining, and whenever Grzymek noticed one that did not seem perfect, he shot at and smashed all the windows of that house. The most dangerous thing was his personal inspection of house after house and room after room. If he thought a room was not tidy enough, its inhabitants were immediately shot. If he came across anyone who was not at work, the unfortunate victim was taken away, and the family had to mourn a new death.

From now on, all illegal inhabitants of the ghetto had to stay in their hiding places throughout the day. Large posters appeared everywhere exhorting people to cleanliness. Soon the pavements were so clean and shining that you could have eaten off them. In this way a measure, which was commendable in itself, was literally flogged to death. On the other hand, no attempt was made to improve the terribly unsanitary conditions within the houses.

There had always been diseases in the ghetto, especially fostered by insufficient nutrition. But now typhoid fever and dysentery were on the increase, and a new ruling was made: anyone who became ill must at once go into a hospital. For stricter control four Jewish policemen and one doctor were assigned to several blocks at a time. If they found a sick person, or heard of someone lying sick, and failed to arrange for immediate hospitalization, they had to face immediate execution. Consequently, there were extremely strict inspections, and everyone lived in constant dread of falling ill. Everyone knew what to expect at the hospital—it was certain death. Toward the end of February both my brothers came down with typhoid fever and dysentery. The all-important thing was to move them to a good hiding place. I dug a spacious hole in a sewer, where they might lie undisturbed throughout the day. Returning from work at night in a state of exhaustion, I had to wash clothes, to cook and prepare everything for the next day. This required the utmost effort, and I was often on the point of collapse. But I knew I had to carry on.

Shortly after Grzymek's arrival, "actions" on a larger scale began at the ghetto gate. This gate was the only opening in the nine-foot-high fence which surrounded the whole ghetto. German nationals did "special duty" there as gatekeepers. Groups of them patrolled the fence and the camp itself. Actually, these German nationals behaved worse than the Germans from the Fatherland, but there was one good thing about them: they could be easily bribed with liquor and money.

Grzymek would stand at the gate in the mornings as the work brigades were leaving. He used to stop people who, in his opinion, did not march well enough, or whom he noticed for some other reason. Sometimes he ordered entire work brigades to stop. These "rejected" persons were sent to prison, from which they were then taken and shot. People did not dread going out into the street within the ghetto so much now, for passing through the gate was by contrast much more dangerous. Everyone envied the workers whose jobs kept them in the ghetto.

Whenever there were new rumors of an imminent Aktion, feverish activity ensued. All the people dug hiding places as fast as they could. I took the opportunity to earn a little money by working for other people doing such work. True, I hardly got any sleep at all now, but we were badly in need of money, and I shelved all other considerations.

Early in March a major Aktion began at the gate. A few work groups, who had noticed in time what was going on, refused to go out, and instead went into hiding. When the Germans noticed that fewer men than usual were going out to work, the Aktion spread to the ghetto itself. This was the first time that there were clashes between the SS and Jews. Shots were fired from 72 Zamarstynowska Street, and two Ukrainian policemen were killed.

The workshop where I labored was in the basement of a house the courtyard of which was used as a center for all arrested persons. From our cellar window we could see those who had been arrested reeling and falling under the blows of the SS and Ukrainians. We were unable to come to their assistance. Suddenly one of the victims broke away and jumped through the window into our basement. In feverish excitement we bundled him into some hiding place. Shots were fired, and bullets buried themselves in the walls. Grzymek and some SS men rushed into the cellar. We had to line up, and the SS turned the workshop upside down. The fugitive was quickly discovered and dragged upstairs under a rain of blows. Miraculously, we remained unharmed in the general confusion.

Again I looked out through the window, worrying about my brothers. It was as if time had stopped and evening would never come. At last I was able to rush home. Thank heaven, they were still safe in their hiding place. What a relief!

21

IN MID-MARCH of 1943, the Germans announced that a special roll call
would be held to count the "workers of the settlement," those who
wore the triangle badge. We all realized the meaning of this. The
Germans had intended, we knew, to keep the number of these workers
at about one hundred. But there were seven hundred of us. This
disparity had happened because Mansfield, the former chief of the
ghetto workers, had been selling badges at 5,000 Rm. (Reichsmarks)
each. Now he was gone, and Grzymek, his successor, did not intend
to respect this arrangement. There were six hundred men too many—
no one had any illusions about their ultimate fate. All of us now were
in a state of tormenting uncertainty and fear, for no one knew whether
his name was on the "legitimate" list of one hundred men. I, however, calmly attended the roll call, for I kept telling myself: If I am
among the one hundred men everything is okay. If not—everything is
lost anyway, and I shall at least die a quick death.

A large number of SS men turned up for the roll call, among them
my former commanders from Janowska Camp, Gebauer and Wilhaus.
Both knew me quite well. I tried to hide behind the others as much
as possible, for of course I was supposed to be dead as far as these two
men were concerned. The roll call began. The first of the Elders of
the remaining Jewish community arrived with Ghetto Chief Grzymek
and called up the names on the list. The men whose names were called
went up in front and were given a new badge by Grzymek, a "W."
I was not among them. The remainder were divided into two groups,
one of which was to be transferred to Janowska Camp, the other to
be shot at once.

Everyone tried to be accepted for the camp. I was assigned to this
group, but deliberately joined the death candidates. They would
recognize me at Janowska, I thought, and I knew the camp methods
only too well. Slow death by torture was their way with escapees. I
preferred the chance of a quick death. The thought of death was by
now so familiar that I felt no emotion, except sorrow for my brothers.

Apathetically I glanced round the parade ground, at the separate
groups in formation, and at the rows of the selected one hundred men,

among whom was Grzymek, still distributing badges. Suddenly I realized that there were fewer than one hundred of them, that a few men were missing. My apathy left me. My brain worked feverishly. I approached the camp Elder, who was speechless with astonishment. Weakly, he gave the sign "Passed." In inward triumph I reported to Grzymek and received my "W." Once again I had been saved by a miracle.

But the greatest of miracles could now be only temporary. Two weeks later another Aktion was carried out on an even larger scale. Again the yard outside my working place was the center, and it was crowded with Jewish prisoners. There was shooting in the streets and in our yard. By evening the streets were full of bodies. As I was going home, a woman threw herself from the fourth floor of a house just in front of me. Later I learned that her husband had been assigned to the death group at the ghetto gate. Ever larger groups were taken from the hospital, usually at night, to be shot immediately. We all realized that the end was near. There was a brisk trade in prussic acid. Quite often, however, it was not the real thing at all—an unreliable substitute. Nevertheless large quantities were sold and bought.

Toward the end of March one of the most evil SS men among the Germans was shot and killed by a Jew in Czwartakow Street. A few hours later scores of SS arrived in the ghetto and called up the Jewish police. They chose twelve policemen at random and hanged them one after another from balconies in Loketka Street. Their bodies remained there for forty-eight hours, dangling above the heads of the passersby.

On my return from work one evening, a Jewish policeman stopped me and ordered me to come along to the ghetto commander's office. I knew I was innocent of any wrongdoing, and calmly went along. Two other Jews were already waiting at the office. The commander politely offered me a seat. Half an hour later two SS men arrived, and we were aghast to hear the commander announce, "Three men ready for camp." Hardly had we grasped the meaning of this when we were hustled into a truck that was taking the familiar route.

Had my lucky star quite forsaken me? I could not, would not, believe it, if only for my brothers' sake. Without hesitating I jumped from the moving truck. My star had not deserted me. The truck did not turn back, and the bullets they sent after me missed me. A few hours later I was back home.

Now I had become one of the "jumpers." There were quite a few of us in the ghetto—men who somehow had managed to escape en route for Belzec, the extermination camp. Some escaped at the last moment. At the station the victims were made to undress completely, and were then crowded in groups of eighty to a hundred into cattle trucks, the tiny windows of which were covered with barbed wire. SS men with guns stood in the guards' boxes and kept watch during the journey. Although everyone was aware of this, it occasionaly happened that the barbed wire was torn off a window and a prisoner would jump. Few, of course, succeeded in their escape bid. Most were shot dead or broke their limbs in the fall. Those who did escape, though, returned to the ghetto—where else could they go?—and were then called "jumpers." Some of them had "jumped" three or four times already.

The following weeks were a little quieter. But this could not deceive us, and we all knew that we were marking time. Everyone dreamed of escape; nothing else seemed of importance. But many would not abandon their families. One day, during a search at the gate, a Jewish man was found to be in possession of a gun. No action was taken. This was new proof that things were moving to a climax. Flight, too, was impossible: the town was surrounded by SS men. All of us were just waiting for the end.

On the night of June 1st, sixty cars full of SS men entered the ghetto; this was the beginning of the end. No one's job made him safe now, and the best of hiding places could offer only delay. I wondered if I should hide in the sewers, but changed my mind, for I should have had to abandon my brothers. I stayed with them in our house. At six o'clock in the morning the SS took us away. We were taken to the spot which had seen so many thousands of Jewish victims. SS commandos drove men, women, and children in front of them. Most of us were calm and composed; many women were singing. We were loaded on tram trucks and taken to Janowska Camp. There we were herded into the parade ground, the last gathering place of so many thousands. We remained there for a day and a night, guarded by SS and Askari. At night searchlights were turned on us. The least movement provoked shooting. New crowds kept arriving. Finally we numbered about eight thousand. I felt happy that I was able to spend these last hours with my brothers. Jacob, the younger boy, was no longer frightened. He was sure that no harm would come to him as long as I was there. Close to us sat a father with his frightened little daughter. He was trying to reassure her:

"Have no fear, my little one; no harm will come to you. Soon you will be in Heaven with your beloved mother and brothers, and the angels will be your playmates. Soon we shall be at peace, and no harm will come to us."

He kept talking to his little girl until she grew calm, and said, "Yes, daddy."

Suddenly there was a shot, and a women beside us fell dead, hit by a bullet. The little girl sobbed aloud again, and her father said, "Look here, darling, that woman has gone to Heaven now." The child looked at her father, wide-eyed, and was quiet.

About 10:00 A.M. of the second day, Wilhaus arrived with several SS men. "Don't be frightened," he said; "we are not going to shoot you. You will stay in the camp." Then an order: "Grownups over sixty and children under five step out!"

All knew what this meant. Mothers stayed with their little ones and stepped up with them. A few children tried to flee. SS men rounded them up. The victims had to undress, and were taken away.

Next: "Grownups over fifty and children under eight step out. The rest will go to the camp." The same scenes followed. A man and his wife next to us took prussic acid. But it was not the genuine article, and they brought it up again. (The husband survived and is still alive.)

My youngest brother, Jacob, tried to hide, and crept up to the fence. He tried to make himself quite small, hoping the SS men would not notice him. But they did. They shot him.

Then it went on again: "Over such and such an age, and under such and such an age, step out! The rest will stay in the camp."

The order was repeated many more times. At last, eight hundred Jews were left, out of eight thousand. Just eight hundred, aged from fourteen to thirty years. We were divided into two groups, one on the right, the other on the left. I was separated from my brother, Aaron, the last of all my brothers and sisters. I was never to see him again. Then I realized the purpose of this arrangement. My brother's group was led away for execution. His eyes turned to me. He gave me a last nod, and was marched off with the others on the road so many thousands had gone before, the Road that Father, Brother, and all our family had trod. He carried his head high. Then I lost sight of him.

Someone gave me a push. We marched into the camp.

PART V

The
Death
Brigade

22

During this part of my imprisonment I was able to keep a diary. Thus I am able to give, to some extent, and as far as it proves useful here, a day-by-day account of what happened to me. Of course, if I had been caught keeping such a record I would have been shot. Later I shall explain how it happened that I was able to keep this journal of my experiences in what we inmates called the "Death Brigade"— that group of Jews the Germans forced to burn the bodies of their countless victims.

Perhaps I should say here that on my return I found Janowska Concentration Camp much larger and far more thoroughly organized for work than it had been when I had escaped. Now special work brigades were sent into the city daily under complete guard to do all manner of work. These brigades were returned to the concentration camp each evening. Other brigades worked in shops within the camp. Instead of going to work, however, often a whole work brigade was taken out to be shot. There seemed to be no method or reason for such executions—work ill done, the members too weak to carry on, and so on. The Germans seemed to decide such matters completely arbitrarily. Every male individual in the camp never knew when he woke up in the morning whether he would be going to work or to death that day.

Only infants and children, the old, the sick and, for the most part, women, could be certain the Germans would kill them as soon as they arrived at Janowska. For these there was for the most part no respite.

But now to begin my diary, the step-by-step account of how I got into the "Death Brigade" and what happened therein.

June 15th, 1943.
Reveille sounds at 4:00 A.M. This means getting dressed quickly and rushing out of the barracks where we sleep through the crowd of bedraggled, emaciated inmates. Everybody hurries because soon it will be time for formation. On the way voices call out in all directions; these are the voices of prisoners hawking their wares. They yell: "Hot coffee"; "Sugar"; "Salami"; "Bread." Because of the lack of money among the

"business people" as well as among the customers, bread is sold in portions of about three ounces. This portion is the standard ration that an inmate received per day.

With the others, I am in a hurry to take care of the necessities. A long line has already formed at the toilets. The situation here is chaotic. It is a struggle to get in and a struggle to get out. At last I am able to get inside, where there is more confusion than at the entrance. There is a constant yelling: "Dont piss on me!" "Don't knock me over!"

Close to every temporary toilet occupant there is a long, disorderly line. Everybody who waits in line is holding his pants, ready to go. They quarrel over who came first. In unison they yell at the one who is squatting: "Hurry up; you can finish it later at work!" A few even threaten him: "If you don't get up right away, I'll push you right into it." Or, "If you don't get up right away, I'll piss right on you."

The next line is preparing to squat when someone suddenly says to the man in possession of a toilet hole, "I'll give you a piece of paper if you'll give me your place." An agreement is made, and the bickering starts anew.

Finally I manage to leave the latrine and begin pushing through the mob to the washroom. Here there is nothing but confusion. For a few groszys (pennies) one can buy a canteen of water from a ragged inmate who has managed to push through the mob at the camp's single water faucet several times to obtain an extra supply. He cannot keep this water for his own needs, but must sell it for the few pennies that it will bring him. Three ounces of bread and a quart of watery soup with a few beans in it daily are not enough to keep him in working condition, so he helps himself in this way. He is helped, too, by the fact that he works in one of the "camp brigades" (the people who work outside the camp and can smuggle things into the inmates). When the man has a "good day," and gets his hands on five or six canteens of water and also finds customers with enough money, he can earn the price of a portion of bread.

I buy a canteen of water and wash myself. After washing, I buy a portion of coffee for half a zloty. Standing in line to get coffee is impossible. The very poor have monopolized this line, and it is necessary to buy from them. Even by passing near the kitchen one can get hit over the head by the camp police, who assume that you are trying to get to the kitchen window for the second time. The very poor are willing to run this risk.

Now I hurry to find the foreman of my work brigade to get my bread ration, since he is in charge of the supply for his whole group. I find the foreman (a prisoner like myself, of course) in the yard, where the inmates are formed into groups of five. Each brigade has its arranged place. The camp police, with rubber truncheons in their hands, herd the inmates to formation.

"Foreman, please, my bread portion," I say.

"You didn't get it yet?" He checks a piece of paper where he has the names of those who have received their portion—for some try to get a second helping.

I get into formation, and at the same time I start to eat. I hardly have the first bite in my mouth when an inmate begs me for some. He doesn't care that the formation has started and he is liable to get hit over the head with a club.

Finally the men are organized in formations. An ominous silence prevails. We are standing in fives, in separate brigades in the form of a U. Everybody is facing inward.

On the right side of each brigade a single inmate stands alone; each has a yellow, blue, red, or white armband on his left arm. These are the foremen of the different work brigades. From the faces and clothing of the men one can easily recognize where and what kind of work the brigade is doing. The brigade that is working on the *Ostbahn* (East Railroad) always looks black from the soot, and they are very lean. The work there is very arduous, and the men are constantly beaten. Because it is very hard to do any "business" on the railroad, they have no additional income and must subsist on the standard camp rations. Other brigades look better dressed and cleaner. They work some place or other in the city and under better circumstances. Impatiently we wait for the moment when we shall be leaving the camp.

Outside the gate music starts to play. Yes, we have an orchestra, made up of sixty men, all inmates. This orchestra, which has some known personalities in the music world in it, always plays when we are going to and from work or when the Germans take a group out to be shot. We know that for many, if not all, of us the music will someday play the "Death Tango," as we call it on such occasions.

At last the gate opens, and three SS men come in with Tommy guns on their left arms and whips in their right hands. They are accompanied by a large dog.

We hear the command "Attention! Hats off!" Like a precision drill team, we all take off our hats with our right hands and hold our breath, waiting for the next command. Everyone's face is frozen; for one motion or simply for a caprice of their own, these murderers can shoot tens or even hundreds of people.

Suddenly we hear the command, "Down!"

Everyone falls down. We are commanded to get up again. Then down. This is repeated many times. After this, there is a long pause, and we hear the call for the first brigade to march out. After the first comes the second, third, and so on.

Everyone is waiting impatiently to leave the gate behind him. At last we are in line, and we hear: "Left turn and forward march!" We march like soldiers. After we go through the gate, the brigade I am in hears, "Brigade, stop!" My brigade stops. The murderers are standing in front of us. There is ironic laughter on their faces. Next to them the Askaris are standing in their black uniforms, looking into the face of the concentration-camp chief.

Wilhaus is still Chief of Janowska Camp. He still has the secret smile always on his face. At a given signal from Wilhaus, the Askaris may very well, for no reason at all, suddenly encircle a brigade and lead it off to be shot. They had done it to thousands before us.

We are lucky this time; it doesn't happen. Our foreman now reports the number of inmates in our group. One SS man checks to see if the number is correct, and we get our command to march forward. We march to the place where they assign us to work. There a few brigades are already waiting. I am one of seventy-five selected from all the waiting brigades. We are told to wait for a truck that will take us to build a road between the towns of Kulikov and Zolkiew. We wait for a few minutes, but the truck does not arrive. We get an order in the meantime, to carry bricks, and are instructed that when we hear the call, "Highway construction, Zolkiew," we must gather at a designated place. Our new foreman is a well-known heavyweight boxer named Gross; he has been saved from death several times by Wilhaus, who favors him.

It starts to drizzle.

I go to the plumbing shop where I usually work. The foreman allows me to work there instead of carrying bricks, but when the truck comes I will have to go on it to build the road. This is just a temporary respite.

Now I discuss with others in the shop the possibility that in telling us we are going to the town of Zolkiew to work the Nazis may be up to some kind of trick. I keep looking through the shop window where I can see the place we are to gather, but the truck does not arrive. Through the window I can see my comrades walking in a line with bowed heads and sad faces, each carrying five bricks. I can also see the hands of the clock, which hangs above the camp gate, moving slowly forward.

Time passes. The lunch hour is nearing, and it is still drizzling, The raindrops are falling on the faces of the men carrying the bricks, and they roll down their checks like tears. It looks as if nature is crying through these people.

It is twelve o'clock. The foreman gathers everybody for lunch, and we shuffle back toward the camp. Suddenly we hear the word *sechs*. It means an SS man is approaching. Within seconds, without turning our heads, we form groups of fives. We hear the voice of the foreman, "Attention! Hats off!" We take off our hats, and march like soldiers. After a short while we hear, "Hats on!" We put our hats back on, and for a while longer we march in formation until the SS man disappears.

Back at the gate through which we had gone earlier, the guard counts us and gives the foreman a slip with the number to be fed. We return to that part of the camp yard where we live and eat. It is clean everywhere. The barracks in which we live are surrounded by small gardens. Here and there one can see the cleaners; they carry sticks and are in charge of keeping the camp spic and span. One can hear the tread of our feet. The roads are made from headstones from the Jewish cemetery. You can see the lettering on these stones. The so-called *Friedhofskolonne* (cemetery brigade) works at the Jewish cemetery, bringing the gravestones that are used here for road construction.

We approach the building where the kitchen is. Here we line up in front of a window with our canteens in our hands. The foreman stands beside the window, checking each one so that nobody can return for a second helping. Everyone is staring at the cook's soupspoon to see if one is to get a bean or a piece of potato.

I have my soup now, and I am hurrying to see if I can buy a piece of bread. The soup is nothing but a pint of boiled water, but very few of us can afford to buy anything additional. Then, too, it is hard to get anything to buy. At last the Cemetery Brigade comes back. I buy a piece of bread from one of the marchers. In the meantime, my "soup" has cooled off. Like everyone else I sit down on the ground near the kitchen building, and eat. An inmate passes by who succeeded in getting a second portion of soup; he is looking for a customer who will buy his soup so that he in turn can buy a portion of bread. I finish eating my lunch and go to the washroom to wash the canteen. It is empty here now, too. I hang the clean canteen on my belt, as everyone else does. The half-hour lunch is over. We gather to leave again for work. We pass the gate. Here there is a tower that contains a guard-house. Across one side of this guardhouse a boy about eighteen years old is spread-eagled. He is black and blue, and silent. He is tied so that his feet do not touch the ground; he hangs in the air. Before he was tied up he got twenty-five lashes. This is his end; as a result of his punishment he will be unable to work; he will be *kaput, shot.* Everybody goes back to his morning job; but before we leave, our foreman reminds us that when he calls us we should gather quickly so he will not have to wait for us.

I return to the plumbing shop. Here I discuss again what I should do, go with my group or not. Is this a trick? If they are going to take us to the "sands," why haven't they done it, as with everybody else, in the morning? Why do they need a truck, and couldn't we walk to the "sands" like everybody else?

Everyone advises me to go with my group because they know that at the first opportunity I intend to escape. They know me of old—I had escaped before. Leaving camp and the city, the truck will give me my best chance to escape.

While we are talking in the yard in front of the shop, two trucks arrive. Our brigade gathers and we start to board the trucks. I look out of the window of the plumbing shop; I can see what is happening, and again I ask myself, Should I go or not? I finally decide that if Gross, who has been saved from death so many times by Wilhaus, is going, I, too, can take the chance. It is a fateful decision.

I run out of the shop to where the trucks are loading, and board the same truck that Gross is on. A tall, slim SS man with the rank of Scharführer steps out of the cab and asks which one of us is a carpenter. Everyone raises his hand and yells what he is, a carpenter, bricklayer, a painter, and so on. From another side I hear a voice say, "Enough! Enough!" I look at the man who has spoken. He is a heavy, good-looking man with the rank of Untersturmführer. He is to be our future boss. He counts us, but instead of being seventy-five we are only forty-four. He says, however, that he has enough men for the time being and that tomorrow he will get more. He gets into the cab of the truck and we start to roll.

The heavy iron gate opens in front of us. We are now on the main road, but no one is certain whether we are actually going to Zolkiew. It is still drizzling. Everyone tries to figure out where the truck is taking us. At the approach of Pilichowsky Street, which leads to the "sands," the directional signal of the truck shows that we are turning into that street. We begin to stare at each other, and simultaneously say, "Let's jump!" Gross, our foreman, jumps first. After him a second man, then a third. I have one foot over the tailgate of the truck when out of nowhere a large truck appears carrying about eighty *Schupos* (German soldiers on police duty in occupied territories). We hear shots, and our truck stops. The two men that jumped off the truck after Gross leap back on the truck. I ask myself why they have come back when we are being taken to the "sands" anyway? Isn't it better to be killed attempting to escape than to get undressed and see in front of you the fire that consumed the previous victims—for we know that the Germans burn our bodies right after they shoot us. The truck moves forward, the Scharführer standing on the step of the cab, pointing his pistol over our heads. The truck with the Schupos follows. We are trapped.

Raise your head, man, and spit into the faces of these murderers! Nobody does; it will bring only torture before death. Still, perhaps one shouldn't give up so easily. Miracles do happen, and we may be saved. Hundreds of thousands have waited for a miracle in the past two years, but it never came. Stop hoping!

During the truck ride all kinds of thoughts go through my head. What is my guilt that I have had to witness the deaths of my parents, my brothers, and sisters first? Why didn't I go with my two little brothers instead of now, all alone? Was I a coward, afraid of death? Had I "saved" myself, watching as my two brothers undressed themselves to be shot, only to end up here, twelve days later?

Torturing questions. Yet, like everyone else around me, I bless every moment that I am still alive, and hope each second for salvation.

It is still drizzling. The truck stops. We are at the "sands." The Schupos and the SS men with machine guns surround us. The

Untersturmführer gives us the command, "Get off!" Everyone jumps off the truck, and we fall into formations of five. A thick, greasy black smoke rises from a deep ravine that is over a thousand feet long. We look into the ravine. It contains an open mass grave with thousands of bodies visible to us. On the side of the hill are large piles of wooden logs. At the bottom of the ravine stands a machine, operated by a Schupo in a black fatigue uniform. The machine is connected by a hose to a barrel of oil. The machine pumps oil through pipes into the fire. The fire is hissing. Perhaps the burning bodies are hissing? Perhaps they burn these people alive? In a few minutes I shall know.

"Don't be afraid," the Untersturmführer begins his speech. "You will work here, and when the work is finished you will go back to camp."

We listen to him with mistrust. We know these speeches by now. Weren't all those who were killed told they were on their way to work? We are told that we must give up everything we have in our pockets except our handkerchiefs and cigarettes. They tell us that they know how to search and where people hide things. They advise us to give everything up and not to risk being shot. We throw everything on the ground in front of us, even our handkerchiefs and cigarettes, because we are sure that we are going to be killed. We are then asked, "Which one of you has been a foreman?" One young blond youth, Herches, in his twenties, our future *Oberjude* (Jewish brigade leader), steps out, and another man, named Lustman, about forty years of age, comes forward.

Who doesn't know the Germans' tricks? There are two fires. I am sure that one man will lead one group to one fire and the second to the other fire.

"Which one of you is a carpenter?" the Untersturmführer asks. Without thinking I raise my hand. I have nothing to lose. Maybe they will send me to Pelczynska Street, where the headquarters are, to work; dead bodies don't need a carpenter. Later on, I shall think about taking the next step. In any case I shall not be there long, as I shall attempt an escape at the first chance. A few of the other inmates raise their hands along with me. Because I am the tallest one in the group, the Germans choose me first and then select two others. Guarded by two Schupos and the Scharführer carrying a Tommy gun, we volunteers are led to the working place, leaving the others behind us. I have been wrong in volunteering, I suddenly realize. Nothing could be worse than this! Now it will be impossible to escape!

We stop.

"Here," explains the Untersturmführer, "we shall build the bunker where you will live."

The spot he indicates is near the edge of the ravine. Enclosing half of this spot are the sides of two very steep hills about fifty feet high. Flat terrain extends for a few thousand square feet between the two hills and the ravine.

When we get there we notice that somebody has already started to build; part of a bunker has been set up. There were three brigades here before us, but none of them had worked more than three days (I was told this in the concentration camp). Now I know exactly where I stand. The Scharführer tells us that we must build carefully because we shall have to live here. I know the whole truth now— we shall build as much as possible in three days and then we shall be burned to death. After us, a new brigade, new victims, will be told that they are going to Zolkiew or Boberik, and they, too, will end up in this accursed place.

We are issued tools and given general instructions by the Scharführer as to how the bunker should look. We look at one another questioningly. Our looks say: Maybe you are a carpenter? It seems that everyone had the same thought in his mind when he volunteered: Perhaps the other man will be a carpenter and I'll be able to pass as a helper." But not one of us is a carpenter. Suddenly one of the men addresses the Scharführer, who has discovered by now that none of us has the slightest knowledge of carpentry. The man tells him that one of the other men in the brigade is a real carpenter. The German asks the name of the man, sends for him, and in a few minutes he arrives. Under his supervision we begin to build. The new man doesn't know too much about carpentry either, but somehow we make some progress. We are all curious to know what has happened to our other comrades, but we are afraid to ask since we are forbidden to speak. We hear the carpenter murmur, "It's hell back there in the ravine."

Suddenly the Scharführer tells us to interrupt our work and gather up the tools. We form a line, and under guard we go down to the ravine, to the huge open grave, in formations of fives. The fire is burning; the smoke stings our eyes and the smell chokes us. The fire crackles and sizzles. Some of the bodies in the fire have their hands extended. It looks as if they are pleading to be taken out. Many bodies are lying around with open mouths. Could they be trying to say: "We are your own mothers, fathers, who raised you and took care of you. Now you are burning us." If they could have spoken, maybe they would have said this, but they are forbidden to talk too—they are guarded. Maybe they would forgive us. They know that we are being forced to do this by the same murderers that killed them. We are under their whips and machine guns. They would forgive us, they are our fathers and mothers, who if they knew it would help their children. But what should we do?

> Father, if you came here
> Couldn't I have gone together with you
> And have everything behind me?
> I wouldn't have been standing alone
> on your grave
> And burning your body before my death.

We are standing between the bodies in puddles of blood. We wait, but for what? Perhaps we are waiting for death, or perhaps we shall be sent back to the "Death Cell" where we will sleep as the brigades before us have slept, waiting only for death.

On the hill the Schupos are standing with Tommy guns in their hands. They are armed as if they were waiting for an attack. We overhear one of them ask the other, "Do you have enough bullets?" We stare at one another. Do they mean this for us?

Our leader, the young blond boy Herches, reports how many of us there are. The number is forty-two. We hear the command "Right turn!" Everyone turns to the right. The turn is not so precise as in the concentration camp because of the bodies we are standing on.

There is a command, "Link arms!" In fives, we climb back up the steep, slippery ravine. They tell us if anyone releases the arm of the other he will be shot. In a little while we are at the top of the ravine where we were three hours before. Now, however, we have courage enough to breathe. The commander of the Schupos gives us instructions we must adhere to while walking. For the slightest error we can be shot.

1. Each must link arms with the other.
2. The distance between each group of five must not be more than one and a half feet.
3. It is forbidden to look around.
4. Everyone must walk with bowed head.
5. It is forbidden to talk.

The head of the Schupos reminds us again that for the slightest infraction of these regulations, or even any suspicion of it, we shall get a bullet.

Now we are counted again, and the head Schupo yells, "Forward!" He adds to it—"but slowly." We are walking with slow step, in fives, on the slippery clay and road. With bowed heads and arms linked we shuffle as if we were walking after a hearse. We are not going the same way as we came this noon, by truck. The road we are on is the one that connects the concentration camp with the "sands." The road is hilly, and contains puddles of water. The whole place is a mass grave.

We move forward. It is still drizzling. One can already see a camp tower on which an Askari stands. Maybe they are taking us back to sleep in the concentration camp? In that case they won't see me anymore—somehow I will escape.

We approach the concentration-camp yard. Here we find inmates sitting on the ground, sorting potatoes.

Among the inmates are some who were supposed to go to Zolkiew with us but had been smart enough to get out of it somehow.

We are told to turn our heads the other way. The Germans have forbidden anybody to see the faces of inmates who have seen the "sands."

We stop in front of the barbed-wire fence of the concentration camp. Then we are led into a special part where I had not been before. The barracks in this section are about three feet apart, all in one line. This is where the women prisoners live. They work in DAW (Deutsche Ausvuestungswerke—German Army Supplies) and in the laundry. Each barrack is about forty-five feet long and eighteen feet wide, and each in turn is divided into three sections. Each section has a door and three windows. The windows of the first barrack facing the gate through which we entered have gratings of iron bars. This is the so-called "Death Cell." The Jews caught in the city are brought here, where they wait until the next morning. Shooting usually takes place in the morning hours, and when enough people have been collected.

Anyone who lands in the "Death Cell" is certain to die. These barracks stand on pillars, so that there is about a twelve-inch separation between the floor and the ground. There is a space fifty feet long and ten feet wide between the barracks and the barbed wire. Here we are told to sit down on the ground, in the mud, with our feet tucked under us.

I think: Should I try to escape right now by crawling under the barracks? No. I decide to wait until late at night. I plan to pull out a piece of board from the barracks floor and crawl out in the space under the barracks. I hope that the guard won't stay with us all night and that they will lock us up and leave.

One Schupo leaves to get water so we can wash up. We sit and wait. From the second and third sections of the "Death Cell" barracks, frightened inmates, their eyes blackened, their faces swollen and with black-and blue marks all over them, can be seen looking out through the iron bars of the windows. These are people brought in from the "Aryan" side. (The whole city is now, in reality, the "Aryan side"—the Jewish side is now the concentration camp.) This means they had been caught hiding in Lvov, trying to pass as non-Jews. When captured they are brought to the concentration camp, where they are questioned and tortured until they lose consciousness. When the victim falls on the ground, nearly dead, the Germans revive him, and when he gains consciousness the torture resumes. The Germans want to find out if the victim knows where others are hiding. While we sit there one SS man, tall, slim, with only one arm, by the name of Heine, rank of Scharführer, brings over a tall, heavy-set prisoner. One can see that he had once been elegantly dressed—though his clothes are now in shreds and he has been beaten to a point beyond recognition. Heine is known by all as the worst sadist here. His greatest pleasure is derived from cutting people up with his dagger. He is the chief interrogator here.

The Schupo who had gone for the water returns. With him are two women carrying buckets of water for us. These are from the group who clean the women's barracks. They stop for a moment and stare at us, with that special look given new victims. We wash. While sitting, we strip from the waist up and in formations of five we go to the basins and wash. The second group of five does not approach the basin until the first group has finished and is seated.

Now we are finished washing. Our dinner arrives on a wagon. It is placed outside the barbed wire because the drivers are forbidden to come in. The dinner wagon leaves, and four of us go out, under guard, and bring the food back. One of the Schupos commands, "The fire tender and the tabulator will give out the food." I think to myself that I know practically all the occupations here, but I never heard the names of these two before. I am to find out.

Everybody receives half a gallon of soup, much thicker than the soup in the concentration camp, a five-ounce portion of bread, and a spoonful of marmalade.

We finish dinner and go into the third section of the "Death Cell" barrack. It is empty. The door is locked behind us.

Our cell is about seventeen feet wide and twenty feet long, and it has three iron-barred windows. Because the wooden partition dividing our cell from the one next to it doesn't reach the ceiling, it is possible to climb from one cell to the other. Around the walls are sacks filled with straw. Near the door are two buckets. Everyone rushes to the buckets, since none of us had taken care of his needs since lunchtime. We had been afraid to ask for permission. In a few minutes the buckets are overflowing, spilling all over the floor. The whole cell becomes one big puddle. We hear the voice of the Schupo: "What is happening here? Instant quiet!" Two shots are fired that hit the ceiling of our cell. "Everyone lie down immediately!" An ominous silence prevails in the cell. Two of us share one straw sack. We lie silently. From the other side of the wall we hear children crying. Perhaps they are crying because of thirst or hunger. We hear men and women moaning. They cannot sit, stand, or lie down because they have been beaten so badly. They have been in the cell for three days already, and now they are just waiting for the SS men to bring them to the "sands."

After a few minutes I begin to talk to my neighbor. He has a foul odor about him because of his work with the corpses. We can't even smell the stench from the buckets because the smell on the clothing of the people who work with the bodies is much stronger. (When we came into the cell we had heard from the neighboring cell: "Pfew, it smells!" "What smells so terribly here?")

I start a discussion with my neighbor with the question, How can we get out of here? Little by little we fill each other in on details of what had happened in the ravine. He had seen much that I had not, because I had worked on the construction on the top of the ravine.

"It was real hell," he says, and tells me that when his group had got to the bottom of the ravine two among them were called back up the hill. There was a truck, and on it was a corpse riddled with bullets. It was Gross, our foreman. Two of the prisoners were told to take Gross by the legs and pull him down the ravine and toss him in the flames. At the same time, my companion went on, a doctor who was in his group committed suicide by taking a capsule of cyanide. He died instantly. So of forty-four persons only forty-two were left.

They then were put to work in earnest, my neighbor now told me. One group worked with shovels—this meant digging out the bodies that had been buried or partly buried after former mass murders. Another group worked with the corpses directly. This was a terrible job. One had to grab the hands or feet of a corpse and pull it out from a veritable mountain of dead bodies. Very often the corpse slid out of their hands, or the skin of the body came right off and was left in their hands. Voices from the top of the hill constantly screamed, *"Los, warum so langsam!"* "Quicker, why so slowly!" "Come here quickly!" The one called was frightened, and went up the hill quickly. He knew that twenty-five lashes were waiting for him. It was not his fault that the corpse slid out of his hands. But there were no excuses. So in twos they pulled the corpses out, one holding the hands and the other the feet. Each corpse weighed 150 to 200 pounds. These were relatively fresh bodies—about two weeks old. That meant they were from the final liquidation of the ghetto. I think: Perhaps my two brothers were among them.

The bodies were tossed into the fire, my neighbor says. On one side the fire tender was standing. (He was one of us prisoners, too.) His work was to see that the bodies were put in right and that the fires burn at the right heat and are not extinguished. He must add wood and shovel away the ashes. On the other side of the fire the tabulator was standing. He held a piece of paper and a pencil in his hands. His task was to keep count of how many bodies were burned each day. This is a top-secret job. It is forbidden to tell even the Schupos how many are burned each day. In the evening the tabulator reports the exact number to the Untersturmführer. Even the tabulator must forget the amount after he reports to the Untersturmführer, my neighbor tells me. When the Untersturmführer asks him the next day, "How many bodies were burned yesterday?" the tabulator must answer, "I don't know."

The corpses are called "figures" here, my neighbor continues. To toss in the bodies one has practically to go into the fire oneself. Those on this job have their hands, face, and hair singed. Once the first body is thrown in the fire, they run for the next corpse, because even fast walking is dangerous here. Everyone is afraid of hearing the familiar phrase: "Faster! Why is the work going so slowly?"

"Another day like today and nobody will be able to endure it," my neighbor says. "They won't need to shoot us."

He falls silent. We look at each other. Neither one of us has the courage to interrupt our silence now or the other's thoughts. Perhaps he is thinking of his parents or family. These are always the last dreams of the doomed men. If the Germans were to ask any of us for a last wish, I am sure it would be to see once again our deceased father, mother, wife, children, brother, sister.

Mother . . . Mother, you who sold your gold teeth to buy food to send packages to the concentration camp so that your son might not hunger.

From a distance we can hear the sound of music. The Germans always play it for the inmates who are returning from work. Slowly one and then another of us gets up and quietly and carefully starts to move around the cell. Some of us cannot lie down any longer because we are starting to feel the pains from the whippings we had received that day. Nobody chases us away from the window. The head of the Schupos is gone. The Schupos, once they are alone, come near the windows. They look around to see if any of the SS men are watching them. They give us cigarettes and try to calm us down. They tell us not to worry, that we will not be killed.

Maybe they are telling us this to prevent us from trying to escape?

Across from our cell are the women's barracks. Women look out of their windows. They would like to pass something to us but are afraid of the Schupos. The Schupos notice this, and approach these women, asking if they want to give us bread. We indicate with our hands that we do not want any bread but that we would prefer cigarettes. Some of us call out our names. We want them to give our names to friends or relatives in other parts of the camp.

Night falls. Everybody lies down in his place. Two Schupos keep guard around our cell. Should I try to break through the door? They will start shooting. But there are only two guards and only some of us will be shot; the others will escape. But what will happen after we get out of the cell? We have the barbed wire to contend with. This barbed wire is closely woven, and about ten feet high. Two feet from the first fence is another identical fence. It would be hard to climb over it. Every six or seven feet there is a pole with a searchlight on it. And if one could break out of this section, there is still another where the workshops are located. It is very well lighted, and on each corner there are guard towers.

But we *have* to do something! For we are certainly going to go from this "Death Cell" to the "sands."

The two Schupos are still guarding us. Perhaps later they will leave. With these thoughts I fall asleep. I dream about my father and mother. They are crying because their last child is going to be killed by the same assassins that killed their other children. I awaken. I must try to escape. I approach the window and I hear the Schupos talking. I try to wake up my comrades, but they are sleeping soundly. Lying down again, I think about what could be done. After a while I fall asleep. I dream again about my parents, about my mother, when she was taken away to be killed. I dream about her telling that she is leaving seven children. In my dream I know it is eleven months later and that I am nearing the same end as all her other children. I dissolve in self-pity and I start to cry. I wake up and fall right back to sleep, continuing to dream about my mother, my father, my brothers, my sisters.

23

I WAKE UP: day breaks. The night has passed—the night in which I had vowed to escape, the night that was my last hope. Now, surely, I am lost. Slowly everyone starts to wake up. One can hear moaning everywhere. Again the cursed day. Oh, God! What did we do to deserve this? If we could have died during the night!

It will be a day of new torture and surely a day of death.

I am near the window. Through its iron bars one can see the concentration-camp kitchen. The usual morning there. Ironically I think to myself: No more of those toilets, and no more reveilles. I don't have to be afraid of the "Death Gate" anymore. Today is the day I die. Of that I am certain.

It is seven o'clock. The doors are opening. We hear the voice of the head of the Schupos. "Out!" he yells. Everybody gets out. We sit down on the ground, as we did last night. The head of the Schupos counts us. The number checks. In front of us is a large container of coffee and bread. We receive a double portion of bread (about six ounces) and a quart of sweetened black coffee; as the proverb goes, "The sweetness before death." Breakfast is given out in the same manner as last night's dinner. We finish breakfast, and get up.

With arms linked we start marching, and the Schupos remind us of the regulations we have to obey while marching. We are forty-two, and the number of Schupos guarding us is forty. Every one of them carries a Tommy gun with a finger on the trigger ready to shoot.

We go through the small gate we used yesterday. On the other side we stop. We wait. From the direction of the concentration camp three Scharführers are coming. One of them is Heine, who manages to be present at every execution. Behind them a group of Askaris follows.

The people we saw last night in the second and third divisions of our cell join our group. The men are separated from the women and children. The guard is enlarged to about one hundred Schupos. Forty isn't enough?

Now we know that we are going to be killed, because women and children surely are not sent to work. Some take off their overcoats and jackets, dropping them on the ground, so that the undressing on the "sands" will be quicker. Perhaps in their fright they feel hampered by their clothing. We walk the same path as yesterday. About 150 feet before the ravine, the guards hold back the women and children, leaving them behind with the Askaris. The men, who number forty-three, are going with us.

These are newcomers from the city. They have just been arrested. Now they leave their wives, children, mothers, and other members of their families, with whom they had been hiding until now, behind them. Most of these new prisoners are from a concern called Feder und Daunen (Feather and Down) in Lvov. The director of the business had pretended he would hide them; he took away all their belongings, and afterward betrayed them to these executioners.

We go to the bottom of the ravine where we worked yesterday. The Schupos stay up on top encircling us. In the ravine we sit down on the corpses as if we were sitting on benches. We remain like this for a while. The putrid bodies wet our trousers. Presently two cars arrive in the ravine. Two SD* corporals step out of the cars along with one private, two sergeants, one warrant officer, and our chief, a second lieutenant.

We rise. They count us. We are eighty-five. The Scharführer who was in charge of the construction of the bunker yesterday calls us up and enlarges the group building the bunker to twenty inmates. We twenty are ordered to go up the hill in fives. We mount the hill and go over to the place where we worked yesterday. Today there is a good carpenter among us. The new carpenter explains to the Scharführer that our work yesterday was worthless, and it is decided to start the work anew. Under his supervision we take everything apart and we begin to build all over again.

Today a young fellow about nineteen years old, tall, blond, and in high boots, has joined us. He had been hiding, passing as an Aryan in the city. His first name is Marek. Because of his pleasant looks, the Untersturmführer, we learn, has ordered that Marek shouldn't be beaten. The Scharführer gives him cigarettes, bread and butter, and ham. Everybody likes this boy, and we all consider him one of the lucky ones. He tells us that whenever the Scharführer had asked him if he could help to find other hidden Jews, he would answer with the question: "If you, Herr Scharführer, were in my place, and knew that

---

* *Sicherheits Dienst*—Security Service, which outranked the S.S.

in any case you would be killed, would you give away your brothers?" He informs us that he will not fall into their trap.

The Scharführer is a little taller than average height, good-looking, slim, a builder by profession. He knows a little bit about machinery. He is not one of the worst sadists here, and he beats the inmates less than the others. His name is Jelitko. I believe that was his Nazi-party name, not his real name. Like most of them here, he originally came from Berlin. When any of his colleagues approaches, he pretends to be yelling at us.

Very often a Schupo named Koenig comes over to our group. He is in charge of the oil-pumping machine. He beats everybody, regardless of whether they work or not. He looks very rough, is of average height and on the heavy side, and comes from around Berlin. He will spy even on his own colleagues and report them to the SD, so that even the Schupos have become wary of him. All the officers here belong to the SD.

During the morning I am carrying a beam about twenty feet long, under the guard of Koenig. Two corporals, a sergeant, and the second lieutenant are standing near the construction site. The beam accidentally slips off my shoulder and falls close to two of these officers. They let out an angry yell. I start to excuse myself, but nothing helps. Each of them gives me ten lashes. I am sure they will shoot me, but I don't care; I think: Let them get it over with. Instead of hearing a shot, I hear, "Get up!" With what is left of my strength I pull myself to the bunker under construction. Here I take a piece of lumber in my hands so that it will appear that I am handing it to the carpenter. By feigning work I get by until lunchtime, and save myself, for by then my strength has returned.

At twelve o'clock, at the command of the Scharführer, we stop our work. We move into formation and are counted; the number checks. We go to the ravine. The smell from the ravine gags us. It is hard to imagine this overpowering odor. The neighboring villages, a few miles away, had complained of the stench.

In the ravine the inmates also stop their work and prepare for lunch.

The sweat is streaming down their faces like water. Their hands are caked with the fluids from the corpses so that one cannot differentiate between the flesh of their hands and the flesh of the corpses. From behind the thick, gray-looking layers of dried pus on their hands one can see a patch here and there of their real skin.

The ravine workers stand in formation; we join them; we are counted, and the number again checks. We are eighty-two. But, I suddenly realize, the number does *not* agree. I remember that we were eighty-five this morning. Maybe they forgot? It is none of my business, in any case. After they count us we are commanded to sit down. Ten people are summoned to go up the hill. The first two groups of fives go up. From a truck they unload containers of soup which had been brought over from the concentration camp. They bring the containers down, put them between the corpses. The same two who ladled out food last night do so today, too. One by one we get up and return with our soup. No one can wash his hands. They give us no water. It would be a mistake to think that at lunchtime we will be spared our beatings. Every so often someone is called up the hill and given a few lashes. We, as well as those who do the beating, never know the reason. We are beaten, and that is all. The object, I suppose, is to keep us under constant tension, constantly cowed.

One o'clock—lunchtime is over. We form into ranks again and are counted, and on the command of the Untersturmführer each group returns to its morning job. Our group, under the guard of eight Schupos, returns to our construction work, building the bunker we were told we would be living in from now on.

At five o'clock, on the command of the Scharführer, we stop work. Formation; counting; and under guard down to the ravine, where the others are already in formation. All are counted again—seventy-nine. We are told to sit down as we had during lunchtime. We sit and wait. What for? To be killed? What else? We sit on the corpses. There is the silence of the grave now, and no one moves. Everyone is as if dead already. Everyone has the same look on his face. With bowed heads, our eyes look inward. The impression is that nobody is thinking. We are sitting, and suddenly we hear "Get up!" We all rise, like automatons. No one raises his head. We get the command to go up the hill.

We stand on the top. We are counted again, and at the command of the Untersturmführer we start slowly to walk.

So today is not *the* day either.

We walk the same road as we did this morning. We arrive at the same place where we were last night. We wash up, receive our dinner, and the situation repeats itself. Tonight no one but us is in the barrack. The people who were brought over today from the city, who lived, with forged papers, as Aryans, have been herded into a field outside the wires under guard. In this place the Germans normally gather together large groups destined for death. The jail barrack is too small for them. This field was the place where the Nazis had collected the people during the liquidation of the ghetto two weeks before.

We enter yesterday's barrack, but today we are put into two cells. Forty inmates in one, the rest in the other. Our cell has been cleaned up. But again there is the same scramble for the pails. The mess is repeated, but no one minds it anymore. We lie down on the straw sacks. To my left lies a good-looking man who had been added to our brigade that morning. He is about forty-six years old, and graying at the temples. His name is Brill. Prior to the war he had a flourishing flour business, and lived on Lyczakowska Street. On my other side lies Roth, a young fellow, born, like me, in 1925. He is tall and slender. His birthplace was Bielsko, a city in western Poland. His father, a lawyer, was a representative of an American oil company in Poland. We lie quietly. The silence is interrupted only by the moans from the straw sacks.

I turn to Brill. "What are we going to do?"

"I would like to die," he says, and starts to tell me of the happenings of the day. He talks very slowly and haltingly—as if he were convincing himself that he, Brill, still existed. After each word he sighs "Oi." Often, in the middle of a sentence his voice trails off and he heaves a deep "Oi." Everything that has happened is beyond his belief, incredible. "I worked at the firm of Feder und Daunen at 5 Zrodlanej Street with my two daughters. One was seventeen, the other fifteen. After the liquidation of the ghetto we were hidden in the company's building. The director of this firm took everything away from us. Then the Gestapo came and brought us here; my two children and I." A long pause. "This was a few days ago. Today they took us, together with you, to the "sands," and I was separated from my two daughters." Pause.

He went on: "I, as everyone else, went down to the ravine. After a long time, about fifteen people were selected and taken to the place where we left the women and children in the morning." Pause. "And there—there" (in a terrible moaning voice) "all, and my two daughters among them, were lying dead . . . shot. What girls, beautiful, intelligent —what I wouldn't have done for them. . . . They told us to make a fire, and we threw all the bodies into it, my children, too."

He was saying something more, moaning, gesturing with his hands and feet, like an insane person. But I didn't listen any more. How could I help him? The tragedy was universal, not particular any more.

It is night, and outside it is pouring. It is dark. In the barrack it is quiet; everyone is asleep. In their sleep the inmates are moaning, "Oi," "Oi." From far off one can hear the muffled cry of children; they are sitting on the other side of the wires, waiting for death. I get up and go to the window. The rays from the searchlights are mixed with the streams of rain. Schupos are walking near the barracks, guarding us. I return to my place and ask Brill, "Maybe we should break out?"

"What for?" he answers. "I *want* to die."

After a while I start again. "If we break out we can die with honor."

"What is it to me, honor or no honor; it is all the same—I want to die."

Yes, yes, I thought to myself; yesterday this man thought differently; he thought about escaping. But he was afraid to risk the lives of his daughters. They preferred to die together. Tonight this man is not living; he is only existing. There is no way of winning; they have us.

Slowly I fall asleep. I dream about the Seder night. The whole family is sitting at the table. My mother serves the food, looks into the face of every child with a smile. The candles are throwing a beautiful glow. Father is asking us children different questions. But I don't answer. I am only smiling happily. . . .

I wake up. The rain is beating on the roof, and on the other side of the wire people are sitting in the rain with small children—we can hear their cries. They are waiting for their Savior . . . which will be death.

I fall asleep again. I dream about the place behind the wires. I am sitting there with my two brothers. I comfort my youngest brother, who cries because he is afraid. I try to make him understand that death takes only a short while, and afterward he will be together with Mother, Father, and his sisters.

He answers, "How much I would like that."

Dreams and reality merge. But here is a scene that is real—that actually happens that night.

The Schupos shoot a woman. The woman's child is sitting next to her in a puddle of blood with her head on her dead mother's breast, sleeping. An SS man wakes the child by whipping her. She must go with the other children to the "sands." The child screams in terror, "Mother, it hurts!" The child gets up and starts to run, and the SS man goes after her. The child yells, and the murderer decides to shoot her on the spot. He reaches for his pistol, and shoots.

The shot wakes me up. Later, we learn the story.

24

DAY BREAKS and slowly everyone gets up. We move around the cell very slowly. We stop as the sound of music, the "Death Tango," reaches us. Surely, today they are playing for us. Today will be the third day, and from all previous experience of other groups which had worked with the corpses on the "sands" we know that it will be our last one.

The door opens. We hear, "Out!" We all step out and sit down as we had yesterday morning. We are counted, and the number checks. Now they release the people from the other cell. They sit down behind us. We have our breakfast, and after we finish, under heavy guard, march out to the "sands." At the "sands" forty-eight inmates are waiting for us; they have been added to our group. These people previously worked at H.K.P. (*Hepres Kraftfahrt Park*—Military Car Depot).

And so our brigade is enlarged to 129 inmates. The day passes as usual, and in the evening we return to the "Death Cells." This night one of the inmates hangs himself from a rafter with his belt. Now our brigade numbers 128. In the morning, when we leave for work, four inmates, following the command of the SS man, carry this man out and throw him behind the toilet. An hour later he is brought to the ravine with the other corpses from the concentration camp.

Thursday and Friday pass with hard work. Today our brigade is opening a mass grave that contains 1,450 bodies. Many of today's corpses don't have bullet holes in them. They have open mouths with projecting tongues. This would indicate that they had been buried alive.

In the evening my younger neighbor, Roth, tells me his story of the last days of the Jews in Lvov. Roth was caught on the "Aryan" side. He had been able to pass as an Aryan for the preceding ten months. Then one day he met an old school friend. The man immediately reported him to the Gestapo. They arrested him and his younger sister, who had also been passing herself off as an Aryan. Roth himself had tossed her body into the fire two days ago.

So passes the night. We talk, then sleep, and resume talking again. The topic of escape crops up. In order to clarify our situation and to describe how little chance we had for escape, I should like to describe the exact conditions and location of our working place.

In the western section of Lvov is Janowska Street. At the end of this street, as I've said, is a huge sandy area, called the Janowska "sands." These "sands" have high hills, deep ravines, and cover an area of approximately two and a half square miles. There are signs in Polish, German, and Ukrainian around the "sands": "To enter this place is strictly forbidden. Anyone nearing this site at a distance of less than 150 feet of the sign will be shot."

Every few hundred feet a Schupo stands guard in this area. On top of the highest sandhill stands the observation point. Here is a tent where the Schupos stay and where ammunition is kept. Here, too, is a telephone with a direct line to the concentration camp and the Gestapo's city headquarters. The houses in the "sands" area had been emptied and taken over by the Schupos. The Schupos, who number over one hundred, are divided into two groups. Each group has twenty-four hours on duty and twenty-four hours off. In addition to the Schupos there are quite a few SD men.

After a long discussion with Roth on how to escape, we fall asleep.

At six in the morning we are awakened. A new day of torture begins —perhaps our last one. Once again this day seems the most critical to us because it is the last day of the week.

It starts as usual. Everybody is at his job. From our brigade the carpenter and one of his assistants have been taken to one of the Schupos' houses to repair something. It is twelve o'clock—lunchtime. Our brigade as usual goes down to the ravine for lunch, but instead of twenty, we number only eighteen today because the two have not returned from the Schupo's house yet.

We are standing in formation waiting to be counted. We stand and wait. Why are they keeping us waiting? Probably to kill us. What else? We all know that today is the last working day in the week. We look straight into the fire—our destiny. Let's get it over with!

But nothing happens. Perhaps we are waiting for the others to join us. At last we see the Schupo and the carpenter arriving on top of the hill, but the carpenter's assistant is not with them. We see the two men are now approached by the second lieutenant, corporal, first lieutenant, and the private. They encircle the carpenter. The second lieutenant has a few words with the Schupo and afterward with the carpenter; he then reaches for his pistol and shoots the carpenter. We all surmise that the assistant must have escaped.

In a minute we hear the command, "Two men up!" Two of us run up the hill, carry the corpse down, and throw him into the fire. Now the second lieutenant himself comes down to the ravine. In silence, beckoning to us, he selects four inmates, most, but not all, of them elderly men, over fifty years of age, and he gestures to them to stand in one line. After that he asks, "Which of you complains?"

One man about thirty-five years old steps forward. "I do," he says. And then he adds, quietly, "Maybe at last I will rid myself of more tortures."

The Untersturmführer motions him to join the line, and picks out one more inmate. They now number six. They stand in front of the fire, looking at it; they are turned away from us.

Now the Untersturmführer begins his speech, directing it at us. "One of you escaped. Because of him these people will be shot. From now on, for everyone who tries to do the same, I will shoot twenty of you. If I find out that you are planning an escape, all of you will be shot."

After this speech he turns to the chosen six, and shoots one after another. Each is shot in the back of his head, and kicked so that the body won't fall toward the Untersturmführer. When he finishes, he calls for four of us to pick up the corpses and toss them into the fire.

While the bodies are being thrown into the fire, the Untersturmführer walks around us as if looking for someone else. Suddenly he points at Marek and says, *"Komm."*

Marek asks, *"Ich?"*

"Ja, du, du."

Tears appear in the boy's eyes. Walking toward the point where the other six stood a few minutes ago, Marek asks again, with a tearful voice, "Why me?"

"Don't babble so—turn around." Marek turns around, and a moment later he, too, is lying dead.

"Two men!" Two men toss him into the fire. Before he is tossed in, the Untersturmführer tells the two men to take off Marek's boots. "Let's not waste such a good pair of boots!"

Now we are counted—122 men. We have lunch. After lunch we march back to the barrack.

Today we work only half a day.

25

THE ONLY TOPIC of conversation on Saturday afternoon and evening is the escape of the man and the death of Marek. Everyone prays the escapee will make it. Let one at least be saved from all those here, and live to tell the world what is happening to us. In any case, sooner or later, they will kill us all. We decide that anyone who gets the opportunity to escape should try it and not pay attention to what the Untersturmführer said about killing twenty other people. Marek is our symbol. Even if the lieutenant likes us, promises us a "long life," takes care that we get enough food, our end will be the same as Marek's—sudden death. If at this time we ask, as Marek had, "Why me?" each must tell himself, "Because I am a Jew!" We must not try to comfort ourselves with hope again.

Saturday and Sunday pass, and again we have before us a new week full of suffering and hard work. Who knows? Maybe not even a full week. Maybe only a few days or even a few hours. Again day, again night . . .

Monday, June 21, 1943.
The day begins with breakfast, then we go over to the ravine. Everybody resumes his work of last week. At ten o'clock a truck arrives. We are called to unload it. The truck is carrying gravestones brought from the Jewish cemetery. They are very large and heavy, weighing 500 to 700 pounds apiece. Each of these stones must be carried to the bottom of the ravine. The SS men tell us that if we drop one, they will break our necks.

We carry the stones down somehow, and somehow without an accident. We are made to lay out all the stones in a square, and to fill the cracks with cement. Near this square we level off an area. Here we place the bones that were taken out of the fire—those not completely reduced to ashes. On the other side of the stone square we level another area for the ashes. On the third side we level a place for the bones which could not be crushed fine enough to pass through the sieve, and on the fourth side we build a bench. We have now created a new working place, where a special brigade will work, the Ash Brigade, *Asch Kolonne.*

The work of the ash brigade is to crush the bones that hadn't completely burned with heavy wooden poles to fine dust and pick out all the metallic items, for example, fillings of teeth, gold teeth, jewelry, and so on. These valuables are to be put into a sieve standing near the bench. In the evening the foreman is to bring the sieve up the hill, giving it to the Untersturmführer, who will then empty it into a linen bag which he then carries off with him.

The inmates working in the Ash Brigade come back at the end of the day blackened from head to foot by this terrible dust from the powdered human bones.

Tuesday, June 22nd.

A prisoner sitting behind bars sees people on the outside, and grieves because he is not free; but it is worse for him if he is sent to an island and is completely cut off from the rest of the world. Here where we work, except for the bodies, our murderers, fires, hills, and sand, nothing exists. There is no connection with the community which exists in the concentration camp. One has a feeling that except for one another, and our assassins, we shall never see another living soul again. We, 122 inmates, share the same fate, work, and thoughts. Everyone thinks about being saved in order to revenge the death of our dear ones.

As on every other day, we leave our cells for work. But this is not going to end like every other day—though we do not know it then.

None of the SD's tell us that we shall not return to the "Death Cell" any more to sleep, but two of the Schupos disclose the secret. As usual our group goes over to the construction site. Today we finish encircling the bunker with barbed wire. Under tension we wait for four-thirty, the hour that the working day ends.

At four-thirty a wagon stops at the gate that leads to the bunker we have now finished, and one of the Schupos who normally guards us is on it. Our dinner has arrived, which means we are staying here.

We 122 members of the Death Brigade will live here in this bunker. That is now clear.

Our new quarters are about thirty-three feet long, twenty feet wide, and only five feet high. It seems as if the bunker were purposely built only five feet high so that our heads would be constantly bowed.

To enter the bunker one has to go down a few steps. One of the walls is a natural one—the side of the steep hill; the other three sides are wooden ones, and on the outside mud and sand are piled as high as the roof to secure the walls. From the main road six steps lead down to the yard where the bunker is situated. Our whole living area is encircled with barbed wire.

Directly in line with the gate is the entrance to the bunker. The distance is approximately seven feet, and from the other walls to the barbed wire it is about fifteen feet. The roof of the bunker contains three holes; when finished, these will give us our ventilation and light. The inside of the bunker is divided into two parts, one section twice the size of the other. These two parts are divided only by an aisle about ten inches wide. We are to sleep next to the walls and in the aisle.

We are commanded to enter our new abode. It is much too small. We quarrel over our sleeping places. At last we lie down. We are packed together like sardines; we have to lie sideways with our legs curled up. The openings in the roof have not been finished, and except for the open door there is no ventilation or light. We sweat and choke because of the lack of air. Owing to the limited space, some of the inmates must lie by the doorway, and no one can get in or out.

Fortunately the door is left open by our guards, and one can go to the toilet anytime, though we must report to the guard if we go out. The Schupos stand guard outside the barbed-wire fences. When one has to relieve himself, a guard keeps a light on him while he goes to the open toilet and returns. And he must walk close to the bunker wall and at no time is he to approach the wire fence. About a hundred feet from our bunker is a tent where the Schupos stay when they change guard. The tent is also used to store extra ammunition.

Wednesday, June 23rd.

At seven o'clock in the morning we have formation in our yard. We are counted, and Herches, the young man who had been appointed our leader, reports our number to the Schupos. After the report is given we scatter about the yard. Then breakfast arrives from the concentration camp by truck. Ten men go out to unload breakfast. In addition to our breakfast the truck is loaded with corpses, those who were killed yesterday in the concentration camp. And so, from now on, every morning with our breakfast we shall also receive corpses.

The men carry the bodies down to the fire without waiting for a command. The rest, in the meantime, bring the breakfast. It is given out; we finish it, and form up for our second counting. At eight o'clock the corporal and the lieutenant arrive. Our leader Herches again reports the number, and everyone leaves for his work. Our group, the construction unit, is now redistributed among other groups, except for one man, who has to finish the holes in the roof of the bunker.

Because I am very much afraid to work with the corpses, I start to move around so that I won't be assigned to any group. Without permission I stay around the bunker. I clean it up and put everything in order. What can they do to me? Shoot me? I am not afraid of that.

Twelve o'clock approaches. Today lunch isn't eaten in the ravine. Instead all the groups return to the bunker yard. We have formation, and Herches reports the number of inmates to the sergeant, who is second in position to the lieutenant. His name is Rauch. He is a slim man of medium height, about twenty-eight years old, and comes from Munich.

We finish our lunch. At one o'clock, formation, counting, and then everybody goes back to his morning job. A truck arrives with straw. This straw had been used to cover the potatoes in the concentration camp. It has a foul odor. A few people are called up from the ravine to unload the truck and to spread the straw in the bunker. The foul odor of the straw isn't as bad as the stench the people bring back from work. Their shoes are full of pus and decayed flesh. That terrible odor is absorbed at once by the straw, increasing it.

At five o'clock we finish our work. Again formation and counting. After that, we wash up. Today we receive buckets and basins. We have to fetch the water. Everyone would like to get washed up, but no one is willing to carry the water because the walk to the well is far and difficult and uphill. The foreman corrals ten young people, I among them, who fetch the water under guard. An hour later we return with twenty buckets. Everyone gets a quart of water, and drinks half of it. We are very thirsty. Dinner arrives—180 quarts of coffee, the same amount of soup, and seventy pounds of bread. Everyone gets his dinner and eats it sitting on the ground in the yard.

We sit around the yard until eight o'clock, at which time we again have formation and counting; then everyone goes into the bunker. Eight o'clock is curfew; we are forbidden to be in the yard after that time.

Now it starts to rain. Because of the open ventilation holes in the roof, the rain pours in. We all crouch together because the water is quite high. This is truly a calamity. We are drenched, exhausted, and sleepy.

If, after a hard day's work, one does not get his rest at night, he will not have much strength left for the next day. Being weak, the chances of getting a beating are so much greater, and the probability of being shot increases. In the morning hours the rain stops and we drowse off.

Thursday, June 24th.

The morning passes uneventfully. The Untersturmführer, satisfied with yesterday's work (over two thousand corpses were burned), makes a speech during our lunch.

He is a man of about forty, heavy-set, about five foot nine, with glassy, shifty eyes; he is always drunk but never rowdy. His name is Scherlack. He is originally from Berlin, but his family, his wife and a seven-year-old son, live here in Lvov. He is shrewd, and an excellent administrator.

He begins his speech with the words, which later become our motto, "Be decent and clean." By "clean" he means clean in conscience, too, because if one of us tries to escape, they will shoot twenty inmates. Thus the inmate who will cause the death of his comrades will not be "clean."

"If you will keep these two things in mind, you will live to be a hundred," he tells us—here he raises his hand and points his finger at us, his eyes narrowing, "I will care for you like a father for his children." He asks how we liked our breakfast, and last night's dinner, and assures us that this is nothing in comparison to what we will get in the near future. He promises us that we are going to get clothing and shoes so that we can change after work, and he will provide us with water so that we will not need to carry it so far. As for the holes in the bunker roof and the flooding when it rains—well, that we will have to learn to live with because, "unfortunately," he has no solution for it!

At the gate a large basin of water and Lysol is set up in order that we may wash our hands. A sprayer with pure Lysol is brought over to sprinkle our shoes before we enter the bunker. From now on we also spray the bunker every day.

The driver takes the empty coffee cans back to the truck. He is an SD man with the rank of sergeant. He, with his truck, was especially appointed to this command. His name is Ulmer. He wears glasses and is a bit rotund. He is a truck driver by trade. It is said that he belonged to the Nazi Party for twelve years; this means he belonged to it prior to 1933. When he beats one of us, he beats recklessly until his victim loses consciousness. At the sight of human blood his eyes glow. He is one of those who literally seem to thirst for blood.

An hour later Ulmer's truck brings water, and he tells me to distribute it before lunch and to keep part of it for dishwashing. From now on, we are going to have a routinized "household," and a manager is needed. I am that man.

Twelve o'clock: All the work brigades are returning for lunch. On the command of the Untersturmführer I stand with another boy at the gate stopping everyone, telling them to wash their hands in the basin of water and Lysol. After that, I tell them, they must go to the sprayer to spray their shoes. At the gate I had prepared a scraper, and everyone scraped off his shoes before entering the yard. In a few minutes everyone is standing in the yard in formation to be counted. After that, everyone washes his hands, rubbing them with sand. The stench of the bodies, however, cannot be removed so easily; washing with Lysol, chlorine, or gasoline still leaves one's hands with the stench of corpses upon them even the next day.

The Sturman checks us out today. Having the lowest rank here, he always likes to prove that he is a "good" SD man, which means that he is the worst one for us—the most sadistic. He is about thirty years old, and comes from Bolechów, Poland. He speaks Polish well and also Ukrainian—his name is Reiss.

After lunch the truck brings twelve containers of water that hold about a hundred gallons each, and everyone gets enough water this evening.

So passes Thursday, June 24, 1943.

26

The morning passes routinely. Today one group is ordered to reopen three more mass graves. These three pits are about sixty feet away from the wires of our yard, and contain over seven hundred bodies. This morning, when we left for work, our chief told us that, starting Monday, he wants to hear singing while we march to work.

The pits to be opened are grown over with grass like the surrounding area, but the SD knows exactly where they are located. They have a double-check on these locations, too, for there are some SD's in our group who were present at the original execution. And, indeed, if one only knows the approximate location of the grave, it is easy to locate the boundaries of the spot because the earth around it is cracked and loose.

The disinterred bodies are still clothed. Most lie piled in a heap, covered with about four feet of dirt. But there are a few bodies lying above these others, only about eight inches down. It seems that they were buried after the others. The explanation: These were the prisoners who had buried all the others. So that there wouldn't be any witnesses left alive, they were shot after their task was done and in turn buried by the Germans.

We in this Death Brigade now have nothing to look forward to but the same fate.

We start a new fire. To do this we first level out a piece of ground about five hundred square feet. On this spot we lay the so-called foundation. This is made of heavy wooden logs in the form of a grate so that air can get underneath for speedier burning. On either side of this "fireplace" we erect steps leading up to it.

During the day, all three graves are finally unearthed. Then preparations are made for taking the bodies out of the mass graves and bringing them over to the fireplace.

Stretchers and long hooks, the kind usually used for pulling large blocks of ice, are brought to the grave sites. These hooks will be used to pull out the bodies.

And so passes Friday.

Saturday, June 27th.

Today, after reveille, which was at seven o'clock, Herches, at the command of the Untersturmführer picks out additional men to go to the three pits with yesterday's group. The remaining inmates go to the ravine.

In the ravine, where all the bodies are already burned, the ground is turned over to see if anything is left. After completing this task, we have to report to the Untersturmführer, who checks very carefully to see if the work was properly carried out. In case anything is not thoroughly reduced to ashes, if even a little hair is left over, each of the inmates in the group will get twenty-five lashes with a cat-o'-nine-tails, which is as painful as a hundred whips.

This is how the work at the three pits is done: three men, with a hook, go down into one of the mass graves, and two, with another hook, stand at the top. The three who are in the grave put the hook into the corpse and pull it out of its original position. Afterward, the two on the top pull hard and this sinks the hook deeper into the body. Then they pull it up. One has to be very careful while sinking the hook because the corpse, already in an advanced stage of decay, might break in two. Another group, the carriers, now put two to four corpses (depending on their size) on the stretchers that were brought here yesterday. Two inmates work with each stretcher and carry it over to the nearby fireplace. Here a mass of corpses is accumulated.

The chief fireman now pours gasoline and oil on the wooden foundation, and starts the fire. The carriers, with their stretchers, climb the steps and toss the corpses into the fire. On one side one pair goes up and on the other side another pair goes down. It is worked this way so that one pair does not interfere with the other. The carriers continuously rub their hands in sand, because their hands as well as the handles of the stretchers become slippery from the bodies.

The chief fire tender is black from the soot, and singed, and he has a rod in his left hand with which he stirs the fire and directs the traffic. He also shows where the bodies should be placed, that is, on which side to ascend and toss the bodies into the fire without extinguishing it. God have mercy if one throws the corpse the wrong way! Then one has practically to get into the fire and pull the corpse out and throw it in again. It is a large fire, and the heat can be felt at a great distance. Standing near the fireman is his assistant and the tabulator.

The fireman's assistant shovels the ashes formed of burned bones, and continuously adds more wood.

When all the bodies are pulled out of the grave, a special group now searches the graves. With their hands they pick up each bone or hair, putting it into a pail, and afterward they throw it into the fire. After examining and collecting everything, they report to the Untersturmführer, who inspects the pit. This group now sprays the walls of the pit, which are greenish from the bodies, with chlorine, to kill some of the odor.

Now the pit is covered and leveled. Afterward, we plow the ground, but instead of horses we pull the plows ourselves. The grounds are seeded, and after a few weeks one cannot tell where the pits were. This is the final effect the Germans want. No one must ever know what has gone on here.

Today, as on last Saturday, we work only until twelve o'clock. After lunch, taking turns, we go in groups of ten to bring water.

We wash our clothing, as well as ourselves.

27

SUNDAY, *June 28th.*

Today is our day of rest. Hesitantly, we approach the wires and begin to whisper to the Schupos who are guarding us. They look around to see if anyone is near. They are forbidden to talk to the inmates. But finally we get down to "business." They will supply us with butter, salami, eggs, vodka, cigarettes, and anything else that we need. For these supplies we will pay in gold; we plan to steal it from the gold we have to turn over to the Untersturmführer, the gold sifted from the ashes of the dead. The dealings with the Schupos will be handled by specially appointed men among us. In each case we shall decide who these men will be. Our group starts to form a "government" with power to decide all our policies.

If caught with a piece of gold, one of course will be shot. If the SD discovers that we are doing business with the Schupos, the whole brigade will be shot. It is imperative to know which Schupos can be trusted. At the present time what we want most is cigarettes; we have enough food, but we do not get cigarettes at all.

The Schupos here are not professional police, but are assigned to special duty. Most of them originally came from Berlin, and its surrounding vicinities, and the majority of them are craftsmen. They didn't come here of their own volition; they are a part of the 23rd Battalion sent primarily to do antipartisan work in Poland. It has its headquarters in the city of Tarnopol (a large city in the east of Poland). They are not allowed to take part in Jewish executions. Some of them tell us that before 1933 they belonged to the Socialist Party. They tell us that they don't like their present job, but they have no choice. The alternative would be to go to the front line, which they consider to be sure death. What one won't do to live!

Some of the Schupos even promise us that in case they hear of some change in Germany's policy toward Jews, they will let us know. When the SD men aren't present, some of the Schupos don't care if we work or not. Sometimes they warn us of an approaching SD. Many of them, of course, act like this in their own interest, not from any true altruism. They get 360 marks a day (less than a dollar), and by getting gold from us they will increase their income handsomely. They advise us to look happy, satisfied with our work; otherwise we shall be shot.

Morning passes. After lunch we are inspected by the *Oberleutnant* (lieutenant) of the Schupos. He is checking to see that none of us have arms, knives, or similar weapons. He searches for shovels and sticks inside the yard or bunker. After dinner, we practice a marching song. We shall have to adhere to the Untersturmführer's command to sing while marching to and from work. Our day of rest is over and a new week is starting.

Monday, June 29th.

The morning passes uneventfully. At eight o'clock we go out to work, to the same places as on Saturday. While marching to work we sing the most "anti-song" song we could think of:

"Hej, j—— twoju mat	Hey, S.O.B.
Czomus me rody la	Why did you give birth to me?
Taki zywot, taki zywot	Such a life, such a life
Ne Powereny nas!"	Better if you had had a miscarriage.

This song the Germans called the "Russian Karavan."

It hurts inside, but one sings.

There is no doctor in the brigade, but there is a pharmacist, and from now on he will be on duty in the bunker and will be, Untersturmführer Scherlack declares, responsible for the health of the brigade. Scherlack, the SD in charge of our Death Brigade, doesn't want sickness. Today they bring medicines for us. Tonight, anybody with wounds is bandaged. One of the Schupos is appointed to be in charge of sanitation. His rank is that of *Zugführer* (corporal). He is skillful in first aid, and has a very light touch when he performs small operations, but everyone is afraid of him. Because he has shown that he is a great sadist, despite his skill no one will go to him for help.

It is a very hot day, and this makes the work at the fire even more unbearable, if possible. We strip to the waist, and most of us are near sunstroke. We return from work dragging our feet. The pharmacist tries to help, but with little result.

Monday passes. In the evening, many of us don't eat our dinner— we are feverish. The night is sticky and hot. Some of the inmates are ill and writhing in pain. Eventually fatigue overcomes us, and we fall asleep. At daybreak, everyone moves out of the bunker and lies down on the ground in the yard to snatch a little more sleep. So passes the night.

Tuesday, June 30th.

As usual, the men leave for work. Three of the inmates can't get up. They stay in the bunker with me. I am now in full charge of cleaning the bunker. Our group foreman, appointed by the Germans, tells the Untersturmführer that we are going to have a general cleaning and therefore we are keeping a few of the men in the bunker to help. We hope the sickness will not spread to others.

The work on the three graves, which was started on Friday, is completely finished today. The fire is dying out, and the people can be seen carrying the remaining ashes in wooden boxes to the Ash Brigade.

Untersturmführer Scherlack continually comes over to our bunker to ask if we are satisfied. Everybody knows that if one values his life, one cannot say "No." Now and then the Untersturmführer asks someone why he doesn't look happy; maybe he doesn't like it here, and if that is the case he can be sent back to the concentration camp. But everyone knows what "going back" to camp means—one would be shot, not returned there at all. We recall the advice of the Schupos to look "happy." From now on, and increasingly, we have to act—look happy.

Today we finish our work at four o'clock. As usual, after work we have formation and counting off. Afterward we wash ourselves. Suddenly, the washing is interrupted. They tell us to get into the bunker and to cover the entrance with a coat. It is an air raid, they say. The Schupos warn us that if they notice any of us looking out, they will shoot. Every one of us wishes that a bomb *would* fall here; even if it kills us, the Germans will die, too.

Suddenly we hear hounds barking and then the stamping of feet and the cracking of whips. We listen. We hear the command, *"Ausziehen!"* (Undress!) Some of us peer through the cracks in the roof and report to the others what is happening; there is a large group of people undressing themselves. Schupos surround them, carrying whips, and they are beating them. We hear yelling: *"Los! Los!"* (Faster! Faster!) A sudden piercing scream. One of the victims has turned around, and one of the police dogs has caught him by the leg, tearing flesh from it. Afterward we hear: *"Zu fünf antreten!"* (In fives, step forward!) Naked people, in groups of fives, clasp their hands behind their heads—they are marching toward the fire.

The Scharführer from the concentration camp stands near the fireplace. He holds a handkerchief delicately to his nose to bar the stench. The rows of fives advance. The SS men stand behind the victims and shoot them in the backs of their heads, kicking the bodies forward. Though the remaining victims standing there see what is happening to the other people in front of them, they walk over to the fireplace like sheep. No one puts up any resistance; they are indifferent. Would resistance help them? It would result only in more torture, and prolong their death.

After half an hour, all is over. We hear the voice of the Schupo who keeps guard near the gate: "Herches, quick!" Herches gets out, and then yells, "Everybody out." We all step out, and Herches gets an order to form a brigade of twenty of the strongest men, plus the fire-chief and his assistant. This brigade then has to toss all these bodies into the fire. Four inmates are sent to sort the clothing and search the pockets. The Schupos watch delightedly. One requisitions a pair of shoes for himself, another, a suit. All told, we collect four pails of money, silver, gold and diamonds. Somehow many of the inmates were always able to hide some of their valuables from the Nazis, to the very end.

An hour later all the bodies are aflame. They number 275.

One terrible thing had happened during the burning. When one of the bodies was tossed into the fire, it cried out. The man was still alive!

In all the horror and madness one cannot make certain everyone is dead. The Germans, knowing that we inmates are half crazed doing this work, drive us even faster to finish.

The victims of this latest execution were from company "Zela 19" (a private German company that overhauled cars for the army). They had returned to the concentration camp after work as usual, with no idea of what was awaiting them. They entered through the main gate, but instead of going into the living and eating quarters they were herded through the small gate and over to the "sands." Among them were two brothers who, I had learned, were supposed to join our Death Brigade two weeks ago. But they managed to get into "Zela 19" because their brother-in-law had been foreman of that brigade. It was a hard job to get anyone into this group, because "Zela 19" was a good place to work; and everyone envied them!

Wednesday, June 31st.

At eight o'clock we leave for work. Today a large group is scheduled to start on a new working site, a place located about thirty feet from the ravine. The graves here are about two months old. The ground is moist, and the workers soon find that the corpses have disintegrated. For this reason the work takes much longer. Instead of pulling out an entire body, one pulls out parts of it; usually the heads are severed from the bodies. We count only the heads. Bodies without heads are not tallied—they are too disintegrated for accurate counting. In one of the graves the bodies are completely deteriorated, with only bones strewn about. The work is gruesome. The inmates are up to their knees in puddles of foulness. With bare hands, they toss the remnants into buckets; they carry the buckets over to the fireplace and toss the contents into the fire.

Meanwhile, in the yard, four inmates sort the clothing and shoes. They search the clothing to make certain nothing is overlooked.

The Untersturmführer is present at the evening formation, and makes a speech.

"All these clothes lying before you are yours. Tomorrow morning, I want to see everyone nicely dressed. Everyone must have one suit and a pair of shoes for work, and another outfit for after work so that you won't enter the bunker in your working clothes." His speech is noteworthy, as he continues: "I will take care of everything for you, but you must behave obediently and be clean. I request only these two things of you, and for it I will take care of you as a father cares for his children. But if you disappoint me, I will be merciless!"

As usual, he gestures with his hands, narrows his eyes, and adds, while smiling: "You'll see, you will live twenty years. What did I say, twenty?—you will live to be a hundred. We have enough work. We will even go to Mexico. Only, watch it. Be clean and proper. Hersches, take good care to distribute the clothes."

At the end Scherlack asks: "Did you understand what I said to you? Good."

He waves his left hand goodbye, and leaves. A real father.

Everyone gets shirts, underwear, a suit, and a pair of shoes; the Schupos, of course, taking the best first. We would gladly have done without Scherlack's gift. But had we not donned these clothes, he would have had us shot for exhibiting defiance.

28

From now on, I discontinue my day-by-day account because it is too repetitious. I will, therefore, touch only on the highlights of the life of our brigade. I shall enumerate and describe the working sites and tell of special cases.

Untersturmführer Scherlack attends reveille with a happy face. Everyone is dressed in a "new" suit. He says: "Yes, I will take even better care of you. Only be decent and clean. Let us get to work, to work, children, to work."

We leave for work. Some of us can hardly walk. Disease is spreading among us. Some have typhus. We have been careful to shield our sick from the notice of the Germans. If we could only get them in the Ash Brigade. There they could sit and look for gold among the ashes of the dead, and the healthy ones could do the tasks that required walking. The Schupos notice our sick, but we can handle them; our foreman silences them with gold.

We had tried our best to care for those who had become ill. In one corner of the bunker we had placed extra straw, so they might have a more comfortable place to sleep during the night. I had made cold compresses for them. To every sick inmate I had appointed a healthy one as a nurse, to wash him, obtain food, and so on. Everyone helped the sick men as much as he could, even to risking his own life.

Finally, however, we can masquerade no longer. The sick cannot even stand up during the counting. They stagger and fall. The Untersturmführer asks what is wrong. The foreman explains that because of yesterday's heat, some of the inmates had sunstroke. The Untersturmführer orders them into the bunker and lets them rest for the day. In the evening, at formation, he inquires about the sick inmates. Herches says that they feel better, but when the Untersturmführer enters the bunker, he finds them unconscious, moaning and burning with fever. Without a word, the Untersturmführer sends us all back to the bunker.

Later that evening a truck arrives. The Untersturmführer tells us to bring out all of the sick men and to dress them well because they are going to the infirmary. We grieve for our brothers. They fought the sickness for so long, and with only two or more days of rest might have conquered it.

The truck carrying them backs up practically into the fire, and the tailgate opens. The inmates get down and stand at the edge, facing the fire. The Scharführer shoots them in the back of the head, kicks them, and they fall straight into the "infirmary."

At reveille next morning, the SD man asks us who is ill. They promise to give us medicine, and advise us not to wait until it is too late. They tell Hersches that he is responsible for the sick ones and must report them every morning to the SD.

At reveille the following morning, under the pressure of the Schupos, Herches asks everyone who is sick to step forward. We had decided among ourselves not to report sick. There is always time to be shot. No one steps forward. When the Untersturmführer asks Herches, "Is anybody sick?" Herches answers: "Nobody. I asked, and nobody reported himself." Later on, when the Untersturmführer berates Herches for not reporting the sick, Herches tells him that the Schupos are witnesses that he asked if anybody were sick, and nobody had reported himself.

Untersturmführer Scherlack orders the Schupo in charge of sanitation to check up on the inmates at reveille every morning now to see whether any of them are sick. The Schupo orders everyone to stick out his tongue. Everyone whose tongue is coated is sent by truck to the "infirmary." We lose many young people because of white tongues. It makes no difference if their tongues are coated because of illness or not. But we find a solution to this problem. We now rub our tongues with hard bread before reveille so that everyone in the brigade had a red tongue. "Tongue reveille" from now on shows everyone to be healthy; but at work people again begin to fall down. The Untersturmführer tells us that if the sick won't report themselves and he discovers them, he will not send them to the "infirmary."

On Saturday, just before lunch, he tells one of the inmates by the name of Jaffe, who was clearly very ill and hadn't reported the fact, to undress, and he shoots him right in front of us. Two inmates carry Jaffe over to the fire and toss him in.

In short order only 94 remain of the 122 inmates we had when we started. There are not enough to do the work. So, on one Thursday, I, too, go out to work with the bodies.

29

A NEW WORKING PLACE—the fourth area containing mass graves we have worked in. It is on the road between our bunker and the concentration camp, and about ninety feet from the ravine. It is grueling work. Here one has to dig very deep before one finds the bodies. The corpses are clothed; they were inmates of the concentration camp six to eight months ago. They lie in layers. Every few feet there is another layer of thirty to fifty bodies. This grave goes down as deep as twenty-five feet and is about seventy-five feet long. At the end of the grave we erect high poles and hang a net about fifteen feet high. We fill the net with green branches. Its purpose is to camouflage what we are doing here, for this pit can be seen from the concentration camp.

Do the Germans think that the inmates of the camp don't know what we are doing here? They see the smoke and smell the stench. As we move toward the sides of the pit, we are clearly visible. Also, we sing loudly when we go to work, and can be heard in the camp.

In digging for the bodies we work in a mass-production line. Each shovel of earth goes from one to the other until it reaches the end of the line, where it is dumped. Our work site is a small ravine; two sides of it are hills about six feet high. The fireplace has been erected near the pit in which we are working. Because of the hills on either side of the pit, the smoke is trapped in the ravine and blows over to the pit where we are working, choking us.

At the fireplace the work is done a bit differently than it was before. The foundation is constructed so that every three feet there is a heavy log of wood. They are placed parallel, four in a row. Some of the heavy logs are split into thinner ones, and we pack these across the heavy logs. Now we distribute the bodies, feet to feet. And so we alternate layers of wood with layers of bodies, in crisscross fashion.

This human tower gets higher and higher, looking like a pyramid. At first, we had been capable only of building heaps of five hundred bodies. After a while we managed to pile up heaps of seven hundred and fifty, and now, really experienced, we can stack up heaps of two thousand and more. The carriers ascend to the top of these heaps on ladders with their bodies.

To light the fire, we pour gasoline all over the top and on the sides of the pyramid. Afterward we make a torch and ignite the fire. There is an explosion as the fire catches and the sky darkens from the smoke.

The length of time required to burn the bodies depends on whether the bodies are clothed or naked, fresh or putrid. Clothed bodies burn more slowly, as do those in an advanced state of decay. The difference in time of burning between fresh and putrid bodies is a matter of one day. Children and women burn faster. But success in our work depends on how much experience we have. In the beginning it took us one week, using much oil to burn the same sized pyre that took only two days using one quarter the amount of oil later on. It's a matter of "know-how."

The supervisor of this particular job is Scharführer Mozaiko, a man of average height and with a red nose. Mozaiko is his Nazi Party name. He beats us constantly.

The Untersturmführer often comes over to ask if we would like to return to the concentration camp, and to assure us that if anybody does, he can do so. Perhaps we are not happy? But everyone is "happy." He tells us that he is going to take care that we get new suits again because the ones we have are wearing out. We all know from where the new suits will come.

The large ravine is seeded over with grass. One would never know what lay beneath the ground now. The earth had been soaked through with blood, but the Germans had planted bushes. Only one plot is left unplanted and unseeded. This is the place where the Ash Brigade works, or, as our jolly German Untersturmführer calls its men, *die Goldsuchern von Alaska* (the Goldseekers of Alaska).

Corpses are no longer brought over from the concentration camp. Now the inmates are transported alive. They undress, and are shot in front of the fireplace. Upon arriving at work every morning, we find scores of fresh, naked bodies. The daily topic of conversation is "How many did they bring this morning?" Were these people from the "Aryan" side or from the concentration camp? Does anyone recognize anybody?

If one does recognize one of the bodies, the deceased life's history is reported in its smallest detail; we learn which school he had attended, where he had lived, about his family, and so on. This is our daily news. We almost look forward to seeing a known face among the corpses.

Everyone finally grows accustomed to the work, and on Sunday, our day off, we find ourselves some kind of job to do. In the evening we sing in the bunkers until ten o'clock. We begin to develop our own sense of humor. "I saw a corpse today and I swear that's just how you're going to look." "Don't eat too much; the corpse carriers will have a hard job getting you up on the heap."

How else could we continue to live? In any case, we consider the dead the lucky ones; they have it all behind them, while our end still awaits us.

One morning we see two SS men strolling along toward the small ravine. With them is one of the most beautiful girls in the concentration camp—Hilda, a tall, well-built blonde, in her middle twenties. She originally came from Vienna. We knew that she worked in the concentration camp office and was known to have affairs with SS men. There is one law here: the more one gets involved with the Germans, the quicker the death. It is forbidden for the SS men to have anything to do with Jews; therefore, Hilda has something on them, and because of it she must be silenced. Later, when we arrive at work near the fireplace, we find a naked, dead Hilda. Her clothing lies nearby.

One evening, around July 15th, a Thursday, we see the SD men sitting on a bench outside the Schupos' tent. All of them are drinking. It is about eight o'clock. We assume they must be celebrating a "happy" occasion.

We go to bed, and at about four in the morning we are startled into wakefulness by a voice barking into our bunker: "What is this? You are still asleep?" We jump up—run outside—perhaps this is the end. We dress hurriedly and are ordered into formation to be counted. We are marched out of the yard. About five hundred feet from the ravine we see a heap of naked bodies. This is what the SD men had been celebrating: a mass murder.

We stop, but the Ash Brigade is ordered to keep on marching. We start to sort out the clothes discarded by the dead before the shooting. About ten feet away some of our group start to build a fireplace. There are enough logs, since they were brought over a few days ago. Lower down in the heap the bodies are, as usual, distended because of the pressure. All the corpses are heavy because most of them had been men. At 9:00 A.M. the whole job is finished and all the bodies are stacked up, ready for burning. The pyre is made up of 425 bodies, but its size is as great as that normally built for eight hundred corpses excavated from the pits. That is because the bodies are so bloated. To prevent the pyre from falling apart we weave the bodies together in such a way that the hand of one corpse is put under the next one. The fire is lighted in the usual manner; only the fire chief and his assistant are left to watch over the pyre; the rest of us resume yesterday's work.

Upon returning from work to our yard, we find bundles of clothing and shoes. In a corner of the bunker are packages of bread, butter, sardines, chocolate and so on, "everything" one could desire; even a roasted duck. We now learn that the victims were from Beutepark (a working unit at the airport). Judging from the fact they had taken packages of food, we can see that they were led away under the pretext of moving them to another place of work. They were an obviously well-to-do group; a poor man couldn't have bribed himself into such a good position. At Beutepark they weren't under armed guard, and lived under normal conditions. These victims had not had to tremble with fear of the "Death Gate" between the ghetto and the rest of the city. Still, they had not really been safe.

As after the previous executions, so today, Untersturmführer Scherlack came to see how we "looked." Maybe we are not too "happy," and another execution will be needed. He comes inside our yard (only SD's have the right to enter), looks in one direction, then another. On one side lie the abandoned heaps of clothing and on the other side we are washing up. We hear: "Attention! Hats off!" He continues to walk slowly, looking into everyone's eyes, as if trying to read our minds. Quickly, everyone dons a smiling face. Behind Scherlack, as is usually the case, walks Herches. When the Untersturmführer reaches the end of the yard, he turns around and stops, asking the first one in line, "Are you satisfied or do you perhaps want to return to the concentration camp?" By now, everyone knows this "song" by heart. "But Herr Untersturmführer, I have food and drink here."

"But I know that you want to go back." While Scherlack talks, he narrows his shiny eyes, smilingly wags his finger, and watches how the inmate reacts to his words. But every one of us is up to his tricks. Now the Untersturmführer slowly moves a few steps forward, still looking at and studying each of us; he stops at one inmate he thinks does not look as "happy" as he should. He says that he can see from his facial expression that the inmate is not satisfied. He absolutely wants to hear the truth. The inmate starts to excuse himself, says that he always seems serious when he looks anyone in the eyes. The Untersturmführer complains, shaking his head, states that we are all lying to him. He repeats again that he wants us to be "clean and decent" and that he is like a father to us and will take care that we get everything we need. All he asks is that we show our appreciation. He tells us that he is aware that scenes like today's have bad effects on us, but they have nothing to do with us. It is an order which he, as well as we, must fulfill.

Walking slowly, and continuously stopping to look everyone in the eyes, while we stand at attention, with our hats in our hands, he slowly approaches the place where the clothes are lying and smoothly changes to the subject of the clothing. He reminds us that he promised us clothing and that he has kept his word, even though these clothes should have been sent to the warehouse in the concentration camp. He tells Herches that he wants to see everyone in a fresh suit. Afterward he remembers the food we got today, and goes into the bunker to look it over. Looking at all this fine food, shaking his head and smiling, he continues: "You have it better than we do; we don't have such food. But you must divide it justly between you." Adding again that we must be "clean and decent," and wishing us a good night, he leaves. At the gate he turns around and asks the one standing nearest to him to take two pails and follow him. After a few minutes, the inmate returns with the two pails filled with beer.

After the Untersturmführer leaves, we start to give out the suits and shoes, because tomorrow everyone must be freshly dressed. But we don't apportion the food now, for at present we all have more than enough to eat, because we are getting rations for 150 inmates and we are only 94. And of these, 20 are sick and cannot eat their rations.

We all try to save the best of everything for the sick. Today, when any one of the men in charge of the clothing found anything that was believed to be of some use for the sick, he hid it in his pocket, running the risk of torture or even death. It is strictly forbidden to put anything into one's pockets during the search. The inmates now take all kinds of risks, for between us a real and true feeling of comradeship has grown.

Saturday morning passes uneventfully. At work the Untersturmführer informs us that in the near future we shall get new friends. Our brigade will soon be enlarged to 125. He has been thinking about this problem for many days, he tells us, but he doesn't know if he should add more people. He would like to keep us as a unit, not add any outsiders. The day before yesterday he had decided to add more people, and went to the concentration camp for the men; he asked for volunteers, and there were so many that he didn't know which to choose, so he hadn't taken anybody.

This afternoon, we are told, we will get a barrel of beer. On Sunday we make a table in the yard. We lay out the cakes, chocolate, and small sandwiches left by the Beutepark victims, and we open the barrel of beer and everyone eats and drinks. We also sing. We do this in the yard, so that the Schupos can see it and report our "happiness" to the Untersturmführer.

30

It is Tuesday afternoon, and while we are working in the ravine thirteen inmates are brought over to our yard from the concentration camp to be shot. This morning the camp had been searched and arms were found on a few of the inmates. The others were under suspicion of trying to organize an escape.

Sunday, August 22nd, 1943.
Nine more men are brought over to our brigade. Most of them were hackney drivers before the war. We consider them "tough guys." The son of one of them had been separated from his father and shot in front of him.

In the beginning everything seems awful for death brigade newcomers such as these. None could believe that anyone could endure it here very long, but slowly they get used to it, too. From the newcomers we discover the fate of the carpenter's assistant, who had escaped from our Death Brigade. When he escaped he got back into the concentration camp. In the camp none of the SS knew that one of us had escaped. Untersturmführer Scherlack had ordered the Schupos to keep it a secret because it wasn't good for his reputation. After two weeks in the concentration camp, the carpenter escaped into the woods. He was caught, and shot.

True to his word, the Untersturmführer enlarges our brigade. By the end of August, we number 118 again. But the work of digging up new pits is ceaseless. We are now working in another area, not far from the last. The pits here are about 165 feet long, and there are about fifteen of them with a total of nine thousand corpses. The people in these pits were killed with their clothes on; the corpses are about a year old. Here we find the Jewish police of the ghetto, the men who were hanged in August of last year in the action on Loketke Street. In each pit, about two feet below the surface, we always found a few bodies of men—they of course were used to bury all the others and were then killed and buried by the Germans. In one pit we also found a heap of so-called "black crows." They were called "black crows" because of the black uniforms in which they had been dressed when killed.

There were Ukrainian fascists, in the division of the SS. They had clearly taken part in the execution, and then, to erase all possible witnesses, they were finally killed by the Germans, too. They were buried in their uniforms, and at the bottom of the pit, under their bodies, we found their helmets all in a heap.

How can we even dream that we will get out alive? We are witnesses, too. We erect two fireplaces. When one pyre stops burning, we ignite the other one and start on a new heap of the dead. We now have taken to building pyramids of a thousand or more bodies, and have been told to keep using less and less oil. We can manage to do this, for we are now very skillful at body-burning.

Untersturmführer Scherlack tells us that, with these pits, the job will be finished here and we will move to the far end of Lyczakow Street in the Krzywicki woods on the outskirts of Lvov. The deadline for finishing the work here is September, we are informed. After giving us this information the Untersturmführer leaves for a two-week vacation.

I had noticed from time to time that a few inmates were secretly trading with the Schupos. One of these secret traders was Lufko, a former butcher from Sloneczna Street. Lufko made his contact with a Schupo, Schneider. Schneider was a *Volksdeutsch,* and therefore spoke Polish well; thus Lufko could talk to him and make his needs known. Lufko had taken 1,000 zlotys from corpses after the last execution and had hidden them. He offered this money to Schneider if he would go over to his friends in the city to bring him different things from them.

The arrangement came to the attention of Sergeant Rauch, who was taking the lieutenant's place while he was on vacation. Rauch came into our yard one day at lunchtime with a group of SD men. He then told us the whole story, and warned us that if the lieutenant should find out that we do business with the Schupos, he would kill us all. He then ordered that the large flat block on which we cut our wood be brought to where he stood. Lufko was told to lie on this. His two feet were tied to either side of this rack and his hands to the other side, and the rest of his body lay where the wood is normally placed to be cut. His head hung down over the side.

Now the SD men approached. There were seven of them and each in turn gave Lufko ten lashes wiith a cat-o'-nine tails. After the beating, Lufko was doused with cold water until he regained consciousness, and was then untied from the rack. One has to be stronger than iron to be able to live through this kind of beating. Lufko was. He got up and was ordered to go outside the yard and stop about fifteen feet from the wire. We were ordered to turn and look in the direction where Lufko was standing. About thirty steps in front of him the SD men took up their positions, pistols in hand. Now they started shooting at him. They did not shoot to kill. Instead they aimed at his hands, fingers, nose, ears, feet. After several minutes Lufko was still standing.

After what seemed an eternity one of the officers took out his pistol and shot straight into the victim's heart. Lufko fell dead. Two carriers took the body over to the fire.

Two weeks pass, and the Untersturmführer returns from his vacation. Everything is in order, and he is not informed of the Lufko case. He has come back with a new idea; we must have music, a lot of it, to lift our morale. We must have it when we go out to work and when we return, and we must have it for entertainment in the evenings and on weekends. For this he brings us a fiddle and a harmonica.

The Untersturmführer has another idea too. He now orders the three leather craftsmen in the brigade to make the fire chief and his assistant two hats with horns, like those of a devil. From then on, we march to work with the fire chief and his assistant leading us, wearing their horns and carrying the hooks they used to stir the fire. The two men were always singed from the fire, and this gave them a charred, blackened look. They were tall and slim, and normally dressed in black fatigues and black shoes; and now, with their horned hats, they truly looked like devils. Our Untersturmführer was determined to lighten our mood.

As I have already mentioned, at the first working site of the Ash Brigade, in the large ravine, there remained a gray heap of small bones that couldn't be crushed or burned. For many months we could devise no method for disposing of them. But the Untersturmführer found a solution for this problem too.

One day a machine is brought to the site. It looks like a cement mixer, and is run by a diesel engine. Inside the body of this mixer are large iron balls. These at last successfully crush the bones. At the bottom of the mixer is a sieve that filters out the fine bone dust, holding back the still uncrushed pieces of bone, which are then returned to the mouth of the mixer. The fine dust is strewn in the neighboring fields.

The inmates who are assigned to work the new machine are covered from head to foot by the dust of the bones, which is black. They look macabre. The work goes very slowly. To finish the grinding by September 1st, the day set for finishing our work here, the machine is started at 5:00 A.M. and kept going till 9:00 P.M. Because of the overload, the dust, and the fact that the motor is old and tired, the machine often breaks down. Sometimes it takes a few hours to start it in the morning, and once it takes the entire day. One day the Untersturmführer, nervous that we might not finish in time, makes an experiment. He has us seed some of the very small bones in the neighboring fields, which belong to a Polish farmer. After seeding, we plow the fields over. But the traces of bone can't be completely erased, so we have to have patience and wait for the machine to grind them. The Germans do not intend to leave the least trace of their doings here.

But we keep to our schedule, despite all difficulties. On the last Saturday of August, we finish the work. Everything in this gruesome place is now leveled and seeded; there is no trace of anything. Still, a single fireplace had been left standing. What can it mean? Is it for us? The work is finished, and yet . . . why are we not moving to another place? Maybe the fireplace is for the inmates of the concentration camp?

While waiting to find out the next move of our masters, we go over the whole territory once more, to be certain there are no telltale leftovers. All of us line up with pails in our hands at distances of about two feet apart and walk slowly, picking up all remaining evidence, even a match or a piece of paper. We even search the places beyond our work sites; a wind might have carried something to them. One can't be too careful.

The cleaning of the area takes one week. All that is left now is to clean up and seed the last fireplace and the spot where the bone-crushing machine still grinds away.

In our yard, we sit around, doing nothing, except for the twenty inmates who go out every morning to service the machine and seed the ashes. The fiddle and harmonica hang unused on the bunker wall, waiting for better times.

Two big tents are now brought over for us to be fixed by our three leather craftsmen. These two tents are supposed to be erected at our new working place.

Every day a few members of our camp are brought by truck to our new working site. It will be a spot in the Krzywicki woods. There our comrades are made to erect signs around the whole territory; these say, in Polish, Ukrainian, and German: "Entering this territory is strictly

forbidden. Sharpshooters are posted at a distance of a hundred meters."
After the signs are erected, contingents of our men are sent over to the
site with loads of the material we will need for our work—logs of wood,
oil, and so on. The Krzywicki woods are not guarded by Germans but
by a local forester. Seeing all these preparations going forward, he had
asked the Germans what was afoot. He was told that a circus would
be coming soon and the wood we had brought over would be used by
the acrobats! The signs were put up, he was told, so that the neighboring people would not steal anything brought over in the meantime.
He was promised a job as a doorman in the circus, and meanwhile was
made responsible for the safety of the materials brought here.

The chief topic of conversation now is our new working site—and
how the city looks, for the trucks bearing our workers have to go
through Lvov on their way to the new site. When the inmates return
from the new place everyone surrounds them, questioning them about
how Lvov looks now, and how the new site is. Afterward we talk over
each thing they report among ourselves, over and over again. What
else is there to talk about?

The Untersturmführer is now, more than ever, solicitous of our well-
being. He continuously asks us if we lack anything. We have a cunning
inspiration. To show him that we are satisfied with everything else,
we decide to tell him that, since they bring so many beautiful women
to the fire, why not allow a few of them to be sent here. They could,
we point out, work as cleaning women in our kitchen, wash our laundry
and other things; and, a thing he could appreciate, we would have
women for our sexual needs.

Our plan, of course, is to see if we can save a few poor souls. The
Untersturmführer listens to us, not unsympathetically.

A few days later a truck with twenty-four women in it stops in front
of our gate. The driver has been told to wait there for a further order
from the Untersturmführer, who is due to arrive any minute. Suddenly
we hear shots, and then the truck turns around and drives away in the
direction of the remaining fireplace. After about half an hour a Schupo
comes to our quarters and orders the fire chief, his assistant, and four
carriers to report for duty. In a quarter of an hour they return, having
tossed the women into the fire.

From the Schupos we later find out what had happened to the
women. There were twenty-four girls between the ages of seventeen and
twenty in the truck. They were the prettiest ones in the concentration

camp. Last night the SS in the camp had had a big party. They had brought these twenty-four girls to the affair, a thing that is strictly forbidden. The girls were there all night. In the morning, to rid themselves of any witnesses, the SS men brought them to the "sands." Because of their youth and health, the SS men, who had heard that our Untersturmführer might be sympathetic, wanted to keep them as cleaners for us and the Schupos. But when the truck had stopped to wait for the approval of the Untersturmführer, one of the girls had jumped out of the truck and started to run. The sudden shooting we had heard had been the SS firing at her. The sergeant in charge now saw quite clearly that the girls were not willing to live here, indeed, that they preferred death. He gave the order to take them to the fire.

One afternoon the sergeant comes to our bunker and orders a brigade of fifty inmates to follow him, carrying spades.

They head us up the same road we went in the beginning, toward the "Death Cell." Here, near the washroom of the concentration camp and the tower on which an Askari is standing guard, the sergeant stops us and points to a piece of ground, saying that there are two mass graves here. These are the two graves in front of which I and 179 other inmates were standing last year on June 8th, naked, ready to be shot. By what stroke of fortune am I not, myself, being excavated today! The inmates in the camp, seeing us march in their direction, run into their barracks. We feel hurt that everyone is afraid of the mere sight of us. We don't look so awful. On the other hand, the two fire tenders, with their horned hats and their hooks in their hands, could scare anyone.

We begin our work. First, we erect a wooden wall about twelve feet high, to hide what we are doing from the inmates of the camp. The guard on the tower, made up of Askaris is replaced by the Schupos, because the Askaris, too, are forbidden to see what is going on here. Today we start the digging, and the day is over before we reach the bodies.

The next day we go to work at daybreak. At the camp the inmates haven't left for work yet, for no one is permitted to go outside the barracks before we actually reach our working site. The Germans don't want anyone to see us going to work.

By about midday all the bodies are pulled out, the fireplace is built and ignited, and the two pits are refilled with earth. There are 275 bodies. The problem now arises as to what to do with the bones that haven't burned. The Ash Brigade has already finished its work and the grinding machine has been partially dismantled. There is no time to reassemble and start it, because we have a deadline; we must move to our new quarters. We are made to dig a very deep pit and bury the leftover bones.

31

TUESDAY, *September 7, 1943. Moving Day.*

At five o'clock in the morning everyone goes out to the yard with all of his belongings packed in his own blanket. These are placed outside the wires. One group of twenty inmates goes by truck to the new place to put up the tents, and to encircle the yard with barbed wire. The rest stay here to take the bunker apart, dismantle the barbed-wire fence, and to plow and seed the ground. I had not believed, twelve weeks ago, when we began construction here, that I would live to take it apart.

By lunchtime the bunker and the wires are taken apart; two hours later the whole place is seeded. The land has now returned to its former appearance. In the meantime two trucks have been traveling back and forth, taking everything over to the new site. When we finish our work, we again are made to search the entire surrounding area of the bunker for any leftovers, cleaning it up, even to the last piece of paper.

Now the moving of the inmates begins.

In groups of twenty-one (twenty inmates and a foreman), under the guard of five Schupos, we ride to the new site. I act as foreman on one of the trucks carrying us, sitting on the side, while the others sit in fives on the floor with arms linked. I, too, am forbidden to stand up or look around. I have to sit, as all the others do, with bowed head. Our eyes are dazzled by snatched glimpses of tall buildings, free people. Different thoughts are passing through our minds. How happy one would be to be free! That one, sitting by the church, without a leg and his arm outstretched begging, should be happy. He doesn't constantly see corpses and death before him as we do. He has a right to be with his family. If one should ask that man there, walking with his wife and two children, whether he is happy, he would perhaps say "no." He probably would like to have this or that; he doesn't know how happy he should be to have his freedom, and to be with his dear ones. We cannot even hope for that; we've already lost ours. To jump off the truck will make no sense, because we are well guarded; secondly, as Jews we would soon be caught—there is no real or effective way of disguising ourselves.

O God, where did I err? Why couldn't you punish me yourself, instead of handing me over to these murderers?

Beset by these thoughts while the truck speeds forward, we pass Lyczakowska Street, and we turn into the Glinanskiej Road and approach the Krzywicki woods.

Glinanskiej Road shows changes already. Schupos are looking out the windows of their requisitioned houses; they had moved in yesterday. They must live near the working place, because even when they are off duty they are on emergency call. In case they hear a shot in the night, they must report immediately. They all belong to our command, which the Germans call *Sonderkommando 1005* (Special Command 1005).

A highway leads off Glinanskiej Road, straight through the Krzywicki woods. At the entrance to the woods a guardhouse and ramp have been erected. A private villa in the woods has been commandeered, and it is now the Schupos' kitchen and mess hall.

From the villa mess hall one can see our tents. They really do look like a circus from a distance. The truck stops, and we are ordered to walk uphill; we go about two hundred and fifty yards to the place where our tents stand, enclosed by two rows of barbed-wire fence, one around the other at a distance of about two feet. The two fences have barbed wire woven between them. The height of the fences is about ten feet. They encircle a square. Each side of this square is about seventy-five feet long.

At opposite sides of the fenced-in area are gates, and near them, on the outside of the fence, are two guardhouses; here the Schupos stay when it rains. Inside the fenced-in area, at a distance of about eight feet from each side of the fence, stand our two tents, about ten feet apart, facing the gates.

In one corner of our fenced-in area is a field kitchen. Close to this are benches, and on these are basins for washing. In the other corner of the area is an open toilet.

Each of the two tents is about twenty-nine feet long by twenty-five feet wide. One tent holds eighty inmates. The rest of the men will live in the other; they are our elite, the foreman, the group leader, the men who clean the camp and keep it in order, the three leathercraftsmen, and some members of the Ash Brigade. I am in this group, too. We are the ones who don't smell, who don't have direct contact with the bodies. One-third of this second tent is separated by a wall, forming a shop on one side. On both sides of the wall are double-decker beds. In the middle of the tent is a long table, and on both sides are benches. We have an electric light here. There are searchlights on all four corners of the barbed-wire fence, lighting up the whole area all night long.

About one hundred and fifty yards away from one side of the camp is a hill of white sand several hundred feet high. This very high hill hides our factory, which changes corpses into ashes. On top of this mountain are two bunkers. To each of these bunkers four Schupos have been assigned; two sleep, one is at the telephone, while the fourth marches outside, back and forth. In addition to the eight Schupos on the hill, there are two Schupos who patrol the area all night long.

Between the sand hill and our camp stands the machine for grinding the bones, and close by the machine a place has been leveled for the Ash Brigade. From now on, only the machine grinds the bones; the Ash Brigade merely picks out the precious metals from the human bone dust.

Because the days are getting shorter, we are now permitted to walk around the yard until eight o'clock. After that time we cannot go into the yard without permission. On one side of the tent the flaps are closed, but on the other side they are always open. One inmate sits guard at the door of each tent at night. These inmates have to report to the Schupos, who are constantly on guard outside the fence, anyone who goes out to the toilet or gets out of bed during the night.

Each Schupo is armed with hand grenades and with a Tommy gun that holds three hundred bullets.

At nine o'clock the light in the tent is turned off and everyone must be in bed, undressed. Everyone's clothing must lie in clear view on the benches. A man can't escape so easily in his underclothes.

At a distance of about seventy-five feet from our tents, in the opposite direction from the mountain of sand, is a tent for the Schupos. The main ammunition supply is kept there.

On Thursday, September 9, 1943, we leave for our first day of work at this new site. There are many graves here, one next to another, starting about one hundred feet from our camp. The corpses in these graves have been in the ground for more than a year. In some of the graves, beside the corpses, there are also packages of clothing. We can tell from these packages that the graves contain the victims of the December, 1941, action at the "Bridge of Death."

At the order of the Untersturmführer we try to build a fireplace with iron grates instead of wooden logs, but under the heat and weight the iron grates bend, and all the bodies cascade down. Since this new experiment doesn't work, we return to the "old" system, the one we used on the "sands." We build pyres of two thousand or more "figures," the name the Germans gave the bodies. They call us "figures," too. They say, for example: *"Zehn Figuren heraustreten!"* (Ten figures step out!)

Normally we ignite the pyres on Saturday, and it usually takes until Wednesday for the heap to be completely burned.

Soon all is running smoothly at this new site, and the Untersturmführer is happy.

Five weeks pass.

We now have a musician, imported for us from the concentration camp by the Untersturmführer. He plays the fiddle for us in the evenings.

The shop in the tent now employs three carpenters, five leather craftsmen, three tailors, and five shoemakers. These artisans do work for the SD's, the Schupos and also for us. It is getting cold, and the Schupos are starting to heat their apartments. We cut wood for them, and in the evening we carry the wood to their houses. Thanks to this opportunity for contact with them, trade flourishes. In their houses we are alone with them, and none of us has any fear of being observed.

The work here is approaching an end. According to the Untersturmführer, we are going to go to Stanislav next. But, on the other hand, according to the Scharführer we are going to go to the town of Zloczow; and according to the Schupos to the town of Grodek Jagielonski. These contradictions about our future plans make us restless and worried. We are going to too many places at the same time, and this may well mean that we are really going to the fire.

By October 8, 1943, we are all but finished with the work at this new site—our last pyre of two thousand corpses is ready to be burned. Before we set fire to it, however, our brigade leader Herches gets an order to be ready to go to another site with twenty of the best workers he has by 8:00 P.M.

I am chosen to go with this "elite" group. The whole thing seems very hush-hush, and we cannot figure out why. We are brought in trucks to the sector of town called Wulka. One of the trucks is very elaborate indeed; it looks as if it were air-conditioned, and is, indeed heavily insulated. In Wulka we are put to work digging in a small area of ground adjacent to a beetfield. In fifteen minutes bodies become visible.

We know at once that these are not the bodies of Jews. It is clear that these had been very important people; we could tell by their clothes and their jewelry. Some of them had been buried in tuxedos, others in very fine conservative clothes. When we pull out the first two corpses, two gold watches with heavy chains and a gold Waterman pen fall out. The pen has a gold band round it about half an inch wide, with the owner's name engraved on it.

The grave is only about four feet deep, so that after half an hour all the bodies are out and loaded on the heavily insulated truck that we had come with. I don't know how many corpses there are exactly, but there appear to be about thirty. A few minutes later the place is returned to its former appearance—we leave it spic and span. After we are counted, we climb back onto the truck, and, about 11:30 P.M., we are back in our tents.

The next day, those who worked last night have the day off. The others unload the insulated truck and put the bodies on the pyre. The inmates, inquisitive as to who these bodies were, start to pull out documents from their pockets. The documents show that among these dead are Professor Kazimierz Bartel, internationally known mathematician and former Prime Minister of Poland; Dr. Ostrowski, Professor Stozek, T. Boy Zelenski, and others. There are thirty-eight bodies— the very cream of Poland's social and intellectual life.

On Saturday, October 9th, the pyre with two thousand corpses is ignited; on it now are also the bodies we had exhumed last night.

It is Yom Kippur, the Day of Atonement, and many of us are fasting.

From now on we go out to different places, where we unearth the graves, disinter the corpses, and bring them, in the insulated truck, to be burned. We go to the towns of Jaryczow, Brzuchowice, Dornfeld, and Bobrka.

32

I SHALL DESCRIBE some of the people in the Death Brigade and the social order prevailing in it.

The inmates came from all walks of life. We had a high-school principal (a very high position in Poland), Dr. Levin, a member of one of the leading Jewish families in Poland; we had a rabbinical student; we had artists, lawyers, high-school and university students, artisans, horse traders, petty thieves, and so on. The inmates formed their own groups. The younger ones always had a few very close friends, with whom they normally worked, as in the case of the corpse carriers, those who carried the bodies to the fire, or those who worked in the Ash Brigade. However slightly you might have known someone prior to the war, or even if you had known a relative of his, this tenuous tie was enough to make you become fast friends. This before-the-war tie was almost holy. Still, the collective responsibility of each one of us toward all the other prisoners was also great.

The hackney drivers, horse traders, and petty thieves among us formed their own group, too. They either knew each other from before the war or had some friends in common. This group we called the *Woile,* which meant the "tough guys." Prior to the war they had had their share of trouble with the police. Often, spending a few months in prison had been their initiation to "manhood." In their opinion they were, before the war, the only ones who had really known how to live. They believed that if they were to survive the war, they would be able to make more of their lives than the rest of us; the Woile disdainfully referred to us as *Jolden*—milksops.

Another small group was composed of the subforeman of the working groups; and the head of these leaders was Hersches. They were young, strong men, and some of them a little "smart-alecky."

Actually, the Jolden showed more daring and responsibility to each other than the Woile, as can be seen from the following few examples.

One of the "milksops," known in the Death Brigade as the Opera Singer, had owned a stationery shop prior to the war. He had managed to live on false Aryan papers until he had been discovered and seized by one of the Schupos who was a guard here. When he was caught he was, as was usual in such cases, beaten beyond recognition and afterward attached to our brigade. When asked about his previous profession, he told the SD that he had been an opera singer. Since he had no singing voice at all, this nickname stuck with him. To the SD's he became a kind of court jester. They liked to balance bottles or stones on his head and shoot at them, or place matches between his nails and ignite them. This man would withstand brutal beatings rather than endanger any of his fellow prisoners. He only acted the fool.

One day, the Woile found a spade and a pistol underneath the Opera Singer's sleeping straw. These had originally been smuggled into our bunker by another one of the "milksops," who had then been shot when he had become ill. The Opera Singer took the weapons and tried to organize an escape. The "tough guys," being afraid to keep them, in panic threw them down a hole in the outhouse.

The fire tender, Avrum, originally came from Warsaw, where he had been a shoemaker. He played the complete fool. We used to call him *der Meshugener Avrum* (Crazy Avrum). A little bit he was, too. In any case, he was not completely sane. The Untersturmführer liked him, because he liked that type. Two men were once carrying a body that gave them a lot of trouble because it was badly placed. Untersturmführer Scherlack, seeing this, said: "Why are you so stupid? Why don't you hold the body so that it is not so heavy for you?" Then, turning around to the Schupo who stood nearby, Scherlack said, "If they hadn't been so dumb, they would have died long ago."

We all had, and not only once, to play the fool so as to deceive the Germans into thinking that we couldn't even think, to say nothing of organizing an escape. However, not everyone was good at acting. When Avrum played the fool, one sometimes had the feeling that his jokes were on us as well as on the Germans.

One evening, around the end of September, the Untersturmführer and all of the inmates were sitting on benches around the table in the tent. We were all singing together with him. Suddenly the Untersturmführer interrupted the singing and began his old song, "Clean and decent." Again he told us that if we kept these two rules, he would get us everything. "I will care for you like a father for his children," went the old refrain.

Here Crazy Avrum interrupted. "Yes, Father, we will still go to America; we have still work for another thousand years." He spoke poor Yiddish, thinking this would make it good German.

The Untersturmführer answered Avrum with a serious mien, to hide from us the fact that he was really laughing at us. He told us that he knew that everything that went on here hurt us, but that he could not help us. He said, as if philosophically, "Life is bitter and harsh."

Some of us were religious; others didn't care one way or another. Still others were antireligious, not from conviction but to be "smart." Most of the "leaders" and "tough guys" were of the antireligious group, and they had different ways of oppressing the ones observant of their religion. For instance, instead of giving the religious ones their cigarette ration on Friday, the leaders doled it out on Saturday, when it is forbidden by religious law to smoke. But the religious ones kept to their way of life despite all difficulties.

It was forbidden to take anything into the prison yard without permission from the Untersturmführer. Even if, inside the barbed-wire compound, one were found with a piece of wrapping paper for use in the toilet one would be tortured and then sentenced to death.

The religious ones didn't pay much attention to this law, and when they found a Jewish prayer book in the clothing of the people that were shot, they would smuggle it out and bring it into the tent. This was much more dangerous to possess than money or gold. Money or gold once smuggled into the camp could be hidden. The prayer books or *tefilin* (phylacteries) were used daily, and the people prayed morning and evening.

Among the religious groups who prayed daily were inmates who, before the war, were not religious at all. Many of us underwent a complete transformation here.

On the eve of Yom Kippur in the Death Brigade one could sense the approach of the holy day. When we returned from work, nearly all of us washed up very quickly, ate, and changed our clothes. A few minutes later, in one of our tents, we began, in whispers, but also in a holy and dignified manner, to pray. As collective praying could get us into bad trouble with the Germans, the "antireligious" group kept guard outside the tents, watching for Schupos or SD's who might approach, and also taking care to see that we did not become so loud that we could be heard outside the tent. Many of the nonreligious ones took part in the prayers, and many fasted the whole of the next day.

In our condition fasting was by no means an easy matter. We had to work as hard as on any other day, and because of the terrible thirst caused by the stench and the smoke some of us had to break the fast.

Among us were some who would usually refuse to eat meat, because here, of course, it was not kosher. They ate the soup only because they had to eat something to keep alive, and to die of one's own volition is forbidden by the Jewish religion. As I mentioned before, cigarettes were a rarity, and among the religious people there were some who not only did not smoke on the Sabbath but who wouldn't even take a cigarette to save for smoking later until after the Sabbath.

33

WE HAVE ALWAYS dreamed of escape, but it is at this juncture that concrete plans for an escape first begin to take shape. Of course, an escape is almost utterly hopeless, as it has always been, from the very beginning of the German persecution. From the start we are surrounded by a wall of steel and utter duplicity. Yet, as we now face up to the fact that the Germans intend to do away with us at any moment now, a fierce will to live flares up in us.

Now there is more and more talk of escape. In the yard, in the evenings, one can see inmates walking with slow step, covertly whispering to each other. When they near a guard, they change the subject and talk louder, about food or women. Though they walk and whisper together when they have a chance, every few minutes they enter the tent where the fiddler is playing to sing a few bars to the music, because they want to show the Schupos that they are "happy." Afterward they walk outside again, encircling the tent, laying plans. This goes on until eight o'clock, when we are counted and go in to sleep.

The immediate goal these conspirators must achieve is to convince our own leaders that the hour has come when we must make up our minds, choose the way of death, or perhaps of life. They know that Herches, head of the leaders, has a mother and sister in the concentration camp and that he is afraid they will have to pay the full consequences for any act of his. For this reason Herches tries to delay the time of escape—not to stop it, but to delay it. He claims there is plenty of time.

Finally the inmates come to the conclusion that Hersches is afraid not only for his family but also that he will lose his grip on us. Thus, seeing that pressure on Herches doesn't help, a group of inmates go ahead on their own. They set Saturday night as the time for the breakout.

But Herches, informed of the plan, calls a meeting in the tent between the leaders and the group that planned the escape. At this council it is decided that from now on it will be strictly forbidden, under punishment of death, for any individual group to try to escape. *All* will escape, or none.

The conspirators' promenade about the tents stops. Now when one inmate passes another, he whispers: "We are lost; our end is near."

But such despair is premature. The camp's leaders mean what they say. They plan an escape for the entire brigade. In a few days it becomes clear to everyone that the leadership really is not just thinking of itself; it wants a breakout, but one that will have some real chance of success. And it wants to give everybody a chance to escape—not just a few of us. Hope is born anew. Again the whispering begins, and secret talk of escape fill us once more with hope.

Two factors conspire to fan our escape plans—actually force us to action.

It is October, 1943, and the German armies are beginning to feel the first breath of the overwhelming defeat they are to suffer. We know little of this, but we hear disjointed rumors and chance conjectures from the Schupos, and we put them together. Our captors may yet be beaten. We must live for that: the very thought fills us with indescribable happiness.

The second factor that hastens our plans is that the Germans clearly intend to do away with all the concentration-camp inmates, including, of course, the Death Brigade. This we learn from the Untersturmführer himself, as well, of course, as from the logic of the entire situation. The Untersturmführer comes to our camp regularly to visit us. On his last visit he makes a speech in which he promises us three pairs of shoes apiece, plenty of clothes, almost anything we want. The next day great truckloads of wood arrive. Then we are ordered to put up a huge new fireplace and to dig great trenches for the blood to flow into. It can mean only one thing: the "final" Aktion against the camp. All must be killed now—and we will be no exception.

The new victims, we learn, will not be brought over here the usual way, that is, by truck through the woods, but by way of Lyczakowska Street, directly to the sand mountain across from our tent. By this time a road has been made from the mountain right down to the fireplace. On both sides of this new road, barbed wire has been entwined in the bushes. Sunday passes while the last touches are made on the road.

Monday, October 25th.

It is five o'clock in the morning. Suddenly the Chief Schupo storms into our tent. "What, you are still asleep?" Everyone leaps from his bed.

"In five minutes everyone is to be dressed, and all should be standing in front of the tent."

We don't know what has happened. As usual, in such cases, we think they are going to shoot us.

When we dress and go out of the tent, we see that the road we built yesterday is lined on both sides with Ukrainian police.

The SD chief now arrives by taxi, drunk. The Chief Schupo explains to us that there will be an "air raid," a very long one; and because the planes may mistake our tents as a military site, and bomb us, we are to go to the village, to the slaughterhouse, where we shall remain for the entire day. We don't believe him, of course, but what can we do?

We go to the slaughterhouse. They give us a radio, and we have music. The Schupos, seeing that we are a little nervous, bring us a chess set and playing cards.

We are sure of what is up now: the entire camp is to be liquidated. We can be certain of this, for from the slaughterhouse, we can see the new road that leads from the sand mountain to the fireplace. There is a steady stream of human traffic on it. Groups of forty or fifty people can be seen running down the mountainside—the inmates of the concentration camp. The Scharführer visits us again and again to reassure us. He tells us that he personally is checking each group of new victims to see if the names of any of our relatives, which we had supplied him with last night, are among them. So far, none of our relatives are among the victims.

It is twelve o'clock noon—at long last. We are returned to our camp. The whole place looks indeed like the aftermath of an air raid.

In the area between the barbed-wired fence and the mountain there is such a huge heap of shoes that one grows dizzy looking at it; there are about 2,500 pairs. Not far from this great pile is another mountain of clothing, and a little farther on, smaller assorted heaps of papers, documents, money, handkerchiefs, and similar items.

We are ordered into formation, are counted and then divided into two groups. One group goes out to heap the bodies onto the pyre; the other group, of which I am now leader, goes out to search through and sort the clothing. Herches appoints some people to my group who have become very skillful at hiding money and other valuables on their persons. These valuables will be divided among us when we escape. None of the "tough guys" are in this group.

It is five o'clock. The work is finished. We line up in front of our tents. The Untersturmführer is present during the formation. He tells us that tomorrow he wants to see us all in fresh clothing and shoes. He has kept his promises to us once more.

The Untersturmführer leaves, and we have a secret meeting in our tent at which we count the money, gold, and diamonds, and estimate that the value of everything we were able to steal is about $100,000. We bury all of it in a secret place in our tents. It is to be taken and distributed among us on the day of our escape.

Tuesday, October 26th.

There is now no doubt that the entire camp is being liquidated. We have another "air raid," but not like yesterday's. Then we were taken away from the tents; today we are locked in. We hear the oncoming trucks and the yelling of the Germans: *"Alles herunter!"* (All out!) *"Ausziehen!"* (Undress!) *"Zu fünf antreten."* (Step out in fives!) *"Unterhacken!"* (Link arms!) *"Im gleichen Schritte marsch!"* (Step together, march!)

Today they are bringing the victims in trucks. Each truck stops in front of our enclosure. It stands there until we are commanded to get into our tents for an "air raid." The tailgate of the truck then opens, and the Schupos shout commands. Over the guttural yells of the Germans one can hear the swishing of the whips hitting the victims.

Of course, everything does not always proceed "normally." Most of the time it does, of course; that is, the victims undress quickly, wanting to get it over with as fast as possible, and to save themselves from prolonged torture. Mothers undress their children, and the naked mother carries her child in her arms to the fire. However, sometimes a mother will undress herself but will fail to undress the child, or the child refuses to let itself be undressed out of panic. When this happens, we can hear the voices of the children. "What for?" or "Mother, mother, I'm scared! No! No!" In these cases, one of the German SD's takes the child by its small feet, swings it, crushing its head against the nearest tree, then carries it over to the fire and tosses it in. This is all done in front of the mother. When the mother reacts to this, which happens a few times, even if only by saying something, she is beaten and afterward hung by her feet from a tree with her head down until she dies.

But I should like to emphasize again that usually the people undress themselves quickly and go to the fire without protest. Some of them even jump into the fire without an order to do so. They have had enough. The tortures have been going on too long. Most of them have already lost all their near ones, and everyone feels that the world is his enemy; even the children in diapers feel this. We are taught that people sharing common tragedy become friends in sorrow. This didn't happen at Janowska. The word *tragedy* perhaps is not strong enough to convey what had happened to these people.

Why didn't they commit suicide? I am certain that if in these last minutes one could have asked any one of these victims, while he was standing in front of the fire, whether he wanted to go back and get dressed, even to have complete freedom, he would have answered "No." They were utterly broken, smashed. Too, not everyone has the courage to commit suicide. Again, some who might wish to, couldn't get poison, for poisons were very expensive and hard to obtain in the ghetto. Finally, many people had children, and not every parent can kill his own child.

I should mention here that we have become expert indeed at our work here—just as our German masters have become in theirs. Every day now, different groups of SD's arrive here; they come from different parts of Poland to study the German method of execution and our expertise in the burning of corpses. Normally they stay with us for a few weeks, and afterward leave to open their own places of death.

When we are asked by such "outsiders" how long we have been here, we say "less than twelve days." We have been instructed to say this because, of course, we shouldn't have been allowed to stay alive for more than fourteen days. The Untersturmführer keeps us here secretly, reporting to headquarters that he keeps changing the inmates.

The reason that he keeps us here and tries to give us everything to make us comfortable is that he thinks we have no thought of escaping. We are an experienced group, and as a good organizer he appreciates this greatly. But his chief reason for keeping us alive is his conviction that he has a group now that is safe, that will not try to break out. This is even more important than efficient work. If there were a breakout, the Untersturmführer would have a black mark as an SD man. He could even be demoted and sent to the front lines, and of this he is very much afraid.

What would he have thought had he known of the feverish plans we now were working out for our escape? Would he have thought that we were not "clean and decent"?

34

When the "air raid" is finished, we hear a call, "Herches out!" Herches goes out, and we hear the order "Let the heap fall in!" Now we hear Herches' voice, "Formation!" In a few minutes we are standing in fives. Counting us, reporting the number of inmates goes very fast. One Schupo unlocks the gate, while outside a group of Schupos are waiting for their assignment. The Chief assigns a certain number of Schupos to each group of inmates, handing a given number of "figures" over to their responsibility, and each group marches to its destined working place.

Our marching-out ceremony looks today the same as on any other day, except that today our corpse carriers have lumps of sugar in their pockets; they are for the "living corpses," those who had not been killed by the bullets. Herches has secretly put the care of the "living corpses" in the hands of an inmate, Schoenfield, or, as some others knew him, Tierhaus. He came from Podwoloczyska; he, as I, was from a Chasidic Jewish family, and he had graduated from a rabbinic seminary. Here in the camp he is one of the most religious men, and is, in fact, our moral conscience. No one in the Death Brigade is more respected by all of us than Schoenfield. No important decisions are made by our leaders without his presence. He always cites passages from the Bible or Talmud, and somehow even the "tough guys" among us listen to him.

It is twelve o'clock noon—lunch. Today, as we had expected, we have many "living corpses." Some of them are slightly wounded, some not at all. This explains why some of the corpses we had seen on the "sands," those killed months before, had open mouths and no bullet wounds—they had been buried alive, as these present victims will be if we can't rescue them. Clothing, with sugar in the pockets, is left beside these "bodies." Two of us take two pairs of shoes and put money in them, with exact directions as to how to escape from this place. The entire rescue action has to be well organized. What will happen to us if it is discovered that not only are we hiding money to finance our own escape but are actually helping others to escape?

It is five o'clock; the groups return from work. After formation, we wash and have dinner. This evening we sit in groups on the beds, and in the center of each group is a body carrier. These carriers tell us that this morning 112 women inmates were brought over from the camp. They describe the ones they recognized. Some of them had been alive; others had suffocated. To the living ones they gave sugar. While picking up one corpse, they would push a piece of sugar into the mouth of the "living corpse," pretending to talk to the other body carriers so as to let the "living corpses" know where they had left clothing for them. The clothing left last night was gone this morning, which meant that the "corpses" had escaped. So passes the day.

October 27th.

The day begins as usual by formation and counting. During breakfast word goes through the camp like an electric shock: "They are bringing somebody in—look at who it is!" Everyone's eyes are turned in the direction of the sand mountain.

Led down in our direction is a tall, good-looking man, at his last strength, dragging his feet behind him. His name is Kessler. He originally came from Tarnopol. We immediately recognize his clothing and shoes. He is one of the "living corpses" we had helped to escape. Why are they bringing him in our direction? They stop in front of our gate. They stand silently for a few minutes. The poor fellow falls to the ground. He lies there for a short while, then sits up.

One of the Schupos starts to speak to him: "Look"—pointing at our camp—"in this camp are your comrades. They work here, have it good; nobody beats them; they have enough food and everything they need. To get into this camp one has to be a very fine person, and this includes telling the truth. I am telling you this because I would like to see you live. You are an intelligent, healthy, good-looking man. Everyone wants to live. Believe me, it is better to live than to die. Now, if you tell us the truth—which we know in any case—you will be saved. On the other hand, if you don't, you will be tortured—and you know that we know how to torture. Afterwards you will be shot. Who helped you escape?" The victim answers quietly, in a weak voice, "I don't care anymore what you will do to me."

Silence. The Chief Schupo arrives and exchanges a few words, after which he tells the victim to get up, pointing with his finger in the direction of the fire. He tells him to walk, but when he sees that it will be quicker to carry him over, he pulls out his pistol and shoots him.

The Chief Schupo does the shooting himself, not because he wants to save Kessler from torture, but because he is afraid that he may get into trouble. It would disgrace him if it were discovered that one of the "corpses" had escaped. We are spared for the same reason. It would not do for anyone higher to learn that the Death Brigade had helped a concentration camp inmate to escape.

By the weekend we discover how the inmates had been taken out of the concentration camp; the maneuver was a study in deception and cruelty.

About two weeks before the final liquidation, the chief of the concentration camp, Warzog (he had become the chief on July 1, 1943), let a rumor leak out to the inmates that more than a thousand inmates would be sent to the concentration camp in Lublin. On Monday, October 25th, the inmates rose as usual at four o'clock in the morning, and they noticed that the entire guard in the camp had disappeared. The machine guns that usually stood around the camp were no longer visible. No one could explain this phenomenon, but everyone was glad about it. Wasn't this a good sign?

They made formation as usual, but the ceremony was different. Normally a few SS men with whips in their hands appeared in the yard. This day only the chief of the concentration camp, Hauptsturmführer Warzog was present. Behind him walked a few inmates, workers in the clothing warehouse. They were carrying clothing. They put the clothing down on the ground near Warzog, who was smiling happily. The inmates, too, were reassured, because it seemed to indicate a change for the better. The counting then began. Afterward Warzog made a speech. He said that in his camp the inmates must look well dressed. Winter was coming. Warzog himself called out the first brigade. He inspected everyone. Then he gave each one a pair of good shoes. All received good coats and suits, and they marched out—to death.

The same procedure was observed with all the other brigades.

The only ones spared were the musicians—we got them. The Untersturmführer had kept his word in this, too. He had said we must have an orchestra, and we got one.

Since the liquidation of the camp, we inmates hold secret meetings every evening. The presence of the musicians helps—they play, others sing, and still others dance so as to create much happy noise.

Meanwhile, in the tent shop a small group sit and discuss the planned attack. This group is under the leadership of Herches, and its members include two representatives of the "tough guys," Schoenfield, myself, and some others whom we call in as advisers for specific questions. We decide to strike in the very near future, because, according to the newspaper that we bought from a Schupo for a twenty-dollar gold piece, the Russian Army is rapidly advancing.

Trade with the Schupos flourishes—and this fact is an important element in our escape plan. It is getting colder day by day. The Schupos who stand guard outside the wire build fires. We carry wood for their fires, and for pieces of gold they supply us with cigarettes, liquor, and so on.

I have already mentioned the separation that existed between the Woile, or "tough guys," most of them convicts, and the other inmates. The Woile now number about fifteen—banded solidly together. Now they have begun to call themselves the "hiki-piki." "Hiki-piki" was the name taken by a group of juvenile delinquents in Lvov before the war. They had had their headquarters and hiding place in the old Jewish cemetery, and were professional toughs.

Around November 10, 1943, during the morning hours, the Untersturmführer suddenly calls all the Schupos together and tells them to line up. This is the first time something like this has happened here. We are sure that this means our end. We are wrong, but the event is ominous.

Outside our gate is a large safe in which the gold collected from victims' clothing and from the ashes was kept. When fifty kilograms of gold were collected (about eleven hundred pounds), it was sent to the bank. Cigarettes and alcoholic beverages were also kept in the same safe, and these were doled out to our Schupos. The key for the lock was kept by the Untersturmführer, but one of the Schupos had made a duplicate, and every time he had night duty he would pilfer some of the alcohol. Untersturmführer Scherlack had discovered this, and that was the reason for the lineup.

Because of this scare, we decide that we will escape on the night of November 18th. We will have to wait until November 18th because there will be no moon. Schoenfield, as a religious man, kept the exact moon-calendar time.

35

November 18, 1943.

At last the day is here. Work goes on as usual. The evening seems like any other. The orchestra plays; the inmates sing and dance. Considering where we were, any outsider seeing this would have no doubt that we were all mad. Nine o'clock approaches. Everyone goes to bed, his clothing prepared, so that at a given signal we can dress without delay.

Our plan is simple. When everyone is asleep, one of us who usually deals with the Schupos will call one in to give him some gold. When he is inside, a designated man will throw a blanket over him, choke him, and take away his machine gun and hand grenades. The Schupo, of course, will have left the gate open. After the Schupo is killed, everyone will quietly get dressed and move out.

Herches and two others go now to unearth the valuables we had hidden in the workshop section of our tent. We had planned, of course, to divide it among all of us.

We are horrified. Everything is gone. Except for Herches and myself, only the "tough guys" know of this place. Herches is beside himself, and returns to the part of the tent where the inmates are on their beds waiting. All can tell from Herches' face that something has gone wrong. The place is full of whisperings, sibilant despair. "What has happened?" "What has happened, Herches?"

"You are no longer human beings," he answers, addressing everyone. "You should be shot like dogs."

So ends the long-awaited day of escape.

Next day Herches calls in the "tough guys." He tells them that if they want to escape, all the valuables must be back where they should be within three hours. Otherwise, if he hears anyone even say the word "escape," he will tell the SD's, and that man will be shot.

Two hours later the valuables are found. Some of them are missing, but we pay no attention to that. We don't really want a quarrel with the "tough guys." We want only to escape.

Tonight we have a meeting again, organizing a new plan for escape, but because of the last experience our hopes for bringing it off are not high.

November 19, 1943.

Herches tells me to get some of the more hardy inmates (below thirty) into the shop and to have the older members of our brigade act as lookouts around the tents. All the others are to get into the tent where the musicians are playing, and to sing and dance. We have been singing and dancing for the last few weeks to throw the Schupos off guard, and accustom them to it.

In the shop the meeting begins. The first to speak is our chairman, Herches. He starts the speech with the following words: "Comrades, brothers! The hour of life or death is here. Tomorrow we will be in the fire or free. I speak first about the fire because one should be prepared for the worst. On the other hand, we are not afraid of the fire that is awaiting us in any case. But, isn't it better to be killed by a bullet, not knowing where it comes from, and with honor, for freedom, instead of undressing ourselves, marching in fives to the fire, and serving them to the last minute, helping them to erase their crime— enough of it!"

Herches then tells us the plan for escape. He then begins to appoint the different inmates to their various functions. He is our undisputed leader. He states who should go where and what should be done. He makes it clear that if anyone doesn't feel up to his assignment, he should say so right away, because each assignment is very responsible and risky. Herches divides the inmates in the shop into groups of fours. The first group is to kill the two Schupos who stand guard right outside the wires. They must do it in such a way that the Germans don't have a chance to make a sound: if they cry out, we are all lost. This will be done in the following way:

Two inmates of the first group will go out, with wood in their arms, through one gate. At the same time the two other members of the group will approach the other gate, one with wood in his arms and the other with a pair of high boots. They will give the appearance of wanting to trade with the Schupo, for we often used the pretext of carrying out the wood to disguise such dealings. When these two are outside the barbed-wire fence, the inmate carrying the boots will drop them. The guard will quickly bend down to pick them up because he doesn't want anyone to see that he is trading. While he is bending down, one of the inmates will grab the German by the throat and quickly choke him to death. The two who go to the other gate have similar instructions—they will dispose of the guard there in the same way. All four will then seize the Germans' machine guns and hand grenades. When this has been done the second group of four will follow; two will go through each of the two gates, taking over the arms the first group has seized. Having a clear road, they are now to go over to the Schupos' tent and encircle it; then two of the group will enter the tent. The Germans will be lying on their beds or sitting and playing cards. Their firearms are now lying quite a few feet away from them. (A few minutes ago one of us who went over there, carrying wood, noted and reported all these details.) The two inmates will, with one pull of the triggers of the machine guns, shoot the entire group. In case anything unexpected should arise, they are to throw a hand grenade into the tent. While the second group is leaving for the tent, the third group will leave, taking the main road toward the Schupos' canteen. They will be armed with knives we have had in hiding. If they meet a guard, they are to kill him. This will not be difficult, because the Schupos are used to seeing us on this road, carrying wood or beer to the canteen, so that for a moment it will not be surprising for one of them to see one of us. This split second, until the Schupo realizes that there is no guard with us, will tilt the odds in our favor.

If everything goes smoothly, as planned, the four who have killed the Schupos in their tent will return to our tent. Until they do, six men must remain with the musicians in the tent, singing and dancing while very loud music is played. This noise must override any unexpected noise from the guards. We must not forget that there is another Schupo on the mountain and that he must not be alarmed.

The biggest risk will be that taken by the musicians and the six that must remain in the tent singing and dancing, because they must go on with their job no matter what happens. They won't know what is going on outside until they are told. If there is any change in plans, or if something unexpected happens, they will have no chance to escape.

Now everything has been decided; no one even questions his assignment.

When the group has done its work, it will give the signal. Then all are to go at once to the tent of the dead Schupos, take their guns and their ammunition, and dress in their uniforms. Disguised as Schupos, we will all leave here together. We ought to be able to get a few miles away before the escape is discovered.

As usual, plans appear simpler than they prove to be.

I am assigned to the job of liaison between the groups. I am in the yard to watch for the best moment to start the action. I am supposed to direct the movement of the groups. Herches stays with the inmates to keep them in line, to prevent panic. I stand near the kitchen, appearing to eat while keeping an eye on every movement of the Germans.

Suddenly I see that a Schupo at one gate is going toward it to open it. Then I see that the two who were assigned to take care of this guard are approaching the gate. One of them is holding wood, and the other one, under his jacket, a pair of boots. They tell the Schupo that they have a very good pair of boots for him which they will bring out very soon. The guard agrees to it. The other two men in this group were to have gone out through the other gate, so I dash over there to make sure that they move in time. These two are at the gate all right, but this second guard moves much slower, taking his time and looking around.

The first two are already outside; they walk with the German toward the guardhouse. Now the one with the boots, as planned, drops them on the ground. The Schupo quickly bends down to pick them up. When he does so the inmate who carried the wood jumps on him and starts to choke him. Unfortunately, his grip is not quick or firm enough, and the German yells out. Both men jump on him and kill him instantly.

Meanwhile, the orchestra continues to play and the singers sing as if nothing is happening. When I hear the scream of the German, I run to the other gate.

When I get to the other gate and tell the two inmates that the Schupo on the other side is dead, they approach the gate at which their guard is already waiting for his promised boots. He hasn't noticed that anything unusual is going on, or heard the scream, and he opens the gate.

But the Germans in the tent had heard the scream of their comrade. Seizing their arms, they run out of their tent, grasp the situation immediately, and open fire in the direction of our tent.

One of the two inmates whose task it was to keep watch on this gate had been holding a shovel with burning wood on it because the Schupo wanted a fire started to keep him warm. When the Schupo opens the gate so the inmate can start the fire, the one with the shovel doesn't wait to jump on the German, but throws the fire into his face and then hits him with the edge of the shovel. Standing next to them,

I now jump on the guard and throw him down, stamping on him between his eyes with my heel. He murmurs, *"Meine Herren, lasst mich leben!"* (Sirs, let me live!) In the span of one minute we "figures" have become "sirs." They are the Schupo's last words. He lies at the gate, through which everyone from our tent is now escaping. We trample on him, crushing him to death.

Everyone in the tents has now run out, including the musicians—for the Schupos have opened fire on them. We had decided beforehand that if everything didn't work according to plan, everyone would run in the direction of the woods. But I can now tell from the shooting that the road toward the woods is full of Germans. For this reason I start in the direction of the mountain. Since it is normally the most strongly guarded place, they would expect no one to run in that direction; thus it may now be the weakest point, and, since the Schupos are busy elsewhere, no reinforcements can be sent here.

Not all joined our break for freedom. There were those who didn't want to escape. There was, for example, Jehuda Goldberg, a man in his forties, a former Polish legionnaire, a member of the underground who fought for Poland's independence before and during World War I, when Poland was occupied by Austria, Germany and Russia. Prior to the war, he had been an employee at a public school in Lvov. When told that there would be an escape attempt that night, Goldberg got undressed and went to bed. Others approached him, asking if he weren't aware of what was going on.

Goldberg answered: "I know about everything, and let God be of such help to you that this escape is a success. I pray and hope that He will help you to survive and tell the world, as witnesses, how they murdered a people. But as for me, where will I go? To the city, to hide? Who will hide me? I have no friends among the Aryans who will take me in. I am not young enough to go to the woods with you. I will only be a hindrance to you, and you will be captured because of me. I cannot run like some of you, and if I go with you, you will not leave me behind on the road, and it will be your end, too. When you escape, the Schupos will shoot everyone left here, and I am better off dead than on the road, a hindrance to you. What have I to live for? My wife and seven children have been killed, and I, too, want to die."

He looked at us: "Good night! Good luck! God help you to survive this war, and give me an easy death!"

He closed his eyes, and turned his head away to sleep.

36

I RUN in the direction of the mountain.

The night is a very dark one, so that one cannot even see a few feet ahead. I hear the sound of machine guns, the explosions of hand grenades. I get no farther than twenty-five feet when I am caught by the barbed wire hidden in the bushes. I fall, disentangle myself, get up, and jump over the wire, trying to remember, while I continue to run, the spots where the barbed wire is placed. We ourselves had put it up. I hear a noise from the bushes; someone else is running. I ask in a low voice, "Who is there?" I know it is not a Schupo, because a guard would have had a flashlight in his hands.

From the bushes a voice answers, "It's me—Beck."

I call him over; it is better to be in twos. Suddenly, from nowhere, a third one "grows"—Mojshe Korn. He was one of the Woile, known in the underworld as "Kaczanos" (Ducknose).

Now we run in threes, constantly falling down and getting up, because of the hilly area. We help each other up and continue our escape. We lose Korn. We climb up the mountain, and are already outside the "forbidden area" and on the main road. Here there are two roads, one leading to Lvov, the other to the town of Winnicki.

We stop for a moment. Where shall we go? I am of the opinion that we should go straight to the woods; Beck is of the opinion that we should go to the city first. There is no time for debate, but one has to know in which direction the city lies, and neither of us knows this neighborhood. Should we turn right or left or perhaps go straight ahead? It is a pity that we have lost Korn, for he knows this neighborhood well. We decide to turn right, hoping that it is toward Winnicki.

We walk a few yards, when we hear footsteps. My friend wants to turn back, but I am of the opinion that this is the worst thing that one can do. I tell him, "Let's march forward, talking loudly, like a couple of roughnecks." We march straight ahead. We are near the sound of the footsteps. When we come closer, we recognize our lost friend, Korn, and with him is Lejzer Sandberg, who had been a taxi driver until the war.

We join them. Korn leads us because he knows the roads best.

We walk behind him, step by step, not even asking him where he is leading us. We feel much better now, having someone who knows the roads. We fall and stumble because of the utter darkness; we walk one after another, following the sound of the footsteps ahead. We keep knives in our hands, ready to kill anyone who may try to stop us.

Slowly we leave the inhabited region we have been going through. We are in the fields. Now, when we hear any footsteps, we fall down and lie still until the sound of the steps passes us. Soon we are at Zniesienie, on the outskirts of Lvov, near the Rucker meat-canning factory. We walk along the railroad tracks, in the direction of the slaughterhouse.

Suddenly a railroad guard comes out of the booth and asks in a loud voice, "Who is there?"

Korn, as our leader, answers "One of us."

The guard says, "Don't you know that it is forbidden to walk on the tracks? Go back!"

"We are going," says Korn.

"Stop!" says the guard, after a short while, as if he had been thinking the whole thing over.

"It's us," answers Korn.

"Who's us? Stop! Or I shoot!"

"Don't shoot! Don't shoot! Don't you know us?" As this conversation goes on, we move away.

The guard, seeing that we don't stop, begins to shoot. We break into a run. Korn and I run to the right of the rails, while the other two go straight forward. They are shot. They fall.

Korn and I both run to the right, but we become separated in the dark. I keep going until I run straight into the fence of the oil refinery. The refinery guard hears the noise I make.

"Who's there?"

I lie down. What shall I do? Where shall I go? Into the woods? I am all alone. To the city, to take the chance of walking around there? I'll be stopped by the first policeman who sees me. The local inhabitants will report me as a Jew. Suddenly I hear the noise of someone moving. I ask, "Korn?" A second later Korn is sitting next to me.

"Do we continue to walk?" Korn asks me in a very low voice.

"No," I answer. "We should rest here for about a quarter of an hour; in the meantime the guard will stop listening for further noises, and afterward we'll go on."

Finally we decide to go back to the railroad track. We walk in the direction of Zolkiewska Street. In one direction this street leads to the center of Lvov, and in the other direction, to the outskirts. Korn says he has a plan. If we follow it, we will have to pass through part of the city. But how? It is a main street. The German police use it continuously. It is probable that by now the headquarters of the SD knows about our escape, and perhaps all the roads are blocked. What can we do?

We have no choice but to walk on the main street. There isn't a living soul on it. Everything is quiet, asleep. The moon, which just came out, lightens the road. Suddenly, it becomes light! Headlights are moving toward us. Korn whispers, "We are lost!" He starts to blame me for going through this street. I tell him, "Stop talking, and continue to walk with decisive steps!"

The car approaches. It stops. We don't know why. We grip our knives, preparing for a fight. We are sure that we are lost. After a minute or so, the car drives away.

We take a deep breath and walk toward the back of a nearby house. We want to wait until the car gets farther away. After a few minutes, I walk out alone to see about the car. Shocked, I see it returning. Perhaps to check who we are? I dart behind the house. The glare of the headlights indicates that the car is nearing the house in back of which we are hiding.

The car passes.

After a while we leave our hiding place, and continue to walk. The night becomes lighter, and the moon is reflected from puddles on the road. Through slits in the windows, one can see light peeping through. It is about midnight.

Apartments. How lucky are people who have an apartment! In the apartment with the light under the edge of the curtain, people are probably telling each other of the happenings of the day or planning the future. There is surely a bed there, made up with clean linens— well, perhaps not clean linens, perhaps without linens at all, but at least something to cover oneself with, one's own bed. How lucky those people are! They don't even know it. If only they could put themselves in our position. Before us, we see only death. We would be happy if we could get into a dark basement, even for one night. . . .

The stillness of the night is interrupted by barking dogs. Otherwise we hear only our own footsteps. The whole city is now in a deep sleep. We keep walking, walking, walking, and we are at about the same place. It seems as if we are walking against the earth's rotations. At last we approach Peltewna Bridge from the Zamarstynowska side. We stop. We look down to the river. Here all who escape are supposed to meet. But nobody is here. Perhaps all have been killed, some in the camp and others on the road. There is also a possibility that they had already been here, and gone.

37

KORN: Over six feet tall, long arms, in his late forties, slim, flat nose, deep large-set eyes, blond, with little hair on his head, by profession a horse trader, and known to the underworld as Ducknose, because of the shape of his flat, bill-like nose. Korn has a Polish friend on Kleparowska Street—a horse-cab driver. We are going to him. But how do we get into his house? Other people are living there. It is about one o'clock in the morning; the front door will be closed. If we knock at the main door and someone else comes out, we are lost. I get an idea. Korn must knock at the door. If anyone else except his friend answers, Korn will ask for the friend. Korn must say that he cannot go inside, for he, too, is a cab driver and can't leave his horse and buggy outside. He will ask whoever answers to please call his friend out. I shall not show myself.

We stand in front of the house where the friend lives. At the entrance of the house are a few wooden steps. I hide under the steps, and Korn knocks at the door. He knocks and knocks. At last someone calls, "Who's there?"

"I'm looking for Macieja," says Korn.

"Who is it?" the same voice asks again.

"Please call Macieja, and tell him that someone is waiting for him with a horse," answers Korn.

After a few minutes we hear steps. Not only a man's steps, but also a woman's. We hear her inside, whispering, "I am afraid for you to go out." At last the door opens, and Korn's friend steps out. Seeing Korn, he understands everything, and walks out alone. With Korn, he turns into a side street. Meanwhile, I continue to sit under the stairs, overhearing the wife talking to her neighbor who first answered the door: "Why does it take so long? Maybe something has happened to my husband? Maybe we should go and see what is taking them so long?"

At last Macieja returns without Korn, goes into the house, and closes the door. What has happened? I lie under the steps in a storm of anxiety. After a few minutes the door opens again; someone walks down the steps, turns aside, and stops where I am. I hold my breath. After a few seconds, I hear a whisper: "Come." I get up, and am led

223

to a shack behind the house. There I find Korn. Macieja closes the door, and leaves.

We lie down on the ground. While lying there, we are careful not to breathe too loudly or to make any noise. Every minute is like a year.

Around five o'clock in the morning someone comes. The door opens and our host enters. He brings us breakfast. He starts to speak in a very low voice: "Now, what are we going to do? You see for yourselves that this is no hiding place."

Korn asks him to take us over to another "gentile" whom Korn and Macieja know. Macieja agrees. It is daybreak, but the distance to the other man's house is not great. He is a gardener, and lives alone with his family. Macieja calls the new man out and leaves us with him.

Now we are alone, with Joseph Kalwinski. While Macieja still was there, Joseph had told us that he didn't have anyplace in which to hide but that he would take us somewhere else. He says this because he is afraid of Macieja—everyone fears everyone else.

Kalwinski tells us that he will build a hiding place in the basement but that in the meantime we must stay in the barn. We give him some of our money from the clothing of the dead, and ask him to bring us something to eat. We ask him also to go over to the Peltewna Bridge and see if anyone is waiting there. We sit in the barn, which is full of straw, afraid to move because the straw rustles. At last Kalwinski returns and reports that there was a man of about forty, sitting with bowed head, at the riverbank. After a while he threw himself into the river, and went under. Whoever it was, he had waited too long for his comrades, and had given up hope.

We remain here for three days. After the third day we have to leave without telling Kalwinski, because when we gave him some money for our keep he went to a saloon, got drunk, and never showed up at the barn again. His wife finally told her father-in-law that because of our money her husband hadn't come home for three days. If he didn't return immediately, she said, she would report "his Jews" to the Gestapo. His father became frightened because he was afraid that if the Germans found Jews at his son's house they might also search his house, where he had Jews hidden, a fact that even his own son and daughter-in-law weren't aware of. In the middle of the night, Kalwinski's father came to our barn and took us over to his house. We left the doors of the barn open so that it would appear as if we had left it by ourselves. In this new hiding place, which was a dark cellar of about 130 square feet, we found twenty-two other Jews.

PART VI

The Hiding Place

38

THE BARN in which we were hidden housed a cow, an ox, and a horse. There was also a separate corner for hogs. By pushing aside the straw on which the hogs lay, one came upon a small trapdoor in the floor that led to our hiding place. The hogs were a good cover because the sound of their breathing was very like that of a human being. Our hiding place housed twenty-four people, three of whom were children; five were women and the remainder men, sixteen of us, the oldest of whom was sixty-two. At first it was difficult for me to understand how so many people could fit into such a tiny space—it was about ten feet wide by thirteen feet long—but somehow we managed.

When Korn and I slipped through the opening in the floor into the basement, we were received with curious stares by the cellar's inhabitants. The owner had already told them about our coming. We were brought water and clean underwear by the owner so that we could wash ourselves and change our clothes. From now on we, as did everyone else here, dressed only in our underwear, for in spite of the fact that it was November, and a cold and wet one at that, it was very hot in the basement. One can imagine how hot it must have been on warm, muggy summer days.

After washing and dressing we sat down on the bed and whispered a short version of our story to the others. We answered the few questions put to us briefly, for there was a strict law of silence.

After a bit we heard steps above us—no one stirred. The small trapdoor then opened, and we could see an arm lowering a pail, which one of us took. Then a bag was dropped down. This was our dinner— bread and soup. After dinner we continued our whispered discussion for a while, and then lay down to sleep. Two men stood guard all night to make sure that none of us made a noise in our sleep. The trapdoor was left slightly ajar at night so that we could get a little air. Even the smell of the hogs and the urine and other liquids from the stable dripping down on us through the open trapdoor could not make us forego the precious cool air.

In one corner of our basement hung a curtain with a pail behind it—

this was our toilet. Every night the pail was taken out and emptied by Kalwinski, the owner.

The first night I slept restlessly, dreaming about SS men, hills of sand, and corpses; and I had to be wakened by the guards every few minutes, for I moaned loudly in my sleep. After a few nights I quieted down.

Before I fell asleep the first night, I heard the others complain about me. "He is so big and heavy; in his place we could have taken in two people," one said. And another: "He doesn't know how to sleep. He could be abnormal from the work he has done, and this could mean trouble for us."

I should explain that when I came to this hiding place I weighed about 230 pounds—I am five feet, ten and a half inches tall. This weight was owing to the plenitude of food we had had in the last few months in the Death Brigade. Because food had been so scarce these last few years, one ate as much as possible.

At five-thirty in the morning we were wakened; we washed very quickly. An hour later our breakfast was brought. We had to hurry because we wanted to turn off the light as soon as possible; someone walking past Kalwinsky's back yard might possibly see the light. At this time suspicions were easily aroused. If an unusual light came from a stable, or even if a gentile was noticed buying more bread than usual, it could be enough to make the Polish neighbors suspect there were Jews hidden nearby. The neighboring Poles kept an exact account of who had been taken away to be killed by the Germans. But one Jewish family in the neighborhood had not been accounted for—and this made it even more dangerous, for the neighbors suspected they were hiding. Therefore we kept the light on as little as possible, and lay or sat in the dark. Two of us always had to sit on the "toilet," since it was impossible for us all to lie down at the same time. We took turns, changing guard every two hours, day and night, to prevent those sleeping from making too much noise. It was very hard while on guard duty to keep awake in the heat and the darkness.

At about 11:00 A.M. a pail of soup was lowered. The man on guard duty picked it up, turned on the light, and when everyone was awake we had our lunch. At 4:00 P.M. we had another light meal, and at about 10:00 P.M. we had our dinner. This timetable was not always adhered to—very often one of the meals dropped out altogether or was delayed by a few hours. After dinner we kept the light on for a few hours.

This was possible owing to the 10:00 P.M. curfew. We knew that people couldn't be on the street at that hour, so the risk that someone might see the shaft of light from our basement was minimized.

The old man—we called him Grandpapa—acted as the barber, cutting our hair. After dinner some shaved, while others read the newspapers. At about 11:00 or 11:30 P.M. our host came down. Everyone listened breathlessly to his whispered account of outside happenings. He gave us an exact tally of how many trains had gone through the town that day and also the exact number of railroad cars that had gone east and how many had gone west, and what these cars had been carrying. From the number and direction of the trains we drew our own individual political conclusions. Of course, everyone had a different opinion. The women usually had none—for what did they know about war strategy! Grandpapa and Korn were our experts; they knew more than anyone else, for they had been soldiers in World War I—Korn had been in the artillery.

During these political discussions the man on guard duty had to be very alert to stop the whisperings from becoming too loud, and only one person was allowed to whisper at a time.

Among the occupants of the barn cellar was the Holtz family. For many years Mr. Holtz had been an owner of a bar in this neighborhood. Everyone knew him, and he had many friends. His children had become completely assimilated, and the whole family was considered to be just like anyone else's family—Polish, not Jewish. When there was talk of the big liquidation action in August, 1942, Holtz had hidden in this cellar. Mr. Kalwinski had known Mr. Holtz from childhood on. The refuge was to be a temporary one until after the action. But when the ghetto was created, Mr. Kalwinski agreed to continue to hide him instead of sending him into the ghetto. Holtz had two sons and two daughters, and he had managed to talk Mr. Kalwinski into giving shelter to these four young people, too.

The Kalwinskis had taken Holtz's younger daughter into their own house to help cook and do the laundry for the three Kalwinski men. She worked in the kitchen, and if anyone approached the house she would hide in the kitchen closet that had been prepared for her.

Holtz's other daughter and her two children, aged six and eight, were first hidden in another farmer's house, while the daughter's husband was working in a "good place." They were hidden there temporarily for the "August, 1942, action time," but when the action was over they tried to remain in the shelter longer. They managed to prolong their stay for a few more weeks, but the owner didn't want to keep them indefinitely. Holtz had pleaded with Mr. Kalwinski, and finally the latter agreed to take them in, too.

One of Holtz's sons had been in love with a girl, Malke, who was still in the ghetto. He had begged Kalwinski to let her come here too. A combination of compassion and a romantic heart convinced the farmer, and he agreed to increase the number of people he was hiding to eight.

These people had very little money, and of course Kalwinski couldn't support eight people indefinitely, even though he was well-to-do. The Holtzes then thought of Malke's cousin, Harry Feig, who was single and fairly well off. He, too, joined the group in the cellar. But being well-to-do and having available cash proved to be two different things, and it quickly became clear that someone besides Harry Feig would be needed to support the by now nine people.

A Mr. Held who had a wife and a seven-year-old daughter now appeared on the scene in need of refuge. He agreed to pay all expenses, and now there were eleven in the basement, as well as the girl in the kitchen. Mrs. Held had one surviving brother, Bernard, and he joined the group. Bernard, who was a very quiet man of about thirty-seven years, had lost his wife and child. One day the husband of Mr. Holtz's daughter lost his "good job," and he, too, came to the cellar.

Now everything seemed to be peaceful and complete for the cellar dwellers—except for the fact that the end of the war was not in sight. The German armies were still advancing.

The political situation made Mr. Held restless; he feared his money would not last.

One of Holtz's sons, who occasionally went out to the city in the middle of the night, knew a place where a doctor and a lawyer and their wives were hiding. The gentile who hid them was by then too frightened to keep them any longer, and wanted to be rid of them. But how could this be achieved? If he handed these people over to the Germans to be killed, he, as the owner of the place, would get into trouble for "breaking the law," though probably he would not get a death sentence. If he evicted them they could be caught, and under torture they might reveal their hiding place. If the matter should come out in this way, he could be hanged in the marketplace in the city.

There was a third possibility, and this had the least amount of risk involved—he could simply kill these people.

Once someone undertook to shelter a Jew, it wasn't so easy to change one's mind.

Holtz's son got in touch with this Pole, and took the doctor and lawyer and their wives to our place, keeping it a secret from the Pole where these couples were being taken. The two additional families were able to help the group pay the bill for its upkeep.

Holtz's son-in-law had two brothers in the concentration camp, one in his forties, and the other, a prizefighter by profession, in his thirties. Knowing that their brother and his family had found a hiding place, they escaped from the camp two weeks before our escape, and were hiding at Kalwinski's son's house. Their fate there was similar to ours, and under the same circumstances, and for the same reasons, they were brought here. Korn and I were the last to arrive, and no one else joined our group afterward.

Mr. Holtz, whom we called Grandpapa, was a quiet man, happy that he had been able to save his entire family. He recited his prayers every morning, and because of his seniority he had the best place in which to bed down.

Next was Mr. Held. For a while, being the sole supporter of the group, he had considered himself superior. He was most unpleasant. For example, he would not drink his tea in a cup, but must have a proper glass. He must also have a metal handle for this container, because he might burn his fingers on the hot glass. In addition, he refused to stand guard; his brother-in-law or his wife had to do it for him. He believed that the later arrivals should be squeezed together and that he should keep the original space he had been allotted.

His wife tried to keep all of her husband's obnoxious traits as unobtrusive as possible. Her brother, Bernard, was a very quiet man, who well understood the deadly seriousness of our situation.

The wives of both the doctor and the lawyer came from the same town in the southern part of Poland; both were from rich families, had known each other since childhood, and had been rivals since then. They were attractive girls, married to professionals.

The lawyer was a boy from a poor home who had worked his way through school and achieved his degree. He had married his wife shortly before the war.

To the lawyer's wife the doctor and his wife seemed to have a higher social standing within our group than she and her husband had. We all liked to ask medical questions, of course, and naturally some medical problems arose among us. In addition, the women in the group felt deep pity for the doctor's wife. She had a one-year-old boy whom she had given, for safety's sake, to a gentile couple to be raised. It would have been too dangerous to hide in a basement with such a small child. A few months before our arrival the child had been discovered by the Germans, and killed. One of the reasons for their discovery of the child was that he had been circumcised. Everyone in the cellar, including the doctor, knew about the child's death, but the mother hadn't been told. She half sensed what had happened, but when she asked about it everyone gave evasive answers. Hopes and uncertainties were fearful things to live with, all knew, but they were afraid to tell her because in her first reaction she might cry out.

Because the lawyer's wife felt that the doctor's wife was getting more attention than she, she went about becoming the center of attraction in her own way. First her sleeping place—the doctor's wife had a better one, which she wanted. Though the exchange was finally made, it didn't help because the better place "followed" the other woman. Next she began to have choking fits, but this didn't get anyone's attention as long as the "choking" was done quietly. Because the lawyer's wife knew she wouldn't get far making noise, the next step was to insist that when she felt a choking fit coming on, we should open the small door to get air for her. She didn't care that this would be dangerous for us all.

When, after repeatedly demanding that we open the door, she was at length firmly told that she could either choke quietly or we would help her choke, she stopped. Now her energies were turned against her husband. She said that he didn't care whether she choked or not, that he didn't even take her side, and that he didn't care how much other people took advantage of her and pushed her around. All of us could see that he didn't care about her, she claimed, and that this was why they threatened to choke her. The poor husband not only had to bear her harping but also the fact that the others told him that it was all his fault because he didn't know how to handle her. This mad situation between the lawyer and his wife continued until our last day together.

Another problem was Holtz's son and Malke, whom he loved and had brought here. Their love was not mutual. She looked down on him as being a simple, noneducated, boorish man, and didn't even want to speak to him. Taking into account that he was a member of our "family" here, the whole group was hostile to Malke. Abusive words were directed at her; she could never take part in any discussion, and would be immediately silenced. Her cousin, Harry Feig, whom she tried to rely on, was not of much help.

I don't know how intelligent or how smart Malke was, because in the entire eight months we were together I never spoke a single word to her. I can say, though, that she was neither friendly nor shrewd, and was most inflexible. First the boy began maneuvering to get her to lie next to him; this wasn't difficult, because the family helped. However, when he tried to embrace and kiss her, she tried to escape him by climbing over the other people in the darkness, and this made noise. People were annoyed by the whole thing, and didn't care who was in the right; they knew only that noise was dangerous.

Holtz's whole family soon began to resent her more and more, because, it was clear, the boy really loved her. Wasn't their brother and son good enough for her?

With each new event her life here became harder. Now, when in the dark the smitten boy tried to kiss her she still fought back, but quietly, without trying to escape. When he threatened to scream if she resisted, she gave in. But it didn't end with kissing, and a few weeks later he tried to rape her. Again he threatened that if she didn't give in he would scream, and when she paid no heed to his threats, he let out a loud yell.

Everyone was stunned by the noise; the lights were turned on, while the frustrated lover sat shaking nervously. Silence. No one said a word. Fearfully we lay down again, and the light was turned off. That night, after dinner, when the first shock was over and we were sure no one had heard anything outside the basement, the two brothers who had escaped from the concentration camp stated that if this were repeated they would leave. They refused to remain at the mercy of one man, a lovesick boy. They stressed that if anything similar were repeated, they would leave.

These two brothers beckoned Korn and me to a corner and talked about the advisability of actually departing. From then on, I became a member of the four "tough" ones.

By now my background and schooling had given me a certain "standing" in this society. To leave now, I told the other three, would be a big risk. The owner wouldn't stand for a few leaving because of the great risk he would run if they were caught and under torture revealed his "crime." He might, I continued, be tempted to kill anyone who tried to leave. We four finally decided it would be the wiser policy to stay.

There was another group, not belonging anywhere, and with no "social" standing—Malke, her cousin Harry Feig, and Joe.

Harry, a thin little man about forty, was peculiar. If he didn't like a dish he wouldn't eat it, even if he had to fast for several days. If he didn't like something in the soup, he would fish all of it out and lay it on the rim of his plate. He was very easily offended, and when his feelings had been hurt he wouldn't speak for days. He had set ideas, and nothing could change them. He was very serious, never smiled, and worried not only about the present but also about the time when he would be liberated by the Russians. His hope was that the Russians should suffer a defeat someplace, allowing enough time for the Western Allies to come here even if it had to take another year.

Holtz's daughter, the one working in the kitchen, was in her twenties, lively and pretty. The Holtz family wanted Harry Feig to marry her, yet Harry never exchanged a single word with her during her visits to the basement. The family, of course, realized that Harry and she would not make a suitable pair. The reason they kept an eye on him was that they thought it was possible that no Jewish men would be left after the war, and even though he was clearly abnormal, he was still honest; furthermore, he had real estate. The occupation by the Russians would be only a temporary one. This was not doubted by anyone in our cellar, and we all believed that after the war Poland would resume as a national state with a democratic form of government.

Joe: About the same age as Harry, he was a little under average height, stocky, with a round face wreathed in smiles. Friendly to everyone, even to those who didn't want his friendship, he tried hard to make the Holtz family like him. He showered compliments on their daughter. Right or wrong, the Holtz family was always right in Joe's opinion; but no one paid any attention to his opinions. He was always denigrating Harry, trying to tell the family that Harry didn't know how to appreciate what they did for him. Harry never talked to Joe.

39

THE DAYS passed slowly in the darkness and terrible heat. The monotony was interrupted only by short-lived excitements. From the heat and the hours of lying about we developed big red spots all over our bodies. A few days after Korn and I came to this shelter Korn got sick. In the beginning he had hiccups, but after a while he began to regurgitate his food, and this became progressively worse. We did not know then how serious this symptom was.

To keep my mind occupied, I memorized a few pages from Grandpapa's prayer book and kept repeating them while lying in the dark. The only outside book I could get was a Christian catechism, and so I learned the whole catechism by heart. The idea of survival was still very dim in my mind, practically an impossibility, but at the same time a dire necessity to hold onto. The concentration camp and the Death Brigade showed how little value life had. The thoughts of how my parents had prepared for their old age, how even when my sisters were infants my mother and father began saving for their dowries symbolized the futility of thinking about the morrow. The world as a whole had no reality or meaning.

At certain moments I would try to believe in the idea that you fight your enemy by trying to achieve the reverse of his purpose; in this case by surviving. Putting my memoirs together in order to tell the world what had happened, wasn't this too the normal desire of any teenager to keep a diary? All the goings-on in this hiding place proved to me the tenacity of the will to live.

I recalled listening in the concentration camp to a discussion between a father and his son after they were both put behind the barbed wire, which meant they would, beyond any question, be shot. That evening they got their dinner ration—a little piece of bread. The son wanted to eat it up right away, while the father thought they should divide it, a piece for now and a piece for the morning. The son's argument was that they would most probably be executed by the morning. The father replied, "But we will be taken to the 'sands' to be shot, and on our way there we can still eat it up."

This discussion was much calmer than one between a father and

235

son on how a ballplayer should have handled the ball in a minor-league play.

I didn't think about the future, or what I could do after liberation, if ever I were liberated. Never, during the time of hiding, or for the two years before, had I any dreams or thoughts about the future—after the war. I didn't even know whether I cared about being liberated. For whom and for what? Perhaps a feeling of guilt lingered on in me; why should I be chosen to survive? The few people here in the hiding place didn't count anymore. On the outside everyone was an enemy, a potential murderer.

December 6, 1943; in the evening.

As usual the owner came down, but this time he seemed very nervous. We realized immediately that something was amiss. He told us that in a neighbor's house, the Juzeks, only a few hundred yards from there, thirty-two Jews had been discovered. The hideout had been reported to the Germans by Juzek's own brother-in-law. From the thirty-two, twenty-six were from the Death Brigade, and among them was our leader, Herches. While they were being led to the truck, they had made a sudden attack on the Germans, and twenty-eight of the thirty-two escaped.

Juzek and his wife had been arrested and next day publicly hanged in the market. Our host was very much afraid that the discovery of Jews in this neighborhood would lead to a search of all the houses. A small search did go on during the following few days, but nothing happened in our house.

I should like to tell about the Polish and Ukrainian underground. On the whole, the Ukrainians in this section of Poland, in the beginning, joined the Germans, and took a very active part in the murder of the Jews. After a time, seeing that the Germans were not going to give them an independent Ukraine, a group of them became partisans, under the leadership of one Bandera; for this reason they were known as the Banderowcy. Their fight was not against the Germans but for a "General Peace Conference." Their aim was to prove that they were an absolute majority in this area. To become an absolute majority they had to get rid of the Poles. The Banderowcy would catch an important Pole, cut him to pieces, and place him in a public place for other Poles to see and take note; they wanted to force the Poles to move out of this part of the country. The Jews were even more afraid of the Banderowcy than of SS men.

The Polish underground in our area was a nonfighting group; they published an underground paper, did some radio work, spreading propaganda among the people, but did very little sabotage. Their underground paper was widely read. As a whole, the Polish partisans never accepted Jews, and very often some of its members would hand over Jews to the Germans. The underground paper and radio never came out with strong condemnation of their fellow Poles for helping in the massacre of Jews, and not even against the Poles who informed on the few Poles who were hiding Jews. Anything would have been of help to us. The few Poles who did hide Jews got no moral support—not even the cold comfort of believing that, if a fellow citizen informed on him, the informer might one day be punished.

One can see how shocked I was to read in January, 1960, in the political section of a leading American weekly, about the "hero" Bandera, a fighter against Communism, who lived in Munich and was killed there; he was pictured as a hero in this magazine, when he was really a murderer. How fitting for Bandera that the city where Hitler got his start should give him refuge!

Christmas, 1943, was approaching now. It was getting harder for our host Kalwinski to obtain a large enough food supply for so many people without calling attention to the size of the purchases.

Christmas passed. It was now the New Year. At the start of the year 1944, all-night shootings began between Ukrainians and Poles. This made our host very nervous. Each day now we awaited the Russian offensive. We never tired of calculating and recalculating how many days and hours the Russians would need to get from their present front line to Lvov.

At last Tarnopol, only eighty miles from Lvov, was taken by the Russians. But in the next weeks it changed hands several times. These changes led to new rumors, and every time something good happened it was spoiled for us by the malicious gossip of the local people. Stories about the Jews were one of their favorite pastimes.

One story circulating at the time was that when the Russian Army came into Tarnopol a group of Jews came out of their hiding place in a Polish house. A few days later, when the Germans returned, this Polish family was hanged for hiding Jews. This story made our host ponder just how long he should keep us in the cellar after the Russian

Army had liberated Lvov. Other stories about Poles hiding Jews resulted in new searches for Jews by the Germans. All the houses in the neighborhood were very thoroughly searched except our house, and this was due only to the fact that our host was the chief representative of the local farmers to the German officials. We were just plain lucky.

The Russian offensive posed another problem. In some sections the Germans forced certain families to evacute with them. If that should happen to our host, who would then take care of us? In some places people left voluntarily, not wanting to be at the front line. If our host didn't do what the others did, everyone might begin to suspect him. Our minds were not only occupied with the military events of the day but also in seeing to it that we were not killed, not now, not after such a long, hard struggle to stay alive.

In February, the German Army took over many rooms in our neighborhood to house their soldiers. In our house, they requisitioned a few rooms to serve as their headquarters. They even put two horses in the stable under which we were hiding. From this day onward, until they moved out four weeks later, we got a meal but once a day, late in the night, and we considered ourselves very fortunate indeed even to get this. One can well imagine how we felt, constantly hearing the Germans talking and stamping heavily about in their army boots right above our basement. We were afraid to breathe. Because our host didn't come down at all, we now were without any information as to what was happening on the outside.

This too passed. It became a little easier again—the news of the Russians was all good. All of us now tried mentally to prepare ourselves for liberation, for being reborn. We had to remember to keep in mind the "labor pains" which could be deadly for us.

It was April, and the Russian Army was coming nearer, ever nearer.

In the Jewish cemetery twenty-eight Jews, hiding among the tombstones, were discovered by the Germans. The first bombs since 1941 now began to fall on the city. Every day became increasingly longer for us.

May again brought bad news. A group of twelve Jews were discovered on Balanowe Street, only one block away from where I used to live. A daughter informed on her own mother, telling the Germans that she was hiding Jews. The mother was hanged, and the Jews were killed.

Lvov had now become the front line. One day we heard many

German soldiers come into the stable. They were going to use it for some purpose or other. To make it fit for this unknown purpose, they planned to pull out the whole floor above us. We heard the entire discussion. We sat paralyzed, staring into the darkness of the basement. The work began; then suddenly an order came for the soldiers to move out. Again we were saved at the last second.

At last the Russians arrived! Our host rushed in with this news in the middle of the day. The light went on, and everyone sat up and quietly listened to details of the news. We still could not talk loudly or make any noise because we were still afraid that the neighbors would find out that we were hiding here.

No one really knew where he would go or what he would do. We were too estranged from the world to have any plans. Everyone must get out and see for himself where and how to start anew. It was planned that we would leave in the early hours of the next day, so that no one would see us. Even now our host asked us not to come back to visit him, or for any other reason; it would go hard for him if it were known that he had hidden Jews.* Many of the Poles didn't like the idea that even a few Jews had been saved. These survivors could be witnesses that the Poles had collaborated with the Germans in destroying the Jewish population. Others, who had taken over Jewish houses and belongings, were afraid they might have to return them.

The only plan that I could make at the moment was a vague one; I would join the army and fight the Germans.

Next morning, about five, one by one we began secretly to leave the place. It was the first time in eighteen months that I was dressing to walk on the streets. The women and children, as well as Grandpapa, were staying until the next day, waiting for their men to find them a place to live.

---

*How sad was the situation in Poland that when a man proved he possessed high, idealistic qualities, he should be ashamed and unpopular for doing such a great deed!

PART VII

The
Liberation

40

I WAS OUT in the open.

Korn, everyone, had left the hiding place, each going his own ways.

Feeling very weak in the legs, my mind a blank, I walked in the direction of the city's center. The streets of Lvov were still empty, except for a few groups of Russian soldiers I passed, and army trucks lumbering by. I tried to speak with a group of soldiers, but they were not interested in talking to me. When I met a Russian Army officer and asked him where the army headquarters were, he asked me what I wanted there. I explained that I had just come out of hiding, that I was Jewish, and didn't know where to go and what to do. His answer was that all the Jews were killed, that only a few German-Jewish collaborators had been spared, and that I must be one of them; there was no other explanation, for him, as to why I should be alive. When I tried to impress on him that I had been in hiding, his answer was short and simple: One does not hide from the enemy; one fights him, he told me. He gestured with his hand—a gesture of contempt—and turned away from me.

I continued walking, without a destination, for hours. I was getting weaker and weaker—and ravenously hungry. Because I had gone so many months not wearing anything on my feet in the cellar, my shoes blistered the soft skin of my feet, and they began to bleed. Finally, I couldn't walk any farther. I sat down in the middle of the sidewalk, took off my shoes, and could not get up. My feet were covered with blood.

I sat . . . my head in a whirl; I drowsed off for a while, how long I don't know. Passers-by stopped to look at me. Some stopped only for a second, others for a little longer. They talked among themselves. The only thing I heard them saying was, "It is a Jew."

I shook myself out of my stupor. A group of people were standing around me, staring as if I were something never seen before. I spoke to no one and no one spoke to me. They whispered to each other, gaping at me. What should I do? I didn't know anyone in the city. I didn't even have a penny. When we escaped from the Death Brigade I was able to take very little money; part of that I had turned over to

Juzek, at the first hiding place, and the rest to our second host, Kalwinski. To go back to Kalwinski was impossible, for he had asked us not to return. The only place I could think of going to was the apartment where I used to live. After all, the whole apartment house once belonged to my parents. This was the last place I ever wanted to see again, but what could I do?

So, slowly, barefoot (I could not put my shoes on at all now, for they were so swollen), I walked in the direction of my house. The street where I used to live, which was once inhabited by Jews, practically all of whom I once knew, looked completely strange now. It is hard to describe my feelings. When, until yesterday, the problem had been to escape being killed, survival dominated one's every thought; today this was not a problem anymore. Today the anguish for those who had been killed flooded over me.

The tortures of the family, the way in which they were killed, began to prey on my mind more and more. The street looked so barren to me.

I was now guilty in the eyes of the people and of the Russian officer for being alive. The only question anyone asked me was, why was I alive?

With such thoughts I approached the house in which I used to live. I stopped at the entrance for a while and pulled myself together. I walked into the first apartment, where a woman, the janitor, lived. She recognized me at once, and told me to sit down. She asked me questions. I felt as though I were under an anesthetic. She gave me a plate of soup. I ate it. She told me with an authoritative voice that she kept telling her friends all the time that the Germans hadn't killed all the Jews and that there must still be some in hiding. I was proof of what she knew all along, she said. She tried to get me out of her apartment, telling me that the shoemaker who used to live across the street, and whom I should know, was now living in our old apartment one flight up. They were only four people, he and his wife, a daughter and a son, she said, so that I can find space there to stay. After all, she continued, it is your apartment; The furniture that your parents left is still there.

I went upstairs, knocked at my apartment door, and, without waiting for an answer, walked straight in, straight through the kitchen into the living room, and sat down on my own old couch. The shoemaker and his family already knew of my presence. Without even greeting me, the shoemaker told me that this was their apartment now; after all, there was a war on; they had had to leave their own place with their furniture, too. (They previously lived in a one-room basement apartment.) He said I shouldn't think that only the Jews had had a hard time; true, his family had not been killed, but "we didn't have it too easy either." He told me about high taxes and curfews.

I told him that I hadn't come to reclaim my own things, but that I would have to stay somewhere until I could find a place or until I could start to walk. I showed them my feet. They calmed down, and made up a bed that was once my father's, and brought a basin with warm water. I closed the door, washed up, and lay down on the bed. In no time I was asleep.

So passed my first day of liberation—the day that so many had waited for. I had lived to see it.

41

I SLEPT, dreamed, woke up many times. I was still in a state of confusion, dazed. I woke up finally in the late morning hours, finding a basin of water next to my bed, a clean towel and an old but clean shirt. After washing up and getting dressed, I went out to the living-dining room; to get there I passed through a room where the daughter of the house sat at a mirror putting on makeup. I said good-morning, but she didn't answer my greeting. I sat down at the table and was given breakfast. After the breakfast I just sat at the table. I stayed there for hours. My feet were still bloody and swollen; and I was still partially dazed. No one in the family spoke to me, and I did not speak to them.

The silence was interrupted at last by a visitor. When, during their previous occupation, the Russians had nationalized all the apartment houses they had set up a system; they had made one superintendent responsible for every three to four houses; and they had put a general superintendent in charge of twenty-five to thirty houses. This system continued under the Germans. The job of general superintendent was, politically, a very important one because the man in this position would be able to keep a check on all the inhabitants. Anyone who stayed overnight at someone else's house had to get his approval, and so on. Because the houses in our street had practically all been owned by Jews, they remained completely nationalized under the Germans, too. The general superintendent in charge of them under the Russians had been a Ukrainian. When the Nazis came he turned Fascist and was kept on this same job during the entire German occupation. When the Russians returned, those who were in high positions under the Germans were left in the same positions so that everything would keep running smoothly—at least until the Russians had a chance to take everything over.

My visitor was a tall, husky man in his forties; he entered the room briskly, laughing. He came over to where I was sitting, hit me on my back with his heavy hand so hard that I nearly fell off my chair, and in a loud voice, scarcely without pausing for breath, said:

"You should be happy you are alive! I knew they wouldn't kill all of you. Now that you are alive, the only thing for you to do is to fight the Germans. There is no mobilization yet, but each street has to supply volunteers which I have to register. Because some bridges and railroad tracks are torn down, these volunteers have to report by foot to Brody." (This is a town about sixty-five miles east of Lvov.) "It shouldn't take you over two days to get there. You'd better take a few pounds of bread with you so that you have something to eat." Where I was to obtain the bread he failed to mention.

When he finished I showed him my swollen, bleeding feet and tried to tell him that in order to walk sixty-five miles I would need at least a few days for my feet to heal. And who, I asked him, would give me the few pounds of bread for my journey?

He said, harshly: "You went through more than only swollen feet. I want to see you tomorrow morning on the road; otherwise you will be considered a deserter." With this, he turned and left the apartment.

I continued to sit silently on my chair. A while later I was given a bowl of soup. I ate it, and again I went into the bedroom and lay down on the bed. I felt that the room was filled with the souls of my family. Every time I heard steps I sat up and waited to see if some member of my family were coming in. I felt like throwing myself out of the window. "Get away from here," I told myself; but how and where?

Thoughts about my visitor came to me. Was this the representative of the liberator? Should I go to fight for the likes of him? Or perhaps for yesterday morning's Russian officer? If it were up to me, the war could continue forever and destroy the whole world. But perhaps there was still a flicker of humanity somewhere. I decided that I was not going to fight. Who was there to fight for? And with these thoughts I fell asleep. So passed my second day of "liberation"—even more disappointing than the first one.

When I arose in the morning, washed up, dressed, and went into the living room, there sat the shoemaker, who immediately told me that to his sorrow I would have to leave the house. I had heard, he said, what the general superintendent had told me yesterday, and I couldn't ask him to risk his freedom for me.

I was certain the scene enacted yesterday was the outcome of a deal between the shoemaker and the superintendent—a deal aimed not only at getting me out of the house but out of town. I knew, however, that I could not protect myself. If I went to military headquarters, who would listen to me? The Russians would simply ask, "What is wrong with going to Brody to volunteer?" I contented myself, therefore, with asking whether the shoemaker could get me some kind of cane. He was only too glad to supply one for me, and I left the house without breakfast.

In a way I was glad to be forced to leave it. But where to now? I knew that a few houses down the street lived a Pole who used to do some odds and ends around our house. I saw him now in front of one of the houses. I began to talk to him. He told me that he was now the caretaker of the house he was standing in front of. I asked him whether he could find some space for me to stay for a few days until I could get back on my feet. He said he could, but then told me that I would have to get a registration permit from the general superintendent. When I explained to him that this would probably be impossible, he said that in that case I could sleep on the stairway leading to the roof. He told me that at night none of the tenants ever went up to the roof. The front door, because of the curfew, was always locked at about 8:00 P.M.; so, if I wanted to stay there, I should get into the house a few minutes before, and leave not later than six in the morning. Also, he told me I shouldn't hang around the house during the day because this might call the attention of the tenants to my presence there.

And so this stairway became my sleeping place for the next eight days. After our discussion I left the caretaker and continued my walk, supporting myself on the cane. My only possession was a package of papers tied together with a piece of string and fastened to my belt by a short length of rope. This was the day-to-day record I had kept of my experiences in the concentration camp and the Death Brigade.

Every few minutes I had to sit down on a stoop to rest. But, hungry and tired, I walked on and on, hour after hour. What was I feeling? Disappointment? No. I felt completely adrift, uninterested, looking, or rather, staring, without any thoughts, at the ground, not wanting to see the world.

While I was walking, I found a gold ring. Immediately, I turned around and took it back to the man to whom I last spoke—the caretaker. I sold him the ring for about six pounds of bread and four plates of soup. He agreed to dole this food out to me for the next four nights, bringing it to my sleeping quarters on the stairway. Another part of the bargain: he must immediately take my shoes and cut them open a little, so that they would not hurt me so much. At least for the present, for the next few days, I was assured of getting something to eat. So passed the third day of the new era.

Sleeping on the stairs didn't bother me at all. I got up the next morning, broke off a piece of bread from the big loaf the caretaker had got for me the day before, had my breakfast, and left for the center of town. My feet felt much better. I was getting used to walking and was in a better frame of mind than I had been yesterday morning. After all, I had a place to come back to in the evening, and food for the next few days.

While walking through the main streets, I saw a sign on a building stating that it was a Russian military office. On the spur of the moment I entered it and went into the waiting room. I sat down next to a Russian soldier who was holding a rifle in his hand.

We started to talk. He told me that he, with a group of Russian soldiers, had been taken prisoner by the Germans some time before. He had finally escaped to the woods and had joined a band of partisans. Now he had come here to register. He was a young fellow, in his twenties, and looked Latin, but was Jewish. After a while he was called into one office. Then a female Russian soldier came out and asked me whom I was waiting for. I answered that I had come to register.

"For what?"

"I don't know," I said. "What can one register here for?"

"The army," was her answer.

"Maybe you can give me some kind of job or a place to stay?" I asked.

"No," she said, "that is not our department."

"Where can I go for something like that?"

"I don't know."

This ended our conversation. I walked out and sat down outside the door, waiting for the soldier with whom I could at least chat. He came out without the rifle; but though it had been taken away, he was still dressed in his uniform and in the heavy army coat. I believe he was glad to see me, too. He was the lucky one—to be registered in the army. Still, he told me, this didn't give him a place to sleep or any food. He asked me if I knew a place where he could stay, or where he could get something to eat. He had no money.

I told him about my staircase "apartment," and said that I had some bread and even soup which I would gladly share with him. He accepted my invitation, and we started toward my "home."

When we got there, the caretaker, seeing a Russian soldier with me, became very polite and helpful, telling us that there was an empty room on the third floor but that the general superintendent had the key for it. If we could get down to the general superintendent's office in time, he was sure that we could get the room. We went down to the office, but it was too late in the afternoon; the place was closed. We returned to the stairway. Soup was brought up for both of us by the caretaker, and even two glasses of tea. We finished our dinner, talked a little, and went to sleep. We were comfortable, for we had the soldier's big coat to place underneath us. The name of this partisan was Arcadi.

When we got up in the morning we began planning our day. First we would go to the general superintendent's office to get the key to the empty room. But food was a problem; my bread would be finished during the day. Arcadi believed that within the next few days the army or government would begin to take care of him, but in the meantime we would have to eat. We decided that the people who now lived in Jewish apartments and had taken over our furniture owed us at least a meal a day.

I knew some apartments in which Jews used to live. Arcadi would represent a government official; after all, he was in a uniform. I would pose as his assistant or guide. We would go into an apartment and say that we had come to register the Jewish belongings. When an apartment owner protested that he had bought the furniture, Arcadi would then insist he knew nothing but that he had been sent here to register all former possessions of the Jews. In the meantime I would whisper to the present apartment owner that it would be wise to invite us to a meal—that during it I might be able to convince the "official" that there was nothing to register here. With this plan we began the day.

First we went down to the office. There the general superintendent, seeing me with a Russian soldier, became very polite, mentioned nothing about volunteering for the army, asked me about my feet, and, when we mentioned the empty room, said: "Sure, anything I can do for you I will be happy to do. Just let me know."

Now that we had our room, the next step was something to eat. Our plan worked perfectly. After a big meal by courtesy of an apartment owner, Arcadi had to report to the office where I met him yesterday. He had been told to report there every day until he received instructions about his next assignment.

While he was there I tramped the streets. I thought I might encounter some other Jews; if I did, I could invite them to come in the evening to our new apartment.

I did indeed meet other Jews. It was easy to recognize one. Most of them had to use canes to walk; they were frightened, pale, and not dressed for the time of year. Somehow, when we met each other we would use the Hebrew word *amchu* (one of your people) to greet each other. Upon seeing a Jew, one would say, "Amchu." The other would answer, "Amchu." Then we would approach each other, embrace, kiss, and ask questions: Where are you from? What is your name? Where did you hide? From one of the Jews I met I found out that in a certain midtown public school all the survivors were organizing. There everyone could register and even get a pound of bread and a plate of soup.

I went there. People sat around the floor, sorrow and tragedy etched on their faces. Others walked around calling out the names of their near ones, when and where they were last seen. They did so to find out whether someone had seen them at a later date than they themselves had. At the entrance to the school slips of paper were posted, asking the whereabouts and fates of the following persons, giving their final known residences or where they had last been seen. Each slip was signed by a father, mother, sister, brother, son, wife, or husband.

I registered as the 184th survivor. Only 184 of us—and this included the Jews who came from neighboring cities within a radius of sixty miles to this "Jewish Center" in Lvov. In 1941 about 150,000 Jews had lived in Lvov alone. I did not ask anyone about my family; I knew only too well what had happened to them. After a few hours there I went "home" to my unfurnished apartment and to my new friend Arcadi.

The next day we again got a good meal from an apartment dweller by pretending we had to take stock of his furniture. After the meal I started for the center of the city, while Arcadi went to wait at the army center. While walking, I found a fellow I knew from the concentration camp. We had worked for a while in the same shop, he as a mechanic and I as an assistant to a plumber. His name was Beresticky. He was on crutches; his feet were as abraded as mine had been. We embraced each other, and he invited me to his apartment nearby. I went with him. He lived in a very nice apartment of three rooms and a furnished kitchen. It was one of those evacuated by the Germans when the Russians came in.

There were seven in the apartment, two families; one lawyer, his wife and children, and a barber and his wife, a girl in her twenties, and their son—and Beresticky. During the German occupation they had all hidden in the sewerage system of the city with several others. Beresticky had known a Pole who worked for the Sewer Department. All the water from the drains and toilets of Lvov flowed through six-foot cement pipes to a river outside the city. Beresticky, the barber, and their Polish friend entered one of these pipes. They then knocked out a section on one side of it and, in the soft earth that surrounded it, scooped out a cave about five feet deep and five feet high. This made an "excellent" hiding place.*

Beresticky invited a girl named Halina to join them, and the barber invited another girl whom he knew to take up residence with them in the cave. The lawyer, his wife and children were asked to come along too, as they had money to supply potatoes, wheat, a kerosene cookstove, a carbide lamp, matches, and similar necessities. The lawyer was from a well-known Jewish family.

They stayed in hiding about fourteen months, more than once coming close to drowning during heavy rains; in warm weather the danger was from choking to death or being asphyxiated by the canal's odors. Sewer rats were their constant companions. The barber's son was

* On the day set for the final liquidation of the Jewish ghetto in Lvov in June, 1943, over 500 people had tried to escape through the sewer system. The manholes, however, were all guarded, and most were caught while trying to get out in other parts of the city. Over 150 tried to hide in the sewer pipes, but after one week 130 of the 150 committed suicide, among them such notables as Dr. Chamajdes, Editor Halpern, Dr. Julie, Dr. Lowe, Dr. Merkel, Judge Glanz.

In the Beresticky group there were originally twenty people but after one week some could not stand it anymore. These were haunted by a dream of seeing sunlight just once more, and so after four weeks eight of these people left the sewers and were immediately killed. Another one drowned. A tenth person, an older woman, Mrs. Weiss, sickened and slowly died there. Before her death she begged not to be tossed into the water, to be eaten by the rats when she died. No one could make this promise.

The food had to be kept in iron containers to keep it from the rats. But because the rats ate through the iron containers, they suspended the containers from the top of the sewer pipe and placed heavy glass bottles around them so that the rats would slip off the slippery glass surface. A chief form of entertainment during their stay in the sewer was supplied by the acrobatics of the rats in trying to reach the food. Ten people were saved—among them two children, a boy of four and a girl of seven. No one became ill during these fourteen months, and so far, sixteen years later, there have been no aftereffects to be seen. The boy is now in Israel where he is a dental technician; his sister is a physician there. Beresticky, a tailor in Paris, married a girl who survived Auschwitz and has two lovely children. The barber became a caterer in London, while Halina is married to an engineer in the United States and leads a happy life with her two children. Each one is now leading his own life, and has very little contact with the others.

conceived and born in the sewer. Their Polish friend visited them very often, bringing food and news from the "outside world."

The apartment was found for them by their Polish friend who knew many of the apartments freed when the Germans had evacuated.

Beresticky cooked a meal for me at his apartment. When he gave me the steaming plate of cereal, it smelled awful. He was still using the leftover supplies from the sewer, which had spoiled and had also been penetrated by the terrible sewer odor.

He offered to share his bed with me, and when I told him that I had a Russian friend with whom I shared a room he informed me that on the upper floor of the same building we were in there was a perhaps better empty apartment. It had, however, been sealed off by the Russian military police.

Without very much hesitation we then and there decided that we would break the seal. After all, what could they do to us? And I wanted, passionately, to get out of the neighborhood where I had lived before the war.

That evening I went back to my room and talked it over with Arcadi, and the next morning we left for the new apartment, never again to return to, or even to pass by, the street or neighborhood where I had once lived with family and friends.

42

I HAD SOME FRIENDS I could visit now, anytime during the day or evening. They were all home most of the time, because they were still too weak to walk around much.

Now, every day for a few hours, I would go to the school, the "Jewish Center," where the survivors gathered. One day while walking there, I met the lawyer who had been in our hiding place in the stable; with him was another man who looked as if he had just come out of hiding too. His name was Dr. Philip Friedman. We were introduced, and as Dr. Friedman was a historian I gave him my memoirs to read. He seemed very interested in them. We made a date to meet again in a few days at the same place.

Next day I met my high-school teacher, Mrs. Eber, at the Center. She came here daily to find out something about her husband, who had also been my teacher. I knew when he had been killed and when he had been burned. Slowly I found other men who had survived the Death Brigade.

How many of us in the Death Brigade escaped is hard to say; I discovered that one man named Widder, who had worked in the shop in the Death Brigade, was caught shortly after our escape, but was not recognized. He was put into the new Death Brigade from which he escaped again a day before our liberation by the Russian Army. From his account, there were about twenty from our old group in the new Death Brigade. After we had escaped the whole guard had been changed. The inmates worked with chains on their feet. These chains were never taken off; they did not even have a lock; they were welded together. This Death Brigade was put to work in other cities, and near Stanislav (southwest of Lvov) the Russian Army finally caught up with them. The Germans shot the entire brigade; but one of the members, Widder, was not fatally wounded, and lay between the corpses until next day, when he was liberated.

I estimate that in our breakout over fifty had escaped, which, under the circumstances, was a very high percentage.

The fate of forty-four of these people was as follows: Ten were liberated, of whom three now reside in the United States, four in

Israel, and one in Australia; one I do not know of. Korn, with whom I escaped and hid in the stable, died of cancer a few months after liberation. Avrum, the fire tender, and Tierhaus, our "conscience," were also saved. Avrum settled in Israel, and receives a 90 percent mental disability pension. The twenty-six who escaped from Juzek's place on December 6, 1943, were finally captured in April, 1944, and of course killed. The two who had joined Korn and me on the railroad tracks during our escape had both been killed. Four were killed trying to get into Lvov. Still another drowned himself, and two young fellows who worked in the Death Brigade as "carriers," and were very much liked by all of us, were killed by the Ukrainian partisans, while hiding in the woods.*

The next few days followed the same pattern of meeting people and listening to their stories, a pattern that varied little. One of the stories, however, I should like to note here because it seemed to us a particularly tragic one. A group of about thirty people were hiding in a village near Tarnopol; when the Russian Army came in they ran out to greet them. Out of excitement these people ran straight toward the Russian tanks, waving their hands; one of the tank men, perhaps not realizing who they were, opened fire, and the whole group was shot down.

Ironically, the very difficulties we faced helped to make a "smoother" transition from the dark period we had been through to the more normal life ahead. Ironically, too, I believe that if the tragedy had been on a much smaller scale it would have been harder to take, for it would have been pain within limits of endurance. Beyond that limit one ceases to feel anything more. . . . Living with and meeting people who shared a similar fate, it seemed that this was the "normal" life. The non-Jewish world continued to be strange to us. We lived in our own world. We didn't talk about those we had lost or how it happened. One's own family was few among millions.

More often we spoke of how our own "good" non-Jewish neighbors had betrayed us. Why? We didn't expect them to help us, but why did they so enthusiastically help to murder us? I found out where the gentile neighbor who had betrayed my mother now lived, and went

---

* Other survivors of the Death Brigade whose names I have not mentioned before are Max Hoening, who now lives with his wife and daughter in New York and works in the garment center as a cutter; a man named Gleich, who works as a bookkeeper in New York; David Manucewicz, who, with his wife and three children resides in Israel where he has become a successful car dealer. Another, Mandel, lives with his family on the outskirts of Tel Aviv and runs a shoe store.

there. I was greeted with the familiar, "I knew that some of you would survive."

I asked the woman why she had given my mother's hiding place to the SS man after having lived on good terms next door to her for so many years. To this she replied: "It wasn't Hitler who killed the Jews; it was God's will, and Hitler was his tool. How could I stand by and be against the will of God?"

I walked out, stunned. I hadn't expected that kind of answer. She did not feel that she should repent or even deny her deed. She was a woman in her sixties.

One day Halina, Beresticky's friend, met someone who told her about a job at the railroad depot. Halina applied, and got a job in the office. After she settled in, she spoke with the director there and made an appointment for an interview for me to work there as an assistant bookkeeper. I got the job. I was now nineteen, and it was the very first real job I had ever had.

The director was a former army colonel, discharged from the army as an invalid. His name was Filipenko, his age about fifty; his wife was a pretty girl of about nineteen; it was his third marriage. Filipenko, a heavy drinker who did not have the slightest idea of how to run an office, was one of the most false and unreliable men I had ever met.

The office I worked in managed a combination of soup kitchen and store for railroad workers. At this juncture in Russia's development most factories and most worker groups had their own individual stores for general supplies, as well as separate kitchens in which the workers were fed. Our office ran such a "store" and kitchen for railroad workers only. All workers' stores and soup kitchens at that time were under one large governmental bureau called the O.R.C.—Organization of Workers' Supplies.

The people I now met at work were very interesting. There was Zimmet, the head bookkeeper in our organization. During the German occupation he had hidden, along with his sister, brother-in-law, and mother, in the household of a decent Polish family.

A Jewish woman, Mrs. Berger, worked in our organization's kitchen. She was the sole survivor of her family. In the soup-kitchen section, where Halina worked, her manager, Rosenfeld, was a sole survivor too. Rosenfeld and a friend had been hidden during the German occupation in a grammar-school basement by the janitor, who lived with his wife in the same building. After hiding these two people for a while, their Polish savior became frightened. He wanted them to leave the shelter but was afraid that if they were caught they might, under torture, reveal his identity. One day, in May, 1944, he decided to kill them. He came down with an ax and split Rosenfeld's friend's head in two; a fountain of blood sprayed over the whole place; and the janitor, seeing the blood pour from the dead man, lost his nerve and couldn't kill Rosenfeld. After he had recovered a bit he turned to Rosenfeld and said: "I cannot kill anymore, but if I do not kill you, and if you should survive, you will give me away as a murderer."

Rosenfeld promised not to say anything if he did survive. Together they buried the victim right in the shelter. Until the liberation two months later he was locked in so that he could not escape, living in constant fear of being discovered and at the same time, when his host came with food, terrified that he was coming with an ax. Rosenfeld kept his word, and never informed on the murderer. After all, his life had been saved.

Mrs. Berger lived alone in a very nice six-room furnished apartment. We all liked one another, and finally Halina, Zimmet, Rosenfeld, and I moved into Mrs. Berger's apartment, each of us getting a separate room.

Mrs. Berger now became our "mother," and we began a harmonious life together. We called our apartment a "kolchoz," the Russian word for their collective farm system. Many more such Jewish kolchozes appeared in the city.

In the meantime, Arcadi got a job. He was to open and organize a tourist office for the Russian government. It made little difference that even in peacetime few ever traveled in this area as a tourist. A tourist office, however, is a "necessity" in such a big city as Lvov.

Arcadi was the right man for the job. He had a university degree in Physical Education, was very good-looking, played a few musical instruments, was at the start of the war a member of the Russian soccer team Dynamo, and was a member of the Communist Party.

On my job there was not much work to be done. Because our office handled the kitchen and supplies for the railroad workers, at least I received a free lunch, and in addition, as a workingman, the regular food ration the government allowed, which normally consisted of over a pound of bread a day, one pound of sugar, and four pounds of meat or fish per month, plus some fat and other things. Miners, professors, and directors got higher rations, as they are considered very hard workers.

It soon became clear that there was not enough food for the workers' soup kitchens, so it was decided that our office would send out a truck to the provinces for potatoes, wheat, and similar farm products. The farmers, of course, were compelled to turn in their produce to the proper authorities; but there was a transportation problem. By having our own truck, our superiors realized, we could pick up what we needed from the farmers directly.

Nobody wanted to undertake this job, however, because people were very often killed in the villages by the Banderowcy—the Ukrainian underground. Everyone in our office had some close relative living in Russia or in some other country; a brother, sister, or uncle. As I was the only one without relatives, I could be the most easily spared. No one would miss me. For this reason I was put in charge of the food-supply transportation for our office.

I obtained an old broken-down Ziss truck, a driver, and an assistant, and started my new work. I welcomed this opportunity for it gave me a chance to make some extra money on the black market; we all needed this extra income merely to live. The pre-World War II joke, "If you work, how do you live?" was still very apt. To a certain degree our strongest drive in life at this point was—food.

43

Slowly life in Lvov began to grow normal. The Russian Justice Department in town formed a special section to investigate the war crimes—in preparation for the Nuremberg trials.

I was invited to the courts to give testimony about the German crimes, as well as to help round up other witnesses and to go over their testimonies. As a result of this the Justice Department published a report about the Nazi crimes in Galicia in which I was quoted several times.

Because of my close association with the Justice Department, I met several high government officials. During general discussions with them the question arose as to who was really guilty in Germany for all the war crimes. They argued that whereas one shouldn't generalize and say that all the Germans had been guilty, one could not hold *only* the government leaders responsible for crimes of such magnitude.

The officials came to the conclusion that every member of the Nazi Party should be held responsible. Their reasoning went as follows: to become a full-fledged member of the Party one had to be over twenty-one years of age, thus capable of taking full responsibility for one's acts. Becoming a member of the Party was tantamount to agreeing with its principles; these ideals were clearly spelled out in *Mein Kampf* —and they included mass murder.

Joining the Nazi Party, these Russian jurists held, had been strictly on a voluntary basis. There was no known case where anyone was punished for not joining the Party. Thus a Nazi had chosen evil when not under duress. It is true that by being a member one could derive preferential treatment either in his job or social position—but that could not justify subscribing to genocide. Responsibility for the crimes also fell on those who gave only their moral sanction to the Nazi cause, however indirectly, the jurists concluded.

In case there ever had been a unique reason for joining the Nazi Party, one not covered by the above reasoning, it would be necessary for the individual to prove his innocence. I fully agreed with these views.

During this period I met a correspondent and staff member of the leading Russian newspaper, Vladimir Belajev, of *Izvestia*. He impressed me as being serious and intelligent, with deep understanding. He had written a series of articles about the tragedy of the Jewish people under Hitler. He told me that he was now working on a book about the fate of the leading Polish intellectuals during the German occupation. Since I knew how and where and when so many of these people had been killed, would I like to write a chapter for this book? The name of his work was to be *Sudba Uchonych Odnowo Goroda* (The Fate of the Learned of One City). I agreed to do so. From then on, we met quite often at his home, and discussed different things. I told him of my desire to settle in Israel (at that time Palestine). Though he thought very highly of Israel, knowing that I wanted to study he believed I would do better in the United States.

How shocked I was to read in 1959, in the *London Jewish Chronicle,* about a series of articles written by V. Belajew, telling of a couple who had been "talked into" leaving Russia for Israel by the Zionists. However, once in Israel, they had hated it and had "escaped" to Brazil. They are now begging to return to Russia, Belajew wrote. Belajew knows better than to perpetuate the myth that all who flee Russia want to return.

According to Russian law, if there are ten people in a given community who want a religious life, the government will recognize their religious needs. Because there were now five hundred Jews in Lvov, we formed a synagogue with a rabbi. All the remaining Jews from the Polish provinces had settled in Lvov because they were now afraid to live in small towns; therefore, at Yom Kippur, our synagogue was packed to capacity. Our number included those Jews who had returned from Russia, where they had stayed during the war.

A Russian Jew, a retired officer of the N.K.V.D., was appointed by the Russians to head the Jewish Community. We were also informed that some packages with food and clothing had arrived through an American Jewish philanthropic organization and that if anyone wanted to get in touch with a relative overseas, he should go to speak to the new community head. But few availed themselves of this great opportunity. Who would go to a former N.K.V.D. man to ask for something that could be construed the next day as "traitorous"?

Normally, for the "sin" of asking for a "relief" package of food and clothing from overseas, or for attempting to get in touch with relatives abroad, nothing would happen—one's name was simply put on a list. If you were caught for another "sin," however, the two sins together would be proof that you were a true counterrevolutionary.

44

Our office at the railroad station grew. We got a new boss, Sweredenko, who was in charge of all the O.R.C. offices in the western Ukraine, and Filipenko stayed in charge of the local office, working under Sweredenko.

Sweredenko was a hardworking man; he was smart and knew his business. To help us get supplies and food for the railroad workers, he was able to obtain railroad cars for use by our office. As I was doing a good job on the truck, I was now put in charge of these railroad cars. We divided one of the railroad cars into two compartments; one of these compartments would be living quarters for my assistant and myself, for, Sweredenko told me, we would now be traveling extensively through Russia to get supplies. In the living quarters of one of these cars we put up beds, insulated the walls, had a stove to cook on and to keep us warm, and a table and chairs.

My first job took me to Kiev. For this pickup of supplies for the railroad workers, as for most in the future, half of a railroad car was enough. I presented myself to the train dispatcher with an official order to connect my car to a train which would go to Kiev.

The dispatcher, seeing on the order that I was going for supplies, immediately invited me to his private office, where he asked me what I was going to bring back. I mentioned a few items, and he said he could use all of them. He then gave me his private address and assured me of his full cooperation. After this interview our car was given top priority.

I was advised to carry a few pints of vodka with me to help resolve any unforseen problems en route—and I did. Soon my car was connected to a passenger train leaving for Kiev, and immediately the vodka came in handy. The man who checked car wheels with an iron hammer to see if one were cracked ordered my car to be disconnected. I ran out with my pint of vodka in my hands, gave it to him, and at once he countermanded his order.

On this first trip I went alone, as I saw no reason for an assistant. The trip to Kiev, about five hundred miles from Lvov, is only an overnight haul, and I would have very little to pick up. At large stations, where the wheels were checked, I was now ready with a pint of vodka, and in the morning I arrived safe and sound in Kiev.

The first thing I did after I arrived was to go to the place where I had to pick up the supplies. There were, however, no supplies. I phoned Lvov, and was told to wait until next day for further orders. I got my *Komandirowke* (pass) stamped, to show, if I were stopped by the police, that I had reported to the correct office. With this pass I could then go out into the city.

The main streets of Kiev had been completely destroyed by the Germans. The first question I asked, as did everyone else, was, "Where is the black market?" I was promptly directed to it.

At this market one could buy a loaf of bread for 120 rubles (my salary was 300 rubles a month) or a pound of herring for about 80 rubles. One could even buy a "pig." A "pig" was an old Russian gold coin, so called because it had the Tsar's face on it.

At the market I met some people, got into a conversation, and received an invitation to their home to sleep, which I accepted. I did not get a room of my own there; in fact, there were five people sleeping in one room. I was the sixth.

In the early hours of the morning I went back to the railroad station to look for my railroad car. I could not find it!

I ran quickly to the stationmaster's office, and he asked me if I knew no better than to leave a railroad car alone over night. He also told me that, according to regulations, there should have been two men on the car.

It had never occurred to me that a railroad car would be stolen. But it had been, and I must deal with the fact. After hours of running around to no effect, I decided to call Sweredenko to tell him the story, and to put part of the blame on him. He should have known the regulations and sent another man with me. His answer was, in effect: You took the responsibility, and you had better not show up here without that car.

I begged and pleaded and threatened, and finally the stationmaster gave me an engineer with a locomotive to look along different railroad tracks; my car had, after all, to be on some track or other. In the late afternoon we found it. It was on a siding about ten miles outside Kiev. Only the car's iron skeleton was left; the wooden walls, the stove, the chairs, and everything else that could be of any use, had been taken away. This skeleton was towed back to Kiev, and I had it connected to a train going to Lvov. It was a cold December night, about five below zero. The engineer took me into the locomotive, and thus I got home without freezing to death.

Losing the car did not do me any harm, as it developed. In fact it showed Sweredenko that I could take care of something that was entrusted to me; after all, I *did* bring it back. We repaired it, and within a week two assistants and I were ready to go to Moscow for another attempt to get supplies for our railroad workers.

I was able to get a *Komandirov,* my official invitation from Moscow. After I received it I went over to the chief railroad dispatcher with a package of food, and in no time my car was connected to a train leaving for Moscow. At every big station en route we "greased" our way with pints of vodka, and arrived in Moscow twenty-six hours later.

It was night, so I stayed in the car. Next morning I went to the Ministry of Railroads to get my seal on my *Komandirov* and to report my arrival.

I went by "metro" (the subway), and was very much impressed by its beauty and cleanliness. Each station was built differently, with statues and marble walls; everything was spic and span. It was strictly forbidden to drop anything in the stations. At the entrance of every metro station there were always two policemen on duty, and when on one occasion my clothing was slightly soiled with flour I had just been loading, I was not allowed to use the subway. Because the escalators in the metro were constantly being polished by women, they shone like mirrors. The trains ran like clockwork; every three minutes exactly, one came along. Once, when I did not take the first train that came along, a policeman came over to ask me the reason for not doing so. I believe the reason was that they didn't want the station to become crowded with people—for many would have preferred to spend their evenings here rather than in their overcrowded homes.

To my knowledge there was no black market in Moscow proper. To reach the black market one had to go about thirty miles out of the city. Sunday was the big black-market day. Thousands and thousands of people left the city by train for it. Because this place was on the outskirts of Moscow, but still within the city limits, one did not need a special *Komandirowke* to go there. The trains, which left every half-hour, were packed to capacity.

The market was so crowded that it was difficult to move about. I bought some bread there. The price of bread was about the same as in Lvov, and a two-and-a-quarter-pound loaf cost about 120 rubles; but the quality was much better. When I got back to the railroad car, I had only a mass of crumbs left in my bag because I had been so squashed in the crowd on the return train.

A lot of items were much cheaper in Moscow than elsewhere. I was able to get a few hundred pairs of children's shoes, a few hundred yards of clothing material, a few thousand packages of cigarettes, and about one metric ton of American bacon. I also got an extra thousand packs of cigarettes.

To get all this back to my railroad car everyone had to be bribed— even the truck-driver who took my merchandise from the black market to my freight car.

I made "friends" with the Moscow railroad dispatcher (with a bribe, of course), and my car was quickly connected to the first train leaving for Lvov.

In Kiev, where we had a stopover for an hour on our way home, three women came by begging to be taken to Zytomir (about seventy miles west of Kiev). They did not have any *Komandirowke,* and carried bags of merchandise with them to take to the market there. I agreed to take them in my car, for which they were very grateful. Two of them were elderly women, the other about eighteen. When later I offered them some bacon and bread, the two older women thanked me very much for the offer, but explained that for the last fifteen years, as they were Jews, they had not eaten any meat products because these were not Kosher. The three of them had liven all their lives in Kiev, except during the German occupation, when they had escaped to Central Asia.

From this point on, I was kept constantly at work going back and forth from Lvov to Moscow. Owing to my good "connections," I never had any delays.

I was now away so much that Beresticky moved into my room at the apartment. He was a very easygoing fellow. He worked, if one could call it that, at the tourist office opened by Arcadi, and he made a little extra by fixing locks and doing some plumbing. He would never do more work than he needed to for his daily expenses. He was a very short man with beautiful dark curly hair. As such, he liked tall blond girls. He went out every night to dance. To go dancing, one had to buy at least a beer, which cost five rubles. Beresticky would buy the beer, and then take the glass home and sell it the following day on the black market for five rubles. He would then be all set for the next evening.

Another man, named Mort, now became a regular guest in our house. He was over forty, with only a few hairs left on his head; he wore heavy glasses, and never shaved. He was a scatterbrain, though a very honest and religious man. He made money easily, but owing to his wild schemes he lost it just as quickly. He had never married. A cousin of his, who lost her husband and two children during the war (she was in her thirties), found him and wanted to marry him. She was a pleasant-looking woman, and a very fine one, too. When we tried to persuade him that he should marry her, his argument was that other men who had been married before the war were marrying young girls now; why should he, a "young" bachelor, marry a widow?

At this time there was a privately organized group of people who were trying to get back Jewish children who had been hidden in non-Jewish homes during the war. The head of this group was Tierhaus, my comrade in the Death Brigade. He continued to be a symbol of high morality and honesty. Some of the gentiles were glad to return the children to the Jews; others wanted money to do so; and still others, especially those who had taken in infants, would not give them back at all. There was, too, the problem of what to do with the children once they were returned; there were so few Jewish families left to place them with. We, in our kolchoz, took in a thirteen-year-old girl, but since we all went to work, we could not properly care for a teenage girl, who of course needed more than just a roof over her head. She had been in a monastery during the war—one that had been under the auspices of the great humanitarian Archbishop Szepticki.

Mort, the newcomer bachelor in our menage, took a six-year-old girl, and to care for her properly he obtained an apartment and asked his cousin (the one who wanted to marry him) to join him in looking after the child. She was quite a problem child, and needed full-time attention. Her father had been killed when she was four years old, and her mother had found a Polish friend with whom she left Lvov as a non-Jew, putting the child into a Polish house. The child felt that she and her father had been forsaken by her mother, and would react to kindness by misbehaving. Mort and his cousin had the child for about a year before her real mother was found in Krakow. At first the child did not want to return to her mother, saying she hated her, but after a few days she gave in. After a time with her mother, this little girl changed completely, becoming well behaved and sweet.

Mort gave in too—seeing what a fine woman his cousin was and how well she had taken care of "his" child—he married her, giving up his treasured bachelorhood. They now have children of their own, and live in Israel.

In the meantime, Arcadi's secretary had become pregnant, and they got married. Not having a place to live, they moved into my room at the kolchoz. Beresticky moved into the hall. Now when I went home I slept in the hall, too.

On my next railroad-car trip to Moscow, I was given a two-way radio and a big package of different foods to deliver to one of the generals of the railroad in Moscow. (Rank on a Russian railroad is the same as that in the Russian Army.) On this trip the chief book-keeper of our office, who was a Russian, came along with me. In order to be allowed to accompany me in my car he had to act as my assistant, for it was forbidden to have passengers. When we arrived I phoned the general's office. He sent down a truck, and in this we transported the radio and food packages to his house.

He lived in a beautiful big apartment. He inspected the radio, and was delighted with it. As a sign of his pleasure he gave me and my "assistant," the bookkeeper, drinks of a very fine liqueur and two tickets to the ballet at the Bolshoi Theater.

Next evening, we went to the theater. All the surrounding streets were full of police. However, when we showed our tickets, we were not only permitted to pass but were treated with great respect. The theater, I believe, has six balconies (we sat in the first); the décor was red, and the entire place was filled with high-ranking officers. The moment the curtain rose, Molotov and his family came into the center box, as well as Vishinsky and his group and the Foreign Minister of Chiang Kai-shek's Chinese government.

The performance was, if I remember correctly, Tchaikovsky's *Swan Lake* ballet. I had gone to the theater in the only suit I owned. It was a well-worn Kufaika—quilted jacket and quilted pants. This kind of suit was very popular in Moscow because it is very warm and light. I must have looked as odd as I felt. As much as I was impressed with the décor and the performance, I felt no inner satisfaction or excitement. The whole theater, with its audience, was part of a world to which I didn't belong. Normally, if one sees or lives through something unusual, one tries to feel his way into it, so he can relive it at a later stage to tell and share his experience with others—friends and family. In my case it was "other people" who went to see and enjoy a good show; but did I belong to these "people"? With whom could I share this experience—with my kolchoz? Didn't they look at it in the same light I did—"Vanity, vanity, all is vanity." After the show I returned to my railroad car to sleep, and I didn't even think about the show any more.

My railroad car was now running with great efficiency. In fact, certain high officials in our bureau preferred to travel in my car rather than go the usual way in a regular railroad coach. I always got what I was sent for and delivered the items to the proper authorities. Sometimes I would pick up and transport furniture and household goods for delivery to high Russian officials. Such items should have been registered and put into warehouses, for they came from Nazi-occupied territories; and, since I was transporting them without any papers, I was legally liable for my actions.

One day in Kiev my car was searched and undeclared items were found. Fortunately, the chief of the N.K.V.D. liked a desk that I had aboard, and therefore the rest of the illicit items were delivered to the proper parties. For each such illicit delivery I was well paid—in special bonuses of five hundred to a thousand packs of cigarettes; these brought in a nice sum of money on the black market. After all, I took the risk of delivering the items. On the other hand, if I had refused to deliver them I would have lost my job.

My efficiency was finally recognized in Moscow itself; it was suggested by a higher-up that I be transferred to the main office in Moscow and put in charge of "trouble spots." But because Lvov, as the big city in the West, had a high priority in supplies, and also because my director claimed he had no one to replace me at the time, my appointment was postponed.

One of the big happenings during the war was the Repatriation Act for Polish citizens. By this decree all the former Polish citizens who had been sent to Siberia in 1940–1941 (see page 29) were released; now that Poland was liberated they could return here. Among the repatriates a big percentage was Jewish, because, of course, in 1940 all the escapees from the Germans were sent to Siberia. When the act was passed, every Polish Jew, including myself, registered to leave Russia.

Repatriation, however, moved very slowly because of lack of transportation facilities. The war was still going on, but it was clearly drawing to an end.

In April, 1945, a month before the war's end, Halina, Bernard, and Mrs. Berger left for Poland; and so our kolchoz shrank.

I went on many trips in my railroad car, but day by day it became even more clear that the war was coming to an end. The Russian and Allied armies were victorious everywhere.

45

May 9, 1945.
The end of the war!

Soldiers danced in the streets; there were private parties, drinking, and celebrating everywhere. But for us "liberated" ones, the day of victory somehow didn't look or feel different from any other day.

The price of the dollar on the black market jumped in a few hours from 110 rubles to between 240 and 280 rubles—an unusual thing to happen to the money of a country which had just won a great war. But there was a reason for it. In some circles there were wild rumors that a war between England and Russia would break out very soon now.

I don't know whether England would have won a war against Russia, but I can say that I gathered from discussions I had with people across Russia that if the Americans had decided at that time to liberate Russia from Communism, they could have walked through it with very little resistance. If anyone asked a Russian if he or she wanted to leave Russia, they would, of course, vigorously deny it. No one was willing to exchange life in the Russian "heaven" to live under a capitalistic system. Even people I knew (and they were aware that I knew that they would leave the country if they got the chance, even in the middle of the night) would still openly condemn anyone who wanted to leave the Red "heaven." But when the United States was mentioned, and the question asked whether one would like to go there, the Russians opened their mouths, but couldn't close them again to say "No." By now, they all knew about the "land of plenty." The Russian leaders were aware of this, and from the first day of peace a slow, but well-thought-out campaign of anticapitalist and antiAmerican propaganda began.

I was invited to a liberation-day party at the house of the Assistant Secretary of Supplies, a top Party member, a very shrewd man. At this party there were about twenty people, all high-ranking men. The Assistant Secretary had come to Lvov from Vladivostok, with his wife and eighteen-year-old daughter, to reorganize our branch of the railroad service. His apartment was in the nicest section of the city, and though not yet completely furnished, looked very elegant. There was more than enough caviar and champagne, but no one got drunk. I, not being a part of the group and not having much feeling about the victory, didn't know what was going on or what people were talking about the entire afternoon.

When all the guests had left, I sat on in my corner in a half-dazed condition.

At this point I was approached by my host. He started to talk to me about my future. He told me that he knew about my good work and that he would like to have me as his assistant in his office. He also told me that he had spoken to my director and that in a few days I would be sent to the Black Sea with two railroad cars, to bring twenty tons of fish to Lvov. I would, he told me, get a barrel of thirty kilos (about sixty-six pounds) of the finest Russian herring for myself, to sell on the black market. He then took me into the other room, where his wife and daughter were sitting, having a discussion in French, and introduced them to me. By their appearance, as well as by their dress, they looked every bit like the society ladies of "capitalistic" countries, a far cry from their fellow "comrades." I was invited to stay for dinner, and because of the curfew I was given the guest room in which to stay overnight.

Two days later, I was on my way to Izmail, a town near the Black Sea, for some more finagling with the black market and to perform some more "favors" for high-placed Russian officials.

Because there was no direct railroad line from Lvov to Izmail, I had to route my railroad car first to Czernowitz (Bessarabia). We stayed there for two days and then moved on to Kishinev. Hanging onto the stairs of the train, and even onto the top of the locomotive, we found twelve- and thirteen-year-old Russian boys. When we got to talking to them, we found out that they came from different parts of Asia and Siberia. When I asked the boys why they had run away and come so far, they answered with the question, "Don't you see?" and pointed to the heaps of corn lying along the railroad stations. Hunger had brought them here to this rich corn country, far from their homes.

Kishinev, the old town, was a name known to me because of the Kishinev pogrom of the Jews in the early 1900's; it had been a huge Jewish settlement before the Germans came—now there were only about twenty Jews left. We met the "rabbi" here, Jankel, a man in his sixties, about four feet eight inches tall. He had had no rabbinical training, but of the Jews left here, he was the religious leader. He made his meager living from "finder's fees." For example, he would find a place for an out-of-towner to buy a few pounds of wheat—or anything else—on the black market.

Just before I left Kishinev a man came to my train and begged a ride to Izmail. His papers weren't in the right order, he told me, but he *had* to be in Izmail the next day. I took him along. During the trip he told me that he was an engineer. He had been born in the United States and had come to Leningrad in 1932. He was very sorry indeed that he had left America and that he had exchanged the American way of life for the Russian one.

On my arrival in Izmail my assistants and I delivered the "gift" I had aboard (black-market furniture) to the proper parties and also got all our papers officially stamped. Then we set off for the black-market district.

The chief commodity here was wine, and it certainly gave this marketplace a "different" atmosphere. As you walked through the streets every farmer stood next to his wagon, on each of which lay a wooden barrel holding one hundred and fifty to two hundred gallons of wine. Not a single farmer ever failed to offer you a glass to sample. After a few minutes of walking this merry way, you could get as drunk as a lord; in fact the whole market was in a very happy state indeed. I could see old women in their seventies dancing, singing, and kissing each other. After a few drinks I decided to buy a two-hundred-gallon barrel of wine to sell in the black market at Lvov. I had no idea of all the problems involved in such a bulky purchase, but here a man didn't trouble his head about future contingencies, even if they lay only a few hours ahead. He faced them only when they stared right at him.

Our railroad cars were parked close to the Black Sea coast so that the fish I was supposed to bring back could be loaded. One couldn't get into this section of the dock easily; there were so many different items lying around that a heavy guard was kept on duty all the time. Though I had my pass, how was I going to smuggle in a horse-drawn wagon and a huge barrel without getting caught?

I decided to buy the wine in the evening, when the dock guards would be alone; the workers would be gone by then and I could make my propositions in private. I didn't have to promise much, just a few pounds of herring to a few of the dock guards, who not only let my wagon pass but also helped my assistants and me to load it on the train.

I siphoned off a few buckets of wine, and the guards and my assistants and I celebrated the occasion.

Next day I got my consignment of herring and began to load it on the train. The dock at Izmail was a hodgepodge. Goods from everywhere were scattered around in confusion. Great mounds of herring and other fish were lying on the ground, spoiling in the hot sun for want of transportation facilities to Moscow, only thirty miles away, where a piece of herring would have been a great delicacy. I had space on my train for at least another twenty tons of fish but I couldn't get permission to take it. It just lay there in the sun, and rotted.

My fish and wine aboard, I left on the return journey to Lvov. I booked my train only to Kishinev, however, for I wanted to lay over there and I didn't know just how long we'd stay. Who knew what good things might happen? We stayed four days, and after scouting the place thoroughly decided to buy two and a half tons of walnuts and two hundred brooms on the black market. My next stop after Kishinev was Drohobycz, about sixty miles south of Lvov, for I had heard that the prices I could get there for my merchandise were considerably higher than at Lvov. But what was even more important than the price was the fact that there would be far fewer police and N.K.V.D. men at Drohobycz. We weren't afraid of them, of course; it was just that the fewer there were, the fewer "partners" we had to share our profits with.

Trading, however, was not brisk in Drohobycz, and I at length pushed on for Lvov. After arriving, we unloaded everything at the company's warehouse. This meant that we had a new "partner"—the warehouse manager.

Meanwhile my barrel of wine had turned sour because I had opened it in Izmail and then had to leave it standing in the hot railroad car for several days. It was a total loss.

We flooded the Lvov market with our walnuts. But when the walnut merchants found out that we had brought two and a half tons to the market, the price fell lower than the price we had paid for them.

The only thing we made a profit on was the brooms. But two hundred brooms didn't cover our losses by a long shot. The only benefit we derived from this trip were the additional official contacts we made, for many members of the police came to us to "share" our profits with us. We were "big operators" on the black market, weren't we? But our reputations far outshone our deeds.

One of the men who didn't show up for his "share" was the head of the railroad division of N.K.V.D. in Lvov, Kapitan Lyceyenko. In his fifties, he was a man with a hard face, who never smiled. Daily he came into the railroad workers' kitchen to get a free meal. He couldn't make a living from his salary either. Because nobody could trust him, he got few bribes. It was known that when he needed to fulfill his quota of arrests required of all N.K.V.D. men, he wouldn't hesitate to haul in a man who had given him a "present" the day before.

I was to have a run-in with this Lyceyenko shortly, a decisive one.

It was at this juncture that I registered as a former Polish citizen so as to be able to leave Russia for Poland.

I believe my main reason for this decision was that the other Jews were leaving Russia; I was afraid to be left alone in this strange society, so alien to all I could remember before the war. The others who left did so to look for their families, to find a Jewish society, to escape from this hostile world of strangers.

Daily, now, I saw transports of former Polish citizens passing through Lvov on the way back to Poland. (Russia had annexed a good portion of the "old" Poland, and Lvov was now a part of Russia. The new, "independent" Poland began some distance farther west than it had before the war.) These people were repatriates, most of them having been sent to Siberia in 1940–1941 for one or another "sin." At least 90 percent of them were either "capitalists" or refugees. Among them, too, were a small number of former political leaders' families, some of them even families of ex-Communist leaders.

46

AS I MENTIONED in Part I of this book, the "capitalists" were shipped out of Poland when the Russians marched in in 1940. Now I found out more about that exodus.

First the head of the offending family would be arrested by the Russians. Two or three days later the N.K.V.D. would come, always in the middle of the night, and order the rest of the family to pack up within a half-hour, telling them that they were being resettled only a few hundred miles inside the Russian-Polish border and that their fathers and husbands were there already, waiting for them. The family was then brought over to the railroad station by truck and loaded into a cattle train, forty to forty-five persons to a car. These trains were made up of from fifty to sixty cars.

Now they headed northeast. For the first 150 miles the journey didn't seem too bad. The doors of the cars were left open, and the guard riding on the platform at the end of each car behaved very well.

After the train had passed the once-Polish territories, the doors were then locked, and the guards put bayonets on their rifles. The people were forbidden to look out through the small train windows, which were covered by wire mesh, and so the long journey to Siberia would begin.

During the trip adults got about fourteen ounces of bread a day and the children (below twelve years of age) about seven ounces—and water. Nothing more. One of my friends was on a train on which a two-year-old baby girl was alone. The family of the baby had gone into hiding, leaving the baby with a woman to take care of it. When the N.K.V.D. came in the middle of the night to arrest the family, they found no one at home except the strange woman and the child. They released the woman but took the child. The child was "adopted" by a family in the railroad car.

After twenty-nine days the train would arrive at Novosibirsk in Siberia. This seemed to be the assembling point for all trains carrying "enemies of the State." On some days during this period twelve to fifteen trains would come in; this meant that over 30,000 people were being shipped to Siberia daily. At Novosibirsk the trains were sent to different destinations.

Let us follow one group of trains. From Novosibirsk it was sent to Semipalatinsk, about 350 miles south of Novosibirsk; then it went to Genqistova, a score of miles. From here the people were taken by truck about another hundred miles to the main *sovchose*. A sovchose is a collective farm under control of the federal government. (A "kolchoz" is under the auspices of the local government.) At the sovchose the people were told in a speech given by the sovchose director that they were enemies of the State and for that reason they had been brought here, and they would have to remain here for the rest of their lives. They would, he told them, have to make up their minds to get used to the work and conditions. The closing sentence was a proverb well known throughout Russia: *Kak nye priviknesh to Zdochniesh.* (If you do not get used to it, you will perish.)

After the speech groups were assigned to different farms, all of which belonged to the main sovchose. They were now transported in carts pulled by oxen or asses. Soon they discovered that they had been relocated near the border of Mongolia and China—a wild region. All of them were given shacks without any furniture or even floors. Children under twelve and disabled people were freed from work. Working people got about fourteen ounces of bread per day, while the children and disabled received four ounces a day. The young men worked in the fields daily, and received, in addition to the bread, a bowl of soup with a small piece of meat in it, while the others got meat only when an ox or an ass died. The children were not given any schooling. The people were not allowed to leave the settlement.

Summer here lasts from May until September. The rest of the year it is very cold, sometimes reaching as low as 70 degrees below zero.

Because there were no trees, there was no wood for heating or cooking. Here and there one could find a kind of prickly shrub; and after a whole day of collecting these shrubs, one came home with bleeding hands, and only enough shrubs to boil a pot of water.

One group was put to work during the summer months to make a fuel "product," a substitute for coal. This fuel was manufactured by mixing animal dung with straw, and then drying it by plastering it on the walls of the shacks. When dry, it was stored in the warehouse and given to the people in the winter to heat their houses.

In the winter, because there was no work in the fields, young people went to "school" to learn how to handle tractors and how to repair them. Because of snowstorms the meager rations of bread were sometimes delayed in transport for two or three days. At times the people couldn't get out of their snowed-in shacks for days. In general it was dangerous to leave one's house during the winter. Even if the sky looked clear, a blinding snowstorm called a buran could suddenly descend. This buran is a heavy snowstorm accompanied by whirling winds so that one can't see even a few feet ahead to find his way back home. Many of these émigrés lost their lives in such storms.

The families were not, of course, reunited with their husbands and fathers, as they had been promised. None of these families knew where their men were.

In September, 1941, owing to the agreement of the Western Alliance with Russia, all of these people were suddenly told that they were now free. They dispersed, leaving this hard country as fast as possible, by foot or by rail. Those who qualified were supposed to join the Polish Army, and many did.

It was these people who were now being repatriated—sent back to Poland.

It is interesting to know just who the Russians considered "capitalists." Bankers, big businessmen, and manufacturers, we were told. But who were they in reality? I knew one. My mother's cousin, who lived only a few blocks away from us, had had a family of nine children. He had owned a candy factory that employed seven men, that is, six of his own sons and himself, and they just managed to make ends meet. The family of thirteen (it included a daughter-in-law and a grandchild) lived in a five-room apartment, and the father couldn't even afford to send the children to high school, because from the age of thirteen on they had to help in the factory. The Russians arrested the father as a capitalist, and he was accused of living on the sweat and blood of the workers. After all, he had six employees. The whole family, including the daughter-in-law and grandchild, were sent to Siberia for his "crime."

After the "capitalists" had been sent to Siberia in 1940, refugees to Russia from the Polish territories, occupied, under the Hitler-Stalin agreement, by the Germans, were taken away under similar circumstances to Siberia. The only difference between the refugees mentioned above and these latter were that the heads of the families in this second category weren't arrested, and weren't separated from their families. They weren't considered to be "big" criminals. More than 95 percent of this group were Jews, who had escaped to the east from West Poland when the Germans conquered that territory.

As to the political leaders and their families whom the Russians had also sent to Siberia, these were not only leaders of antiCommunist movements, but leaders of leftist groups, too—and only a political theoretician could, in most cases, have separated their intellectual convictions from those of diehard Communists. In Munich, Germany, I had a friend who attended the same school I did. His father, prior to the war, was a high official of the Communist Party in Poland. Before the war the father used to go secretly to Moscow for party meetings. He was caught by the Poles for this subversive activity and was sentenced to "Bereza Kartuska," which, prior to the war, was the most terrible prison in Poland for enemies of the State. He was liberated by the Russian Army when they marched into their part of partitioned Poland in 1940. When at a Party meeting one day, shortly after the liberation, he voiced a dissenting opinion, he was taken away and shot forthwith. His wife and son were sent to Siberia, where his wife died. The son returned as a repatriate.

47

THE TRIP I made to the Black Sea was my last big one for the company. I informed my boss that I had registered under the repatriation law and wished to return to Poland. While waiting my turn for transport space, however, I came to the office daily in order to train a new man for my job.

One day at the end of June, 1945, I got a phone call from Lyceyenko, the head of the N.K.V.D. in Lvov, to come over to his office at 4:00 P.M. that afternoon. His office was in a buidling which housed the N.K.V.D. headquarters. The guard showed me in to Kapitan Lyceyenko's office. As I entered I had the tardy premonition that I shouldn't have come.

Inside the door stood an N.K.V.D. man with a rifle on his shoulder. Lyceyenko sat behind his desk. When I approached his desk and greeted him, instead of answering civilly he got up from his chair and brusquely ordered me to empty my pockets and put everything in them on the desk. After I had done so, I was told to be seated.

The N.K.V.D. man standing at the door now came closer and stood right behind me. Lyceyenko started to pore over my belongings and documents. When he finished he asked me for my Komsomolske membership card (Youth Organization of the Communist Party). When I told him that I didn't belong to any organization, his answer was "It figures." Then, pacing to and fro behind his desk, holding a lawbook in his hand, he began his accusations.

The first accusation he leveled at me was that during the war I had been a collaborator with the Germans; the proof of this charge was that they hadn't killed me. I had agreed with the Germans that after they left I would spy for them; the proof for this charge was that I got a job on the railroad to travel throughout Russia—I had got the job in order to spy.

When I tried to answer these charges, I was hit so violently in my ribs with the rifle by the N.K.V.D. man standing behind me that all the breath was knocked out of me.

Lyceyenko's accusations now went on and on, so long, in fact, that I stopped listening to them. I bent all my efforts to thinking: What does he want and how can I get out of this? If he had wanted me to ransom myself, he wouldn't have had this other N.K.V.D. man in the room.

After each accusation Lyceyenko would open his lawbook and read: According to paragraph so and so of our constitution, for such and such a crime one gets this or that sentence. For one of the crimes he read I could be sentenced to death.

After a while I got bored with this long tirade. I could think of no way out of the situation, so I simply withdrew my attention; he ranted on for the next hour and a half. After the speech was finished a gesture by hand signaled to the guard behind me to lead me out. The guard led me through a long corridor down to a dark basement, pushed me inside, and locked the door behind me.

Alone I sat down on the ground and slowly analyzed the whole situation. There was no doubt in my mind that all of this came about because Lyceyenko hadn't received a sufficient cut from some of the black-market transactions I had made for Russian "higher-ups." I was in a bad spot, no doubt of it. I knew from previous cases that it wouldn't be difficult for Lyceyenko to get me sentenced. He would present his whole case in the court while I would be forced to stay here in this basement. And even if I were taken to court it would have been foolhardy for me to question the validity of charges from a captain of the N.K.V.D. Just to accuse such an official of not telling the truth is enough of a crime to be sent to Siberia. With such thoughts and with visions of myself again jumping from a train or truck, as I had under the Nazis, I fell asleep.

Next morning a guard came in and told me to follow him. First he took me to the lavatory and told me to wash up. After that he took me again to Lyceyenko's office. The first thing Lyceyenko told me was that I was free. All my belongings were then given back to me. He also told me that last night they had caught the "guilty" one. However, because he, Lyceyenko, would need some future statements from me, I must not leave my apartment, except to go to the office. He also mapped out for me the exact route I must use to go from my home to the office. In case I had to go to some other place, I must first phone his office.

When I got home I took the money I had saved from its hiding place under the floor of my apartment. I then sent my friend Mort out to buy some gold pieces and dollars for me. I had about 50,000 rubles. On the black market this amount had a value of about $110. I also got another friend to go to the railroad station to find out exactly what time that very day a train with repatriates was leaving for Poland. He was to do anythng possible to get me on that train.

Ten hours later I was on the train, saying my farewell to Russia.

My destination in Poland was Gliwice (Gleiwitz), a city in Silesia, part of the new, "independent" Polish territories. (Prior to the war it had belonged to Germany.) Practically all of the repatriates went to these new territories, because under government pressure all the Germans had to leave these territories and housing had been made available for us, the repatriates from the east. I chose Gliwice because Rosenfeld, Halina, and Mrs. Berger, my kolchoz friends, were already there.

When I arrived, they took me in and I lived with them for a few weeks until I could find an apartment for myself.

At this time the people felt much freer in "independent" Poland than in Russia. We now began to think of the future. Most of us had hardly settled here before we had begun to make plans for further wanderings. Very few of us even considered remaining in Poland. Most wanted to leave as soon as possible. Those having relatives in Western countries dreamed of being united with them; the others spoke only about Palestine.

Before the war there were about three and a half million Jews in Poland; this accounted for over 10 percent of the Polish population. Because the Jews lived mostly in towns and cities, these often had a Jewish population of over 35 percent. Owing to this large Jewish concentration, the Jews often had their own local governments (*Kahal*) which took care of the Jewish communities, religious and charity needs, furnishing, cemeteries, hospitals, religious schools, free kitchens for the poor, orphanges, and so on. To support all these institutions every Jewish family had to pay income taxes to the Kahal, and the government gave the Kahal full power to collect the same. Every four years the Kahal held elections, and there had always been about a dozen political and religious parties running their candidates for office. These parties ranged from the extreme right wing to the extreme left. One of the strongest parties was the *Bund*. This organization, which was, basically, a labor movement, was anti-Zionist; it believed in fighting for social and labor reforms, in uniting the international labor movement, and in this way achieving rights equal for all minorities. Thus it was believed the elimination of the Jewish problem could be achieved.

As a result of the war, this party, and all the rest, too, with their "solutions" of world problems which indirectly would also solve the

Jewish problem, practically disappeared. None of us had any interest in political movements anymore. There was no question in our minds that if during World War II there had been a Jewish State, our fate in Poland, under the Germans, would have been different. None of us was interested in political ideologies, only in a Jewish State.

There arose now an organization among us called *Ichud* (United), whose members represented all the different Zionist factions, independent of political ideology. Its membership was small, but the Jews as a whole strongly supported its cause. Unfortunately, the life of this organization was short. Its demise was contributed to by American Jewish organizations, by Palestinian leaders, and by a few political leaders who had returned from Siberia.

48

NOW I TOOK my next step—this time toward a slightly more normal way of life. The affirmation of life in us had begun slowly to erase the feelings of hatred against everyone. How can one live despising the world?

At first one felt kinship to all Jews, his comrades who had shared a fate like one's own. And then, gradually, we began to discuss the fact that there had been those who had risked their lives to help us. We talked of the great humanitarian, Cardinal Szepticki; of Kalwinski, the Pole who had hidden me and the others in his stable cellar; or of the man who had helped the Beresticky group, and of similar individuals. News reached us of the heroic deeds of the Danes, the Dutch, and others. This fortified our wounded spirits. We were adjusting to life, taking slow step after slow step, back to a saner, more normal view of people. We survivors began to get married, to have children, to worry about everyday family problems, and to think about the future. While some believed that children shouldn't be brought into "such a world," others came to believe that it was everyone's responsibility to have children to rebuild a Jewish life.

One of the greatest desires my parents had had was to see to it that their children were educated. In my mind the spirit of my parents lived on. Since I believed this, I began to try to shape my life to conform to their wishes wherever possible. Therefore, I decided to fulfill their wish, which I shared, for an education.

Having saved a little money, it wasn't imperative that I start work immediately, so I engaged a tutor to review my high-school subjects, for my plan was to enroll in the Polytechnic Institute recently opened by the Polish Government in Gliwice. In October, 1945, I was admitted, and started to attend this Institute.

The few months there were for me like those of a shy little boy starting school in a completely strange neighborhood. I never spoke to my other classmates; not one was a Jew. I entered the classroom when the bell rang and left it as soon as the lecture was finished. I could not make myself speak to or try to get friendly with the other students.

Only a few of my friends knew about my decision to try to become an engineer. Some middle-aged Jewish people I knew tried to discourage me from this decision, claiming that without any family or other support, and after what I had been through, it would be a waste of time to start because I would never be able to finish. I turned a deaf ear to these people, who would then ridicule me, saying that I overrated myself. This was difficult to take. It was very important to me to be accepted; I had no one left, and this group of people, the older Jews, afforded me my only sense of belonging. Therefore, I began to deny, or at least not to admit, my plans to many of the people I knew. But this presented another problem for me; a young man, not working, not learning a trade, but "dreaming," made me look "peculiar" in the eyes of these people.

The terrible times we had been through had made many of us much stronger characters, while some became weaker. It was like wood in water, where some kinds of wood become hardened while others rot. Sometimes a wood rots only on the surface.

Life had taught us that to achieve something one should not give up easily, and for us "easily" was something more than it would normally mean. We had learned that logic is not always right. Not being afraid of obstacles anymore, Jews now embarked on the "Exodus" ships to fight the English blockade; some of us now had an indomitable determination to rebuild life. Setbacks and hardships didn't count; we were resolved to achieve what we had set out to do. This spirit infected me, too.

A Central Jewish Historical Commission was established in Lodz with branches in all the main cities of Poland. The director was Dr. Philip Friedman, one of the few Jewish historians left in Poland after the war. The purpose of this Commission was to collect documents about Nazi crimes. The Commission also published documents and memoirs that were important contributions to the history of Nazi crimes. One of the first books to be published was my memoirs. Because of limited funds and scarcity of paper, only one part, namely, the "Death Brigade,"* which constitutes Part V of the present book, was published in the spring of 1946. To prepare this book for publication, I went to Lodz a few times. During this time Dr. Friedman and I became close friends, and our friendship continued until his death in 1960.

The fight for life of the small remnant of Polish Jews left was not

---

* The *Death Brigade* was edited in Polish by a close friend, Mrs. Rachel Auerbauch. I shall never be able to thank her sufficiently for the help she gave me.

over. In October, 1945, only a few months after the end of the war, while I was visiting Krakow, there was a Jewish pogrom there; Poles attacked the small Jewish community in Krakow, and quite a few were injured. On the same day there was another pogrom in Katowice; forty-six Jews were killed. While pogroms of a smaller size than these had, prior to the war, shaken the whole world, these pogroms somehow didn't make much impression anywhere—not even on the neighboring Jewish communities. On one hand people were used to killing; on the other it was no shock to find out that we were not safe here. The only effect these pogroms had on us was to make us realize that it was not enough to *think* about leaving; we had to act. But where should we go?

If at this time we had been free to emigrate to Palestine, there would have been no problem; practically all of us would have gone there, even those who had close relatives in the Americas. But Palestine was still closed to us then. The only possibility was to get to a friendly country; there one could wait until he could go to the place of his desire.

Germany wasn't looked upon as a country, but as four zones belonging to the Four Powers. In each of these zones there were displaced-person (DP) camps. These were the only places that larger groups could get to. Very small groups were allowed to go to Italy or France, but all others had to go to one or another zone in Germany.

Most people chose the American Zone. The Russian Zone was not even considered. Nor was the British Zone; the British Government wanted the Jews to stay where they were: more people in the DP camps meant more pressure for immigration to Israel, which was against British policy. The French Zone had very few DP camps. The Americans had the most power to pressure England to permit entry into Palestine. To exert the maximum pressure on the world for a free immigration to Palestine it would be necessary to concentrate as many Jews as possible in the DP camps and as far as possible in one spot. The logical spot was the American Zone in Germany; or, on a smaller scale, the American Zone in Austria.

The Jewish leaders, knowing that one had to strike while the iron was hot, organized an underground organization named Bricha (Exodus). Bricha was very well organized; its goal was to smuggle people to Palestine. Because the countries where Jews were still left, such as Russia, Poland, and Rumania, had no direct route to Israel, the smuggling was done in steps, transporting individuals from country to country. Owing to the strict English blockade of Palestine, only a negligible number could be smuggled into Palestine, while all the others were directed, for the time being, to the American Zones.

The members of Bricha were heroes and idealists comparable to any known in the history of mankind; they were people without compensation, risking their lives, their names never to be known, their work endlessly hard, terribly dangerous. These people, perhaps because of their own strong convictions, couldn't see why everyone was not willing to sacrifice himself, and sometimes they would force other people to join them.

In February, 1946, I left Gliwice for the American Zone in West Germany. With a bribe to the right person of about twenty dollars I was able to get papers, and I traveled by train to Vienna, Austria. There I was directed to the old Rothschild Hospital, which served as a receiving place for Jewish displaced persons. The people stayed here for a few days, after which they were dispersed to different camps. I first registered and obtained a place to sleep in a big hall that housed hundreds of military beds. Next day I discovered that the managing director of this receiving center for Jews was from Lvov, and knew me. Owing to this, I was very well treated, and two days later I was sent to Munich.

On the train near Munich I began to talk to a man sitting next to me, and he told me I could stay in his house for a few days until I found a room. Next day I went down to the Central Jewish Committee to find out how to legalize my stay here. I was given several papers; these directed me to go to different departments in various sections of the city for registration.

The transportation in Munich was at this time very poor. The streetcars were overcrowded, and people clung on, standing on the steps. Because this resulted in many accidents, the police began to fine everyone riding on streetcar steps. The trouble was that this new ruling went into effect on Friday, my second day there, and I didn't know anything about it. I and a lot of others were caught standing on a streetcar step. A policeman stopped the car, loaded us all onto a truck, and headed for the police station. All the German citizens arrested simply paid a fine of about ten cents and were released. Another young man and myself, being DP's, were not under German jurisdiction. We could be fined only by the American Military courts. Because it was Friday afternoon, the American courts were closed until Monday morning.

We two were taken to the city jail, where we were held until Monday. Everything was taken away from us, even our shoelaces. The cell in which we were placed slowly filled up with people, some of them real criminals. There were no beds, and we slept on the floor. My only worry was whether I would be able to go about my business on Monday after sleeping for three nights on the floor in my only suit. The two days passed slowly, and on Monday I was brought before the tribunal. The judge scanned a piece of paper and said, "You know it is dangerous to ride on streetcar stairs; please don't do it again." I didn't have to pay any fine, for after all I was not a German, but a DP.

And so my stay in Germany began with jail. I was not surprised.

49

THAT SAME MONDAY I got a room, and next day I went over to the *Technische Hochschule* (Engineering School) for registration. The head of the Mechanical Department, Professor Foeppl, was a very nice man, one of the few on the faculty who even then were anti-Nazi. I was lucky that I didn't have to lose any time, because the school year was just about to begin. In the next few days I took a placement test, and began my studies.

Here at the university were a few other Jewish students, and we formed a closely knit group, studying and spending our free time together. We were like an island in this German school, always aware of the fact that we had no other place to learn if we wanted to get ahead with our studies. So far no country had opened its doors to us. We were completely absorbed in our studies. On our short vacations we would take trips to the mountains, to get interested in the beauty of nature. Slowly, we became more humanized.

To support myself I got a part-time job with the Jewish Historical Commission, which was a subsidiary of the Central Jewish Committee of Liberated Jews.

I began at this time to hear stories about the cruelty and ferocity of the Jewish *Kapos* at some of the concentration camps. The word *Kapo* was strange to me—we hadn't used it at Janowska. It simply meant, however, "Jewish leader," one appointed by the Germans—the functions of Herches, our leader in the Death Brigade, would fit the word.

I should like to say here that, despite these reports that some Kapos had beaten their own Jewish fellows, informed on them, and so on, in my experience, the leaders I had known had been, for the most part, superior men of high moral quality.

There was, for example, Kamps, our first Jewish leader at Janowska. He was an engineer by profession—a good man in every way. He really never laid a hand on anyone—if he had to admonish a fellow prisoner, it was always for that individual's own good and safety. He was finally shot by the Germans.

And then there was Axer—who became our camp leader in May, 1942. He was rich and prominent, and the son of a leading lawyer in

Lvov. Axer never hit anyone, but he worked very hard to help us. Everyone felt he had a friend in him.

Axer lived in a separate room on the concentration-camp grounds, and very often was allowed to go to the city without any guards. He always returned; but then one day he decided to escape. After two days in hiding, however, he decided to return. He did not get punished for it. Probably the German Chief of Camp, Wilhaus, expected a big present for sparing Axer.

When Axer returned, we asked him why he had done so. He answered that his conscience bothered him when he was free—he felt guilty for trying to save his own life when we in the concentration camp were clearly doomed.

One day in 1942, Axer yelled at Wilhaus for shooting so many people. Wilhaus took out his revolver and shot him dead on the spot.

For Axer, escape would have been quite possible. His family had so much influence that some gentile would certainly have hidden him, but he chose, and one can say voluntarily, to die with his people. He wasn't a man of physical violence. He never stooped to raise a hand or even a weapon. He knew how to die heroically for his people. At one time such was the stuff that saints and martyrs were made of.

After Axer's death, there were other leaders in the camp, but no one paid much attention to them, and they didn't make imprints on our lives, so that the survivors don't even remember who they were or how they looked. But they certainly were not cruel or unfair to fellow Jews.

Our Jewish community leaders—all I came in contact with—were of high moral standards, men who went bravely to their deaths in front of their people, whether they were Dr. Parnas or Rabbi Levin or the many others I haven't mentioned here. Perhaps the only regrettable thing is that because of their high moral standards and moral values, they didn't know how to organize a physical resistance. Physical power may have been too repulsive to them.

Even today, the idea of the "cruel" Kapos is completely strange to me and to all the survivors of Lvov and its neighboring towns.

After the publication of my book *Death Brigade* in Poland in March, 1946, I began getting letters from all over the world: from a man in New York, asking about his cousin; from Moscow, a wife begging for information about her husband, for her six-year-old son wanted to know how his father had died; a Palestinian newspaper editor asking more details about his brother, "Marek," the blond boy whom I had described in the *Death Brigade* and who lasted only a few days. One of the letters, from a father, was of special interest. It read as follows:

20 May 1946

To the Jewish Committee in Munich:

I am taking the liberty to ask you to send the enclosed letter to Mr. Weliczker, who left Poland for Munich about two months ago. If it should not be possible to find him on the basis of registration in your offices, please try to find him through placing this letter on the special "looking for people" board.

With my deepest thanks.

[signed] Dr. Ernest Roth.
Chairman of Jewish Committee
in Bielsko Biala.

The letter from Dr. Roth read:

Dear Mr. Weliczker!

I am the father of Jan Roth, whom you mention on pages 49 and 52 of the *Death Brigade*. Until now I knew only that on June 11, 1943, Jan and his little sister, Eva, were reported and taken away to the Janowska camp. Further checking after them didn't bring any results. I was sure that if Jan had been in the concentration camp he would have escaped as he has done once before in December, 1942. He had a place to hide. I surely assumed that he must have been shot immediately, together with my little daughter.

I feel that you, sir, could tell me much more about him than what I read in the book, where there is no space to discuss the details of each member of the "Death Brigade." I am very sorry that when I found out about you, sir, you had already left the country. I will try to meet you, but in the meantime, I would beg you to write me when and how my son, Jan, was killed. If you, sir, remember any tortures, sicknesses, beatings or exhaustions, please tell them to me. Please, don't hide anything from me.

The data in your book are exact because my son and daughter were taken away on June 11, 1943, at seven o'clock in the evening by Ukrainian police.

If you hesitate to tell me all that you know because you want to spare their mother, my wife died June 30, 1943. I am very much indebted to you for remembering so much about my children. Waiting for an answer and hoping that until I can meet you this letter will be a start for our friendship, I remain

With best wishes
Ernest Roth

A note was included from a woman whom I had once met, asking me to fulfill my duty to this tragically smitten father.

It wasn't easy to answer this letter. What could I say about exhaustion or beatings? Who noticed it at that time? I wrote about the escape, the fate of the ones who didn't escape, a little about myself, and so on. Dr. Roth and I began a regular correspondence.

In his next letter Dr. Roth wrote more details about his children. In this letter he also wrote that his wife had committed suicide on June 30, 1943, by taking cyanide. She had taken all the twenty-five pills that they had, and none were left for him to follow her with. She left a letter asking that her clothing be sent to the gentile woman who took care of Eva when she was a child. Dr. Roth's letters were full of pain, though they were without hatred; they told only about the people who had helped his children until they were discovered and killed. One has a feeling from these letters that he felt guilty for not having been killed himself. In one letter he wrote, "Does a father have the right to outlive his children?"

I should now like to interrupt the Roth story. I shall come back to it later.

The Nuremberg trials had now begun. On the whole, the trials were not much followed by us. We discussed them as though the Nazi crimes were something that didn't concern us anymore. The murderers should be hanged; but the millions were already dead. The Nazi plan should have been prevented by the world before millions of innocent people had been killed. Our discussions centered upon our wonderment at how such people as these had become leaders of one of the most powerful nations of the world. Even now, during the trial, these degenerates fought among themselves, and over such trivia as to who should enter the court first. All of them were frightened; each tried to push all the responsibility for his crimes on the others. Frank, the political leader of the Nazi Party and the Governor-General of occupied Poland, even tried to become a convert to Catholicism. He stupidly hoped in that way to have the Pope intervene on his behalf. The Russian prosecutor mentioned my testimony several times during the long trials. At the end of August, 1946, I visited the Military Tribunal in Nuremberg a few times, but it was a most uninteresting "show." On Tuesday, October 1, 1946, the former German leaders were sentenced. Twelve received death sentences, three life imprisonment, four from ten to twenty years in prison, and three were freed.

In general we were satisfied with the sentences, especially the death sentences to Frank, to Rosenberg, who had been the *Reichsminister* of the occupied territories in the East; and to Streicher, the murder-propaganda man. Streicher was the publisher of *Der Stürmer,* a weekly anti-Semitic paper. The four Powers agreed on the principle that the propagation of hate and murder made the individual as guilty as one who had committed such crimes. Whether we are adhering to this principle is another question.

The trial brought out tons of documents showing that the mass extermination of the Jewish people had been systematically organized. For example, there was the letter signed by Heydrich. It was date-lined Berlin, September 21, 1939, and had been addressed to "The Chief of Security Police in Occupied Territories." The German code number for this letter read, "PPII-288/39 Secret." In it Heydrich had described the exact steps to be taken in the projected liquidation. In his own words, the letter was written to clarify "our final aim and the steps to achieve it." He went on: "The planned measures need solid preparation from the technical as well as from the economic viewpoint."

The letter describes the exact way to organize the Jewish committee, the exact measures to be used to concentrate the remaining Jews in one place, to make sure that the concentration of Jews would always be near a railroad station, and methods of murder. If one compares Part IV of this book with Heydrich's letter, one can see how exactly this plan was followed.

Another "secret" letter of December 2, 1941, written by the German Inspector of the Conquered Ukrainian Territories to Herr General Thomas of the German Infantry, speaks of the Jews as behaving *ängstlich-willig* (anxiously-willing). "They take care to avoid anything that will displease the Germans. It is obvious that they hate us." The letter stated that the liquidation must be swift, because "in big cities they sometimes comprise over 50 percent of the population and they comprise nearly all the artisans as well as the labor groups of the small and middle industries." The Inspector further stated that (in the east) between 150,000 and 200,000 Jews had been killed already. The letter went on to say that the shooting of the Jews was conducted openly with the help of the Ukrainian military, but also "unfortunately very often with the help of volunteers of members of the army. . . . The procedure used in the mass extermination of men, old people, women and children of every age was horrible [*grauenhaft*]. The action was so gigantic that until now even the Soviet Union has never undertaken such an action."

The above letter, despite its tone of horror, is describing an earlier and "milder" time in the destruction of the Jews, in fact its "beginning," on December 2, 1941. The Inspector in the same letter wrote that he agrees that there are certain advantages in liquidating the Jews, but worries over the disadvantages as well—worrying that their loss may affect the German economy adversely. At the Nuremberg trials, as well as at the trials of other Nazis elsewhere, one of the chief defenses was that "no one really knew what was going on!" So much for that lie.

Meanwhile, I was making good progress with my studies. We Jewish students at the Engineering School took practically no vacations, trying to cram one and a half years of study into a year's time.

50

ONE NICE SUNNY Saturday afternoon in June, 1947, a former friend from the Death Brigade, Max Hoening, came to my apartment, interrupting my studies. Completely out of breath, he asked me to rush over with him to Military Police headquarters to identify Haupscharführer Rauch, one of the worst of the Germans, you will recall, in charge of the Death Brigade. On the way, Max said, he would explain the details.

We rushed over, and en route he told me that while waiting for the streetcar on Karlsplatz, in the center of Munich, he noticed a man quarreling with a girl. He knew at once that the man was Rauch. But how was he to arrest him? If he went over to Rauch right then and there, it most likely would attract a group of people around him, and he feared that Rauch would then disappear into the crowd. Max decided to follow Rauch to find out where he lived. While following him in the direction of the railroad station, a jeep with an M.P. in it came down the street. Seeing the M.P., Max caught Rauch by the collar of his jacket with one hand and beckoned wildly with the other hand to the M.P. The M.P., seeing that something was amiss, pulled up in the jeep, made both the men get into it, and drove them over to the nearest German police station and left them there.

To the German police Rauch denied that he ever had been in Poland, much less in Lvov. He also stated that he had never been in the SD or SS. He had papers showing that he had been taken prisoner by the Russians in Czechoslovakia and had been released by them a few weeks ago. His name was not Rauch, he held, but Rausch.

The police inspector explained to Max Hoening that he could only take the addresses of both parties. When Max had more proof he could return, and at that time they could arrest Rauch. Max was very unhappy about the proposed solution, for he knew Rauch would disappear at once. He was able to persuade the inspector to keep Rauch in the station jail until Monday morning. He would accept, he told the inspector, all possible consequences for arresting an innocent man.

Now Max was afraid that Rauch might get out of jail before Monday. What to do? Where to go for help? As we talked, it occurred to Max that the next plan would be to go to United States Military Police headquarters. I agreed. We got to headquarters, but because it was Saturday, and late in the afternoon, there was only a skeleton staff on duty. After running around for hours from one room to another with no one understanding a word that we said (at that time I didn't know one word of English) we left, not knowing what else to do.

We discussed the problem with each other until late in the night. At length we decided that in the morning Max should go to Foerenwald, a town about thirty miles from Munich. There, we knew, another survivor of the Death Brigade lived—in a DP camp. His name was David Manucewitz, and Max would get him as an additional witness. The more witnesses we had, the better our position would be. I, in the meantime, would find some way to communicate the situation to the American authorities. We did not trust the German police much; we even doubted whether they would keep Rauch in jail till Monday.

Sunday, early in the morning, taking my book *Death Brigade,* which contained a portrait of myself in it, I went down to the main office of the American CID (Criminal Investigation Division). One couldn't get by the sentry without a pass. The guard wouldn't listen to me, and even if he had, he probably wouldn't have understood what I wanted. I decided then to stop every man in an American Army uniform who passed me until I found someone who not only understood German but would also be willing to help.

I approached each soldier now with the open book, showing my portrait, gesturing with my hands as a kind of introduction. After about five hours of "peddling" myself (perhaps some thought that I was trying to sell my portrait or at least exchange it for American goods), I met an officer who stopped and actually listened to me.

The officer understood me and my problem. He took me inside the CID building and told me to stay in the waiting room. He returned after a few minutes and took me in to see another officer. This new officer spoke Polish well. I told him the whole story and showed him that my book, which was written in 1943, contained the exact description of the man we had caught—Rauch. The officer called up the police station where Rauch was detained and told them that Rauch should be brought over the next morning, Monday, at ten o'clock to a certain place. I, too, was given the address of this place and was told that my two friends and I should report at the same time. Excitedly I ran over to Max's house and told everything to Max's wife, and left the address of the place where he and David Manucewitz should come the next day.

Next morning Max, David, and I met outside the building where we had to report. I noticed by Max's behavior that he was restless. When I insisted that he tell me what the matter was, he mumbled that perhaps he had made a mistake and that the man might not really be the right one. It often happened that two people looked alike; after all, he did have release papers from a Russian prisoner-of-war camp and he had claimed that he had never been in Poland. Of course, I had not seen the man, so I could not have any opinion on the matter.

We went inside the building. In the long corridor sitting on a chair was—and there could be no doubt about it—the infamous Rauch. A German policeman stood guard over him. David and I recognized Rauch immediately.

David was a strong, well-built fellow in his late twenties; he had, in fact, been the strongest fellow in the Death Brigade. Seeing Rauch, David now became very agitated and, without thinking, kicked him squarely on the chin. Rauch's head hit the wall and he fell off the chair, bleeding. The policeman seized David. We three were then put into the station jail. One by one we were then called out for questioning. I was the last one called.

A German secretary, a young girl, did the questioning; the American officer-in-charge did not even appear. The secretary began by telling me that I must be very certain of what I said. She knew, she said, that I was going to tell the truth, because it wasn't I, after all, who had caught Rauch, and so it would not be I who would be liable if the wrong man were being accused. She knew of cases, she told me, where DP's, wanting to take a girl away from a German, accused the German of having been a Nazi.

This kind of talk infuriated me. I got up from my chair and, smashing my fist on the desk, said to her: "Who are you to question me, to question me at all? I have also heard about cases of love affairs between bosses and their secretaries and that afterward the secretaries run the shows. I plan to find out what is going on here! I know the right people."

I walked out of the office then, slamming the door behind me. I went home, too nervous to talk to anyone, even to David or Max, who had also been released after the "questioning."

About ten o'clock that same evening a German policeman came to my home. He told me that I would have to report next morning at the same place where I had been that day.

Next morning, when I arrived, I was taken into a room and introduced to an American officer. He spoke good Polish. I was the only witness invited today, and I was very well treated. The German secretary came in; she asked me to forgive her for her behavior to me yesterday. She told me that after I had left, Rauch had been questioned and had admitted that he remembered me, that he had been in the Death Brigade, and that his papers had been counterfeited after he had been caught by the Russians in Czechoslovakia. She also told me that she couldn't believe her own ears when he had told them of what had actually gone on in the Death Brigade.

"Such an innocent, young, good-looking fellow," she added.

A few minutes later Rauch was brought in. He and I talked while the officer listened. Rauch claimed that he had been only a chauffeur in the Death Brigade. I stated that I knew he had been the second in command. He admitted that he had been sceond highest in rank and that when the chief was away he took up the reports, and so on. But he still maintained that he had been only a chauffeur. He said that in 1932, when he was eighteen, he had joined the Nazi Party. During the war he had been assigned to the concentration camp and he had been very happy that he had not been sent to the front line instead. I was anxious to hear more of what he had to tell, but his next statement stopped the discussion. "You know, sir," he said to me, "that the Poles and Ukrainians were worse than the Germans."

The American officer was a naturalized American citizen of Polish descent. When he heard Rauch say this, he immediately got up from his seat and walked over to the door. While standing there he beckoned me over, saying in Polish that there was an iron bar near the window, but that I should remember that if I killed Rauch or created visible injuries I could be put on trial. He further told me that he would be back within minutes, and then he left.

I didn't know what to do. To beat up anybody, even a murderer like Rausch, was repugnant to me. It then struck me that if I didn't react "normally," it might later be construed that perhaps Rauch was after all "not so guilty." With this in mind, I hit him a few times with my fist until he fell to the floor. A few minutes later the officer came back; we shook hands, and I left.

51

I WAS MAKING very good progress with my studies now. On July 10, 1947, I applied for a scholarship to L'École Polytechnique Fédérale, in Zurich, and on October 10, 1947, I received a letter through the Central Jewish Organization telling me that not only had I been awarded the scholarship; I had also been accepted at the Polytechnique. I applied for an entrance visa. This was turned down by the Swiss border police on the basis that I was a stateless person. So for the time being I had to stay on in Munich. As for Rauch, I heard no more about him for some time.

Then, in late December, 1948, my landlady told me that in the evening, while I had been out, a man had come there looking for me. She had told him to come back at about seven o'clock in the morning, before I left the house. Next morning, about six forty-five, a man in his thirties, of about average height, came to my room. He introduced himself, telling me that his cousin had been killed in the Dachau Concentration Camp and had left a wife and three children. Knowing that I worked with the Historical Commission, he asked me if it were possible to find more details of the case because the children would like to know the circumstances as well as the date of their father's death. I told him that it would most probably be extremely difficult to get any information, but that since I knew some people who had been in Dachau, I would ask around. We agreed to meet again in about fourteen days.

I inquired here and there, but no one had heard the name the man had given to me; after all, Dachau had been a very big camp. The man didn't show up in the two-week period as he had said he would, and I slowly forgot about the case.

It wasn't until one evening about six weeks later that the same man came to me again. Instead of asking me about his cousin, he asked me if I knew who he was and what he really wanted. I said No. He then told me that he was the brother-in-law of Rauch and that when first arrested Rauch had been interned in Dachau. After about half a year he had been sent to Poland and was now in a jail in Krakow. Rauch, this man told me, had been doing very well there. He wrote home very often and had got some witnesses who were ready to testify on his behalf. Then Rauch's brother-in-law came to the point. Rauch wanted me to write to the court in Krakow and state that I had never seen him actually kill anyone. As for the rest, they were certain they had enough connections to get him out of jail entirely.

The brother-in-law told me he had already spoken to Max, and Max had told him that everything depended on me, because I was known in Poland. I realized at once that Max, having a wife and child, and seeing that Rauch's family knew his address in Munich, had clearly become frightened of reprisals, and had pushed all the responsibility onto me. I listened to everything, being glad to find out that Rauch was in a Polish prison, for there, I was sure, he would get a fair trial. On the other hand, I was bothered by the new witnesses Rauch had drummed up and the "pull" his family had. We, the real witnesses, were here in Munich. I decided that I should find out as much as possible about the Rauch case through his family, so I told the brother-in-law that I would do everything that I considered to be right and fair. I added that I would like to hear from him again. Of course, I didn't clarify what I meant by "right and fair."

After the encounter I immediately wrote to Dr. Roth in Poland; I have mentioned him earlier. He was also an interested party in the Death Brigade. I told him the details of how Rauch was caught, about the meeting with Rauch's brother-in-law, and of the fact that Rauch was now in Krakow. I asked Dr. Roth whether, as a lawyer living close to Krakow, he felt that he should look into the case, seeing to it that there was no miscarriage of justice—through the use of false witnesses or "pull."

To this letter I got a swift answer. Dr. Roth told me that he had got in touch with the court in Krakow at once and that the date of the trial had not yet been set. It had been put off because affidavits from the witnesses, most of whom lived outside Poland, hadn't arrived. He further wrote: "I am going in the near future to Krakow to get permission to see Rauch because I would like to ask him if he could tell me what happened to the members of the Brigade after the escape in November, 1943.

"From your letter it seems that Rauch should get the heaviest sentence but from your book one gets the feeling that he sometimes had some human instincts."

When I received this letter saying that Rauch had "sometimes had some human instincts," my blood began to boil. Dr. Roth was a father who had lost his only son and daughter at the hands of these killers; his wife had committed suicide because of it; his son had had to burn his baby sister's body; and yet the father still tried to find something "positive" in this murderer. I immediately wrote him a letter in this vein.

In the meantime Rauch's family visited me again. His mother, in her sixties, a thin little woman, his older sister and the brother-in-law came to my apartment. The brother-in-law introduced us, and I asked them to be seated. The mother began to speak. "As a mother I can't bear approaching another Easter holiday with my only son not with us. You must understand that he was a young boy when he was in the camp. You once had a mother, too."

"Yes, and she was killed by people like your son," I interrupted.

"But where will the world end?" she continued. "One is killed by another. Now the other is killed by a third one, and so on. There must be an end somewhere. One must be above this. You, sir, will know what it means to have members of your family killed. Here speaks to you a mother. A mother's heart, whose one wish is to have her only son for Easter—"

"And we will make it up to you financially, to compensate for the loss of your family," interrupted the sister.

While Rauch's mother was talking, my heart was full of pain for my own family. My mother didn't ask to be with her children for any holidays; she asked only that they not be tortured or brutally killed; and here I, in the name of my family, the victims, was being asked to be superhuman. We Jews, on the whole, were not even allowed the rights of an animal—the right not to be cut up while still alive, the right not to have the suckling ripped from the breast of the mother before she and the suckling are killed. These animal rights were in the Seven Laws of Noah, eons before "civilization."

I told them that I would do my best, that the trial's date would be set as soon as possible. I also told them that their defense lawyer should ask the court to obtain the statements of us, the three chief witnesses, right away. I was afraid that if the case were delayed any longer, I, in the meantime, would have left Germany in one direction and Max in another; David had already left for Israel. It would be hard, if we were all three out of the country, to get our written statements.

That same night I wrote another letter to Dr. Roth, asking him to find how Rauch managed to write home so often, who the "good" witnesses were, and why the trial had been so much delayed.

A few weeks later Max and I were called down to the Polish Consulate, where we gave our sworn statements about Rauch.

The next letter I got from Dr. Roth was dated July 5, 1949. It read:

DEAR MR. WELICZKER:

I was in Krakow and saw Rauch two days before his trial on June 24. I am sorry I didn't read the court record before I saw him, but the judge was at a trial. There were three preliminary trials before the last one, and reading the court record I can understand why Rauch was so relaxed and sure of himself when I met him.

I was mainly interested to hear from Rauch what happened to the members of the Brigade after the escape on November, 1943. He claimed that because the night when you escaped was foggy and dark *all* escaped. The guards didn't even fire a shot, being fearful that they would shoot each other. This was obviously a lie, as was everything else that he told me. Otherwise it was a very educational discussion for me. Perhaps after the verdict of guilty he will finally fully realize his heinous crimes, because from our conversation I don't know if God himself could find the slightest trace of feeling in him, not to speak of a painful conscience. After reading the court record I had such feelings of revulsion for him that I couldn't bring myself to go to the trial, even though I had previously arranged to stay in Krakow for it.

On the last day of the trial a new letter arrived for Rauch from his sister; it was addressed to *"Allerliebstes Brüderlein"* (to my most beloved baby brother), and was full of love for the brother, who was being prosecuted by the devilish Jews, who themselves committed crimes and because of those crimes were afraid to return to Poland. I showed this letter to the Prosecutor who was awaiting your sworn statement from the Polish consulate in Munich, which in the meantime had arrived. Your statement and a witness here, Edward Gleich, who stated that he himself saw Rauch shooting a small child, brought the death sentence which he got on June 24, 1949.

In the court record there were papers signed by a man, Hriorij, now living in Munich, who in my opinion was a *Volksdeutch,* that Rauch was never a member of the Nazi Party and was a fine man. Another statement from the Weihbiship said that there must be a mixup between this Rauch and Brigadier General Rauch.

With best wishes.

[signed] E. ROTH

Dr. Roth has since married a widow, whose husband and daughter had been killed by the Nazis. They now live in Israel.

I will end my story here—with Rauch's end. More famous Nazis had been hanged before him, but he was more intimately connected with the fate of the people I had known so well.

From this point on, normal life began for me. And, in the summer of 1949, after getting my Ph.D. in Engineering, I left for the United States. In this country I was to dwell among strangers no longer. Here I was to start anew, and to find myself completely.

But that is another story.